EVERYDAY INTUITION

EVERYDAY

WHAT PSYCHOLOGY, SCIENCE, AND
PSYCHICS CAN TEACH US ABOUT FINDING
AND TRUSTING OUR INNER VOICE

INTUITION

ELIZABETH GREENWOOD

HARPER

An Imprint of HarperCollins*Publishers*

HarperCollins books may be purchased for educational, business, or sales promotional use. For information, please email the Special Markets Department at SPsales@harpercollins.com.

FIRST EDITION

Eye art courtesy of Getty Images/ filo

Library of Congress Cataloging-in-Publication Data has been applied for.

ISBN 978-0-06-337569-7

25 26 27 28 29 LBC 5 4 3 2 1

For Susannah,
For going on the errand with me

Whoever cannot seek
the unforeseen sees nothing,
for the known way
is an impasse.

—*Heraclitus*

CONTENTS

INTRODUCTION

If the family that raised me had a motto, it would be: *We're fucked*. The origin of this credo stems from an incident trying to exit a mall parking garage when the parking-machine ticket was lost for all of three seconds. In those three seconds, trapped by the mechanical arm, our lives as contributing members of society were extinguished. Now we would live inside this garage forever. Goodbye, cruel world. We'll be huddled by the Nordstrom entrance in zone B6 for the rest of our days.

We laugh about this story because it possesses a deep truth about the worldview of its protagonist, the woman behind the wheel of the car, the one who could not locate the ticket: my mother. The shortest line between A and B is not "The ticket must be here somewhere." It's "Game over." That moment represents a pervasive anxiety about the inevitable doom nipping at our heels and, worse yet, the belief that we could not meet that doom and deal. We'd be fucked.

We laugh because of how ridiculous this is on its face, of course. But also because of who is saying this. My mom is one of the strongest, most resourceful, most courageous people this world has ever known. And she has been led by her intuitive sense. My grandmother was Mennonite, and my mother grew up in a Mennonite-adjacent religion, Church of the Brethren, in rural western Pennsylvania. They believed in pacifism, austerity, and humility. The women in my family are seers—they connect with the dead, they get visions in dreams, they know when someone is pregnant before they have been told. My mother's mother loved to lead us on walks through cemeteries. Since she died, she has come to my aunts and cousins in the form of songs on the radio, in deer standing in special spots, in rainbows at family reunions.

Being plugged into these experiences is powerful, and yet in Mennonite culture one's own power is to be met with suspicion, especially for women. The diminishment of the individual in favor of the good of the collective is a central tenet of the faith. It also results in knee-jerk self-deprecation, so much so that having a bit of self-esteem is synonymous with pride, a sin. On my mother's side, this ranges from no one being able to accept a compliment to outright declarations of one's own stupidity. Intuitive experiences contradict those messages. Also, you come into this world steeped in original sin, which makes it tough to trust yourself. And experiencing intuition within an orthodox religion is complicated, too. Because what is that voice? Is it God? Or your own inner voice? How to square personal knowing with abiding faith? That special knowledge became the source of shame for a great many women in that culture. And shame is such a tough adversary to tangle with. It's so bone-deep that few of us can even name it. As Taffy Brodesser-Akner writes, "What is it about shame that always feels like the truth?"

Intuition is considered a little bit shameful whether you are Mennonite or not. We are taught that knowing without knowing why is irrational, fanciful. Being plugged into the spiritual is often reductively considered "woo-woo" at best, superstitious at worst. And yet we know from experience that taking the intuitive route can have the greatest outcomes for our lives. Against all odds, my mom listened to her intuition, which led her down a very different path. She was the first person in her family to leave her community and go to college, where she started out studying chemistry (practical, rational) and changed tracks to history—not the most lucrative or pragmatic. In her career, she followed the breadcrumbs of her curiosity to magical discoveries that had positive repercussions for the living ancestors of the people she animated in her scholarship. She is kind of an intuitive genius. She didn't so much subscribe to five-year plans but to following the next exciting step. Like an incantation, she told me and my sister, Susannah, to always trust our guts.

That proof is in her life and her achievements. And yet lurking in the shadows is anxiety, the constant companion. As someone without pedigree, she suffered from impostor syndrome in the rarefied institutions she earned her way into. When I was eight years old and Susannah was one, she became a single mom. She felt a sense of scarcity and precarity. She did a great job—I was a somewhat feral latchkey kid but also took weekend art classes and went on family vacations. And yet, with one false move it seemed like the whole house of cards could come tumbling down. *You lost that parking garage ticket? You, my friend, are you-know-what.* No wiggle room, no grace. In addition to intuition, I think anxiety was the ubiquitous pressure that propelled her.

Both of these voices were ingrained equally: *Trust your gut. We're fucked.* This is a battle royale between anxiety and intuition. Anxiety wants to keep you small; intuition wants you to expand. Anxiety pokes holes of doubt into all your dreams; intuition wants you to trust that whatever happens, you can handle it. These two are in a constant tug-of-war. So which voice wins?

To people living in the twenty-first century, paradoxical messages are no surprise. There's so much noise, our heads are spinning. Am I supposed to flatten my stomach or embrace my curves? Rest or mobilize? Unplug or build a platform? Be flexible or boundaried? Parent my children gently or let my kids free-range? We've become separated from our intuition and, worse yet, taught that it is a faulty faculty, an ephemeral, emotional thing, when it is really so much more.

I became a mother during the first Trump administration, and all I wanted to do was read my horoscope and go to psychics. Nothing made sense anymore. I wasn't alone. Never before have tarot readers, astrologers, mediums, and other purveyors of supernatural intelligence been more popular or more mainstream. Psychic services is a $2.2 billion industry, with a growth rate of 2.6 percent in 2021. So many women worship at the altar of Gwyneth Paltrow and her coterie of intuitive practitioners, from medical intuitives to psychic mediums to dream interpreters. Intuition is a wing of the wellness industry, a component of self-care. A 2021 Pew survey found that 29 percent of Americans say they have no religion—a 6 percent increase from 2016—and 28 percent of Americans describe themselves as spiritual but not religious. Millennials and Gen Z have replaced religion with spirituality. People are hungry for a different, more personal, less hierarchical way of knowing. We crave spirituality that doesn't make us feel dumb, and intellectualism that doesn't discount the spirit.

In the spring of one of those Trump years, I attended an evening workshop in my neighborhood for women experiencing burnout. We journaled, we thrashed around the room, we screamed, we cried. We planted seeds of intention. Almost every woman said she wanted to learn to trust herself. We've been conditioned to second-guess and gaslight ourselves, to mortgage our inner authority to experts, institutions, and social norms. Learning to trust our intuition uncovers another script, a more encouraging voice. How do we find our way back?

Like blood, intuition is something you are born with. It is an ancient, adaptive ability designed to keep you alive. When your body knows something is amiss before your brain can catch up, that is intuition. It's a knowing, without always knowing why. The *why* isn't super important—it's the knowing that matters.

People experience intuition differently. Some people receive it as a feeling, some in images, some in a push or a pull. For me, it's the vibe I will have about something, anything, and before I can even begin to articulate it in words, my body says *No, that's a bad idea*, in the form of constriction, or *Yes, that's a good idea*, in the form of expansion, relief. For me, learning to listen to and to trust that inner voice has made "intuition" synonymous with self-belief.

And yet since the Enlightenment we have been indoctrinated in the belief that "rational" ways of knowing are superior to the intuitive. The information age in which we are living fetishizes data. It suggests that there is but one way of knowing: material, visible to the naked eye, quantifiable. But intuitive data doesn't map easily onto an Excel spreadsheet. Yet it is data nonetheless.

Claiming intuition as a valid system of knowledge is revolutionary. To be right in this world is to be male, white, rich, straight, linear. It is to fit into hard right-angled boxes. To be wrong is to be not male, not white, not rich, not straight. Spirals, cycles, and complexity just don't fit the constraints of our culture.

How do we learn to trust ourselves in a society that tells us we are wrong? Intuition tells you that you are right. If your way of knowing doesn't align with the dominant form, you are not wrong.

One of the funny paradoxes about intuition is that it is both derided as not real and then trotted out in the highest-stakes moments. When faced with the choice between two jobs or two apartments or two romantic partners that both have an equal ledger of pros and cons, where there is no clear winner, what do you do? You go with your gut. It's a fine idea, in theory, but why should you trust your gut at these critical junctures when you haven't practiced using it in the day-to-day? We need to cultivate everyday intuition.

Intuition has been polarized, with feminized love-and-light airiness on one side and hard-nosed "go with your gut" business-speak on the other. It has been placed on a high mantel of the esoteric, where you gain insight through silent meditation and retreat. For most of us, that is just not a thing. I can barely use the bathroom without my kids banging down the door. And if you go to any airport bookstore you will see two books about intuition on the shelves, and they say contradictory things. *Blink*, by Malcolm Gladwell, argues that you should trust this so-called rapid cognition. *Thinking, Fast and Slow*, by Daniel Kahneman, says you shouldn't, and that quantifiable data, rubrics, and spreadsheets are king. The intuition I'm talking about is not either/or; it just is. It's the pull of history, the vibe you get walking into a room, the decisions we make, big and small, that don't always make sense on paper but make sense for us. It's the feeling of being guided, of a voice so resonant that it can feel almost outside of yourself and yet so essential, the deepest part of you.

You *should* trust your intuition. But first you have to figure out what intuition is to you, its true character, not the protective mechanism that masquerades as intuition: avoidance, anxiety, procrastination, whatever fear gets in your way. Intuition can be very difficult to disentangle from anxiety, and even harder to hear. And even if you don't experience anxiety yourself (who even *are* you?), there are a lot of blocks to intuition. Perhaps it's distraction, or numbing out, or ideology around the supremacy of certain ways of knowing. So how can we tease apart true, expansive, authentic intuition from its more nefarious doppelgangers: reactivity, bias, and just plain bad ideas?

What I am advocating for in this book is for you to trust yourself, and to realize which voices are worth trusting and which are not. An intuitive impulse is one that pokes an opening in the fabric of the everyday, a curiosity that will beckon you down a different road, ultimately toward your greater good. Hitler and any other number of madmen throughout history trusted themselves and it didn't turn out well, nor do the inner voices of self- or outward destruction that tell us to harm ourselves or others. That's not intuition, and that's not what I'm talking about here.

Our unconscious biases can wear the mask of intuition as well. We live in a racist, sexist, classist (you name it "-ist") society that fills our brains with trash ideas. Even if we rationally *know* some ideas are garbage, they percolate up because it is the water in which we swim. Take the popular genre of true crime, one micro example that reflects a greater truth about bias. In countless documentaries and podcasts, middle-class white women are centered as the victims of violent crime. You might get the idea that this demographic suffers the most from violent crime, and it might inspire hypervigilance and paranoia at becoming the next victim. In reality, young men of color are disproportionately the victims of violence in the United States.

When you skim poorly sourced articles and social media accounts that attempt to provide alternative theories about facts, be it the rotundity of planet Earth or the link between vaccines and autism, then what "feels right" has perilous consequences for both the individual and society at large. It's crucial to interrogate the trickier, dangerous side of intuitions.

The self-trust for which I'm advocating doesn't mean that every intuition you follow will be correct. But an intuitively led life is a framework and a process, not a zero-sum game. Say you married the wrong person. One way of looking at it is that you had lousy intuition when it came time to choose a partner. But from another angle, your intuition is actually quite good, because you realized you were with the wrong person and got out of that marriage. Like opening the heart, you can't choose to accept only joy. With an open heart can come great sorrow. The same with intuition: it isn't always going to be easy, seamless, or "right." But you can train it to be open for the next experience. Learning to trust your intuition is a way of being in the world.

Intuition is not weak. It's actually pretty hardcore. When you begin to start tuning out the many voices and messages that surround us, it can become an act of defiance. What do *you* want? Intuition will rarely tell you to buy or consume something. More often, it will tell you to lie down. Do nothing. Watch. Wait. Developing intuition doesn't cost a lot of money, but it does cost effort: the effort of noticing, presence, and discernment. It is the effort of data collection, except this data is about how you feel, and the yardstick is your quality of life. When you begin to tap into what you really want, your life might actually get harder in the short term. Your intuition may tell you what you already know and what is hard to act on: that the relationship isn't right, the job isn't good, your life needs changing. But as one intuitive master, Oprah Winfrey, once said, "Difficulties come when you don't pay attention to life's whisper. Life always whispers to you first, but if you ignore the whisper, sooner or later you'll get a scream."

In disentangling anxiety and intuition, you can begin to uncover all the good stuff that is here, too. Your intuition can lead you to tiny joys papered over by the doldrums of the everyday. It won't stop bad things from happening. As psychic Nelly Reznik says, "Intuition won't fix all your problems. But it will make you a more active participant in your life."

I cast the widest of nets to figure out how to do just that, ergo the subtitle of this book, and I look to psychology *and* science *and* psychics. Intuition is such a huge question that not just one of these disciplines can begin to answer all of its mysteries. All of these schools of thought have important things to say, and frankly I need and want them all. I interviewed neuroscientists and psychics, entrepreneurs and psychedelic ceremonial leaders, ER doctors and hypnotherapists, economists and tarot card readers, statisticians and psychologists, all of whom study and use intuition in their respective fields. Themes emerged. Though the methods and tools they employ to get at the truth are indeed quite distinct, the ideas about intuition that they advance are not always so different. Most importantly, I interviewed regular people who have mastered their intuition—they know when to listen and how to trust it. If you're reading this book with a pen, their words are the ones you should underline.

This book is structured like a swimming pool: we begin in the shallow end, where you can touch the bottom, conceptually speaking, by examining intuition through the lenses of science—the sciences of the brain, society, and the body. From there we progress into deeper waters: the notion of women's intuition, ways of accessing the unconscious, premonitions, and psychic ability. Trying to capture this slippery concept can feel like trying to staple Jell-O to the wall. But moving from the most grounded examination of intuition to the most ethereal, it becomes clear that intuition touches most every facet of life.

Intuition as a concept has some essential qualities, as we'll see, but each person's experience of it is very personal. I have made myself my own laboratory to test different theories. My experience is not the be-all and end-all, and your mileage may vary. I'm not a spiritual teacher or a mental health professional. I'm a forty-two-year-old mother of two. I want to watch Bravo and go to bed by 9 p.m. I'll always have more questions than answers. I get it wrong a lot. I gnash my teeth and blame everybody but myself. Sometimes I stop trying for a while and go on my phone and smoke cigarettes and polish my resentments and water my grudges. Then I try again. I wrote this book to fill a gap between the pithy bullet points of self-help and the dense tomes of academic studies translated into pop psychology. I suspect that this book shouldn't fit neatly into either genre, but into a third: something intellectually rigorous but at the same time pragmatic, polyphonic, and also personal.

When I set out to disentangle anxiety from intuition, I did not know the difference between them. They both simmered in the same stew of urgency. Today, as I write this, I do know the difference. They might live on the same cul-de-sac, but their homes are quite distinct. Still, just severing the two conceptually is not enough; I have to remember again every day, and try anew every day. I let myself be changed by this research. This is how I got there.

The following is an invitation. And like the many Paperless Post invites clogging your inbox, you don't have to RSVP yes to all of them. Take what works, leave what doesn't. This is just one woman's attempt to try to trust herself in a world, culture, and familial inheritance that says she shouldn't. The following is a yearslong quest in trying, and trying again. The quest is also a homecoming. These are questions about intuition and shame and anxiety that women in my family and beyond have been wrestling with for generations.

Intuition is something we all possess. Harnessing it as your guide can become an orientation toward life. It can be your north star, and the foundation for everything. Best of all, it can make you feel less alone, less wrong. It can be grand and mystical. It can also answer the simple question "What needs to happen next?" If we can escape the noise of our egos for a moment, we can find the grandeur in the small. These intuitive hits are the fractals of majesty reflected in the mundane. They are an energizing current through daily life. In the most pragmatic application, intuition is triage, prioritizing the next right step—to drink a glass of water, to take a break, to stop and wonder. And through the accumulation of those tiny moments, like a flurry that turns into a snowstorm, it can lead to something awesome.

And somehow, in our mixed-up world, there are people, extraordinary people, who have learned the language of their intuition, its vernacular and its cadences. They are lessons hard-won, usually. You probably know some of them, and the question is always: How? How do they come with such energy, presence, and confidence? How did they learn to trust themselves? As I set out to make my days more transcendent and to build a more trusting relationship with myself, I knew the perfect person with whom to commence my investigation.

EVERYDAY INTUITION

CHAPTER 1

EVERYDAY INTUITION

The scene: an apartment building in the South Bronx, New York, 1973. A family comes home. The young girl is with her grandparents. They are her caretakers, because her mom and dad are in the grip of addiction.

The grandfather has a favorite chair, as grandfathers do. He goes to take his usual seat in the corner, by the built-in bar. But the girl, no more than five, issues a warning.

"Don't sit there," she says.

"Why, *mija?*" He chuckles and takes his seat.

"No, please don't sit there," she repeats.

She begins to cry. The little girl's tears sway him. "*Ay, no llores,*" he says, laughing, as he moves to appease her.

Moments later, a crack ruptures the ceiling above the grandfather's chair. Moments after that, the crack gives way, raining down plaster and cement. The ceiling—in the spot exactly above where the grandfather would have been sitting had his granddaughter not compelled him to move out of the way—caves in.

—

Melissa Coss Aquino, the little girl from the Bronx, grew up to be a professor, novelist, and mother of two sons, both now grown. She is the kind of person who, once you are around her, you only want to be around her more. You could call it presence, or energy, or a vibe. She is constantly fielding phone calls from friends, family, and former students seeking her counsel. She listens, she connects, she plays surrogate mom, auntie, big sister to many. Her light fills any room. She has long, curly hair and a full-throated laugh, which she often employs to laugh at herself. She is dropped in, enough so that she somehow, at age five, saved her grandfather's life.

Ever since that ceiling collapsed, she's felt guided by her intuition. It has kept her and those around her safe in ways she cannot explain with logic alone. She listens to that inner voice—most of the time. Even the most intuitive among us are still subject to the chatter of the brain. You know the sound: the critical bully that cuts your intuitive impulse off at the knees. The one that says, *Why are you overreacting? Don't make a stink, you'll look foolish. Just do what you've always done, you silly idiot.* None of us are immune. But Melissa has made it her life's work to try to follow a quieter voice, one born of instinct, survival, and a little bit of magic.

"I live according to my intuition," Melissa tells me matter-of-factly. She isn't a psychic or peddling her wares on social media. "I'm just a *bruja* next door!" she says, laughing. Rather, she has taken that faculty that life has given her—that she believes life gives all of us—and made it her north star. What I love about Melissa is that she has this magic yet is still a serious person. She has a doctorate and a job as a professor of English at Bronx Community College; she pays her taxes. She is no ding-dong, as our data-driven, rationalist, left-brain culture would have you believe. Melissa has figured out a way to integrate her intuition into everyday life.

—

It makes a perfect kind of sense that the time and place I first encountered Melissa was steeped in magic. We met at an all-women writers' residency on an island in Puget Sound. We'd go for long evening walks, watching otters flop around in the marsh, having the kind of meandering, luxuriant conversations that occur when you're suspended from everyday responsibilities. Melissa, to me, seemed to have an otherworldly type of knowledge in the midst of harsh life circumstances. She told me about growing up in the Bronx in the seventies and eighties, her parents' addictions, and the solace her grandmother provided. She mentioned feeling protected by something larger than herself, or something within herself. It seemed as if she had a force field around her. "There were times when I was a teenager and I was about to get into a car with a guy, and I would feel a hand on my chest, physically stopping me from getting inside," she said. To feel that sensation is one thing. To actually heed its warning and not talk yourself out of it is quite another.

One night she took a picture of me, then six months pregnant, in the late summer light. On the brink of becoming a mother, I could feel myself moving into a new, visceral knowledge. You could call it hormonal, or evolutionary, but I know it was more than that. It was intuition, an impulse, and a knowledge that came from a place that was not my thinking brain. And here in my path was someone who seemed intimately familiar with it. I lapped up Melissa's stories and attached myself to her like a barnacle, hoping to become her friend and learn her way of being in the world.

———

Melissa still resides in the Bronx, in a rambling three-story home on a hill in Kingsbridge Heights with her husband, Fernando, who also holds a PhD in political science and teaches at Lehman College. The couple married in their early twenties, after six weeks of courtship (hello, intuition!). One morning, four years after we met on that magical island, I meet up with her down the hill to try to re-create one of those sprawling conversational walks.

Her life wasn't always so settled and prosperous. "I grew up in a benign neglect that would put you in danger," she tells me as we cross over a highway to Van Cortlandt Park and its expansive wooded trails. "I say 'benign' because the older people themselves were in danger too, everybody was in danger," she says. "And you're the only person with your head about you, even though you were five. How many times I had to pull my mom back from a car crossing the street when I was a kid!"

Melissa credits the influence of two important family members for her ability to notice and to act: her maternal grandmother and her father. "By the time I was seven, I was alone with my grandmother. That's not the same as five or six people in the house," she says. The grandfather whose life she saved from the ceiling cave-in died a few years later. That solitude the two shared came in the form of quiet. "My grandmother and I bond over how much quiet we need. Everyone I've encountered who learns to listen a little more learns to listen to silence," she says.

That silence was punctuated by appearances by her father. "He was a man who wore a pinkie ring and cowboy boots in the South Bronx," she says. "That's a lot of personality going on." He retired from formal education in ninth grade, as he had an undiagnosed learning disability. But he was smart and driven, and made the city his school: "People called him the Philosopher. He would joke about having a PhD in streetology. It was all-encompassing—intellectual, spiritual—but not academic. He was incredibly aware, but he didn't have any degrees, so he wasn't valued as a thinker. Even though he was super *machista* with his wives and women, he was super feminist with his daughters. He'd say, 'You have to go to school—I don't want to hear about wedding gowns, I want to hear about caps and gowns!'" Melissa laughs. His spiritual intelligence was one he came by honestly. "His grandmother read cards, read leaves. They hid their Indigenous spirituality in Catholicism, in the saints," she says, describing the traditions and practices her family brought from Puerto Rico. Even though her dad never explicitly taught her about their spiritual lineage—and much of that knowledge has been lost because of colonialism and slavery—he provided a model for what an intuitive life could look like.

He was a bundle of contradictions, but his words resonated with Melissa. He wasn't always present in her life, but he wanted to protect her. "He always said, 'Do your thing, make sure your name is on the lease, don't let anyone fuck with you,'" she recalls. "At one point he sat me down and said, 'You're attractive, you're smart. But you have to know that if you get involved with certain dudes, or go down certain roads, not even I will be able to help you out. So choose carefully.'"

—

She did choose carefully. She was the first in her family to attend college. She spent a semester abroad in Brazil, where she was confronted with the kinds of choices her dad had warned her about.

"I was nineteen, studying at the University of São Paulo. I was hanging out with some women who were going to take a trip to Rio that some older men were funding. A part of me was like, *I've seen it all before. No one is going to mess with me.*" She took a bus to Rio to join the others. "But when I got there," she recalls, "I could not for the life of me pick up the phone and call the person who was supposed to pick me up. I sat on the beach in Copacabana, in the rain, for hours. The message at that moment was very clear: *You can go, but you will pay. And it will be big.*"

In the end, she never made the call. "I sat on that beach for so long that it was almost a fugue state. Then the fever dropped and I was just very clear: *I need to get on the bus and go back to São Paulo.* And I left, as if I'd always known the answer, but I didn't. I had to get shaken up."

I recall a more recent time Melissa got a big no like that.

"Do you remember last summer you were going to drive down to see me in Brooklyn, and then you texted me right before like 'Nope, sorry, I'm not'?" I ask.

"And then there were cars floating down the Major Deegan?!" Melissa laughs. The Major Deegan Expressway is the road Melissa drives from her house to mine. "I don't even think it was raining when I texted you that!"

It wasn't. It was a perfectly normal sunny day in August, not a cloud in the sky. But that clear sky would later turn dark and pour down torrential rains.

"I trust you on this stuff now," I say, "but walk me through that decision. How did that information come to you? Explain it to me like I'm a golden retriever."

"I think a golden retriever would resent that," she says, laughing. "I'm super verbal," she explains. "When I was younger, it was more physical, my stomach would clench at the sight of a person that would put me on guard. Now it is literally the voices in my head. I'll hear a *Don't fuck with that.* And I'll say back, *But c'mon, why can't I have fun?!*" Understandable. But even more critical to the whole intuitive endeavor is this: "There's a part of me that has to check in and make sure that's not just fear speaking."

———

This is the million-dollar question. How can we differentiate when the impulse to stay away is a wise intuitive download and when it's a neurotic pattern of fear? When is the voice anxiety, my constant companion, and when is it true intuition, my new and sometimes flaky friend?

For people living in the twenty-first century, anxiety is the very air we breathe. It's the push notifications on our phones, the climate crisis, inflation, the threat of fascism if you're liberal, the threat of the other if you're conservative. Coupled with the trauma of COVID, anxiety is very real and very debilitating. Everyone's anxiety is different. My anxiety is pretty mean. It tells me I am never good enough. Anxiety will often stop me from saying what I need to say for fear of hurting someone's feelings and making them feel bad, which wouldn't be setting an appropriate boundary and advocating for myself—*no, no, no*—but would be shameful. My anxiety doesn't do a great job with scale. An argument with my husband and I'm living on the street. An unreturned text and my friendships have all been lies. My anxiety can twist any compliment into the most withering insult and shade any accomplishment into a reflection of my inherent mediocrity. In a more generous interpretation, my anxiety has been adaptive: it has powered and propelled me forward. But that energy source is a bad one, like nuclear runoff. It has awful implications for the living beings in the surrounding environs. Anxiety is an endlessly renewable resource, but it is toxic.

———

I recently came up against this precise clash of shame versus intuition when debating whether to apply for a teaching position at my alma mater. On paper, I am qualified for the job, but academic hiring is notoriously political and subject to opaque criteria known only to the hiring committee. My relationship with the institution is fraught, to put it mildly: tens of thousands of dollars in debt; adjuncting as a lecturer teaching classes to students I care for deeply while being passively abused by the administration; never feeling quite like I belong or that I am good enough. The opening was for a job I'd love, plus the opportunity to go from part-time wooden marionette to full-time real-boy faculty, with health insurance and an office to boot. But to put myself in a position to be rejected would reinforce the bad stories I tell myself about myself, about not being good enough. "I have Stockholm syndrome from that place," I texted a friend. "I know they are bad for me, but I want them still. Or my ego wants them."

Back and forth like this for days. It felt like selling myself short not to apply and like flirting with self-harm to do so. I was afraid of being rejected and reinforcing the narrative of *not good enough*. Is that self-protection or self-defeating fear? Or would applying just mean I was looking to fill the hole inside myself (inside all of us) which is more like an abyss? The abyss of being human? Or would I—could I—get the job?! Is it an anxious, avoidant behavior to opt out of even trying, or is that a wise intuition? You can see the knots tying!

When I laid out the calculus of the problem for friends, they inevitably had their own conundrum of anxiety versus intuition. My friend Helen told me about the specter of an apartment she didn't rent that she now thinks about all the time. She read meaning into the application process itself: she opted for apartment number one, but when she tried to pay the security deposit to the landlord via Zelle, it wouldn't go through. Then the landlord of apartment number two called her and said they'd waive the broker fee.

Of course, the knots we tie ourselves into around decisions like these are never just about a job, never just about an apartment. They are repositories of our histories, our generational traumas, our life choices that might have never been choices at all. Housing is fraught for Helen. She's an unfettered Sagittarius, for one, so putting down roots is tough for her no matter what. Her Jewish ancestors were forced from their homes and homelands. And signing a lease is no joke when you're a writer and an adjunct professor whose source of income isn't predictable or permanent. Helen is aware that these factors are all at play no matter where she decides to live. These thorny inheritances are perhaps the most difficult (and most important) sites to discern our intuition. But she couldn't get that other apartment out of her head. Ultimately, she went with apartment one. But apartment two, and perhaps the alternate life she would have lived inside it, obsessed her enough that she left a handwritten note to the current tenants asking them to get in touch should they ever move.

So: anxiety or intuition?

When my friend doesn't want to go on another internet date, is it because she's had bad luck in the past, or is that disinclination some kind of mechanism protecting her from a potential creep?

When you don't want to go to the party that an acquaintance has invited you to, is that intuition preventing some unforeseen social tragedy or anxiety preventing the vulnerability of putting yourself out there?

When I feel nauseated at the thought of driving and want to hand the keys over to someone else—anyone else—is that a big "no" presaging a horrible accident? Or is it because I was actually in a horrible accident decades ago, and painful memories of it are still real in my body?

This is such a ubiquitous conundrum that it often comes up as a meme in my feed: a woman puzzling over equations on a whiteboard, with a caption to the effect of "Is it anxiety or intuition?"

In the end, I didn't apply for the job. My intuition had been pushing me in a different direction, one that felt less fraught. The brass rings I'd been taught to reach for no longer felt like they fit me. I was coming to know myself in a new way, and uncharted pathways were opening up. The days I craved now looked different from what I thought I had wanted. This is one thread of what intuition is for: to align one's external life more closely to the internal. So how can we become more like Melissa, who uses intuition to simply live better? Let's start with the origin point of both our anxiety and our intuition, my friend, my tormentor—the brain.

CHAPTER 2

BECOMING EXPERTS IN OURSELVES

As a goalkeeper, Briana Scurry never looked at her opponent as she approached in a penalty kick. Having played professionally and on Olympic teams, at pivotal moments, she says, "my MO is to not even look and just focus on what I need to do, on my preparation for everything." But in the championship Women's World Cup game in 1999, the US women's team was tied with China and the game came down to a shootout. Scurry had missed the first two kicks. On the third kick, facing Liu Ying, Scurry did something differently.

"As I was walking into the penalty area to present myself for the save, I heard something in my mind say *look*," Scurry says. She heeded the call. "I watched her approach the penalty spot, which is something that I didn't normally do, and I knew right then that that was the one I was going to save."

In that split second before Ying kicked, Scurry says, "time slowed down. Everything she did was slow motion and very clear. She opened her hips up, she approached short from the same side, I saw the inside of her foot she was using, so I knew exactly where she was going before she kicked the ball."

The way Scurry describes the experience, it sounds like magic. And perhaps it was. But Scurry was also relying on something else: her expertise. This is the intuition of blood, sweat, and tears, the intuition of ten thousand hours of experience, of what Malcolm Glad-well, in *Blink*, calls "rapid cognition." To mere mortals, Scurry's save looks like the work of the gods. But to the neuroscientists who study intuition, the save is pattern recognition at the highest, fastest, most optimized level.

—

As I did research for this book, I noticed right away that scientists and psychics alike study and use intuition. Can they possibly be talking about the same thing? While a psychic might contend that intuition is the province of the spirit, neuroscientists attribute it to the brain.

Neuroscientist Patrick House describes the brain thusly: "a thrift-store bin of evolutionary hacks Russian-dolled into a watery, salty piñata we call a head." Our brain's main job is to keep us alive, and recognizing patterns rapidly is an evolutionary asset. So, to neuro-scientists, intuition is pattern recognition and memory retrieval that happens superfast, below the level of our consciousness, and often results in biofeedback (sweaty palms, a lump forming in your throat, a wave of nausea). Our brains process the data and spit it out in sweat and feelings. Our minds make meaning from it. Our bodies are inextricably linked to it all. Attempting to locate an Intuition Central in the brain is kind of a fool's errand (one this fool spent many hours trying to find) because of the complex and dynamic interplay of the human beast.

We'd like to think of our brains as computer processing hard-ware, but it's much more complicated than that. University of Sus-sex neuroscientist Anil Seth describes it this way: "I use the word *wetware* to underline that brains are not computers made of meat. They are chemical machines as much as they are electrical networks. Every brain that has ever existed has been part of a living body, em-bedded in and interacting with its environment—an environment which in many cases contains embodied brains." This is scientist-speak to say that all things are connected, and brains do not exist in isolation, literally or figuratively. But examining some functions of the brain—or, more specifically, how scientists who study the brain think about intuition—provides one level of understanding how we know without knowing why.

Today, neuroscientists divide the brain into three broad regions. The first is the so-called reptilian brain, our oldest ancestral inheritance, located at the very base of the cortex. All vertebrates, from birds in the sky to fish in the sea, share these structures, which are responsible for our most primitive processes and responses. The second is the more sophisticated limbic system, which deals with social and emotional processing. And above the limbic system is the neocortex, where higher-order brain function takes place, like sensory perception, cognition, motor commands, spatial reasoning, and language.

How is intuition different from instinct? Was it Scurry's instinct that told her to look up at the kicker in that fateful match, or her intuition? I ask John Allman, a California Institute of Technology neuroscientist and the recipient of something called a Golden Brain Award. He is an eminence in the field of evolutionary and organismal biology. I spent one of the more humiliating hours of my life asking Dr. Allman to explain the difference between instinct and intuition.

Both take place without a great deal of conscious deliberation. But instinct, he tells me, is "genetically programmed behavior necessary for survival." Dogs shake when they are wet, turtles hatch on the beach and make their way to the sea, birds fly south for the winter. Humans have fight-or-flight responses deeply encoded in the amygdala. The difference for humans, with our instinctual behaviors, is that fighting or fleeing is not always precisely applied, and can cause problems in relationships. (See: conflict avoidance and overly defensive protective behaviors.)

Intuition, on the other hand, also "does not require conscious intervention" but "has a strong learned component to it," Allman says. Here he refers to social intuition and emotional intelligence. His research has pinpointed a group of neurons located in the anterior cingulate cortex and the frontal insular cortex. These are the von Economo neurons (VENs), also known as intuition neurons. They are four times the size of other brain cells and are present in great apes but not smaller monkeys. These neurons essentially allow large mammals to read social situations and cues and inform their owner what to do, intuitively. "The von Economo neurons may relay a fast intuitive assessment of complex social situations to facilitate the rapid adjustment of behavior in quickly changing social situations," Allman says.

Human babies arrive with few VENs and go on to develop them within the first four years of life, acquiring far more than other large mammals. "It is as if the infant is in no need of intuition until they become more socially independent, and only need to learn behaviors that are adaptive in socially complex settings," he says.

Allman studied the brains of people diagnosed with frontotemporal dementia, a type of dementia that results in a loss of empathy—basically, when Grandpa loses all filter and starts telling everyone how he really feels. They become estranged from family and friends and make poor decisions. In looking at these people's brains, Allman and colleagues noted a denigration of VEN cells, suggesting that these large mammalian cells are responsible for our social graces. Similarly, people diagnosed with autism seem to have a deficit of VENs.

Social intuition isn't the first definition that came to mind for me. And yet this kind of rapid knowing what to do, applied in social settings, is an area of intuition that neuroscience concerns itself with, perhaps because it is more readily explainable and measurable. If you were to think of someone who is socially intuitive, some of the adjectives that would come to mind might include *easy, organic, natural, fluid, comforting*, and *knowing just what to say and do*. You might apply the same adjectives to what you consider when you think of intuition in your life, whether that's knowing what to eat for lunch or when to leave a relationship. This information can come in quick, fully formed, and without much deliberation. It speaks to the compelling wonder of the subject that the hardest of scientists, someone with a literal Golden Brain and a lab at Caltech, studies "intuition," as do spiritual charlatans self-publishing in Comic Sans. I admit this is part of the pull for me to try to unpack it all.

Another place in the Venn diagram where the spiritual and the scientific seem to overlap is in the experience of the flow state. Flow is that peak human experience in which your brain and your body are fully united in tackling the task at hand and time seems to dissolve. Unlike just zoning out or hyperfocusing on something, the flow state is ecstatic—people have described their flow experiences as imparting a sense of clarity and of obstacles melting away, and imbuing a lasting sense of fulfillment to life beyond the activity itself. Here we seem primed to experience excellent intuitions. Briana Scurry making her game-winning saves in the 1999 Women's World Cup is an example. Musicians, dancers, chess players, and mountain climbers have all described themselves as entering a state of flow when they are carrying out their work, fully immersed in the moment. Perhaps you've experienced flow performing in a play or gardening in your backyard or surfing in the ocean.

Researchers have found that in order to get into the flow zone, the right activity is crucial: you need to care about what you're doing, it can't be too easy or too hard, it should be something you're good at, and your mindset should be about the process itself, not the ultimate result. I've found flow when riding a bike, hiking, and, on the rare occasion, in my writing. Hobbies are a good place to start: you already like the activity and probably don't seek out distractions, which are enemy number one to flow. Experiencing these activities in your most focused time of day (morning for me) and working in some recovery time to detach from work and responsibilities allow you to slip into flow more readily. Taking stock of when and how flow occurs for you is the first step in integrating more of these moments into daily life.

But on top of entering the downright pleasurable and life-affirming state of flow, this is also a place where we are more receptive to intuition. Some psychologists are building on the state of flow as an "optimal experience," as the originator of the idea, Mihaly Csikszentmihalyi, referred to it. More than just being in the zone, being in flow can be characterized by "a dynamic cascade of insight." In plain English, it is in these receptive yet engaged states that we are more prone to "aha!" moments. It's the reason why you are more likely to come up with a good idea for a presentation when out on a walk than toiling in front of your computer. Effortlessness is a hallmark of an intuitive insight. Psychologist Robin Hogarth defined an intuitive burst as one that is "reached with little apparent effort and typically without conscious awareness. They involve little or no conscious deliberation." It's no mistake that Scurry was already in that heightened flow state when she heard the call, out of nowhere, to break with her typical practice and look at her opponent walking up to the ball. Being in the zone allowed her to receive that intuition, effortlessly, and make a career-defining save.

Intuitions originating from flow seem to be the exception that proves the rule of pattern recognition—here we find ourselves so deeply engaged that we are able to disrupt our habitual, ingrained patterns to arrive at something deeper. Intuition is pattern recognition, yes, but it seems to be something more, too. If it were only pattern recognition, then artificial intelligence should have perfect intuition. When the Writers Guild went on strike in 2023, in part to demand protections against AI taking their writing jobs, a sign on the picket line reflected the problem. Alluding to the famous "I'll have what she's having" line in Katz's Deli in *When Harry Met Sally*, the sign presented an alternate version that AI might have concocted: "I'll have what she's eating." It hits different. It is a wooden translation of human experience. I wonder if this might be because AI lacks intuition, a most human quality.

I speak with Matt Lindauer, a professor of philosophy and psychology at CUNY, who spends a lot of time thinking about how people conceive of right and wrong. He is working with AI companies to get our robot counterparts to consider the same thing. As Lindauer explains, "AI is going to make various decisions. How should those decisions be made? Should they be made in utility-maximizing ways, like what would be best for the world overall? Should they focus on respecting human rights?" Hope so!

When I press him on why AI still feels so robotic, so unintuitive, Lindauer gives a most poetic answer: "We're really a product of all the other people that we've ever interacted with and inherited genes from, and all of the cultural moments and books and of all the things that we've read. Those are the things that give rise to the shared repertoire that we've drawn on in a conversation like this. And so machines can sit on a network, but they can never be a part of the same number of experiences and sightings of the world."

AI is coded pattern recognition. These models are trained to process data and respond based on rules and patterns they have been taught. And yet, while it is getting better by the moment, AI still lacks the natural fluidity that humans possess. Intuition perhaps illustrates the difference between intelligence and consciousness. Perhaps intuition, like consciousness, is an essential trait of being alive. This makes me think that intuition can't be just pattern recognition, or else AI would have it mastered. Intuition must be something else then, too, something that the brain alone cannot account for. Maybe by the time this book comes out, AI will have evolved past pattern recognition, but this current deficit shows us something about what intuition feels like.

———

Margaret Sheridan is a neuroscience professor at UNC–Chapel Hill who studies "scaring small children," as she tells me. She is the director of the Child Imaging Research on Cognition and Life Experiences (CIRCLE) Lab, which uses neuroimaging and interviews to study how early life experiences ranging from poverty to maltreatment to institutionalization impact neural development. One phenomenon she studies is fear learning. "What science has shown is that if you pair a regular stimulus that is not scary, like an orange square, with something that is scary, like a loud noise or a shock, over time when you see that orange square your body will prepare for that shock," Sheridan says. It's like a Pavlovian response in reverse, a clenching aversion instead of desire.

"Your palms will get sweaty at a very low level," she continues. "And it can happen even if you're unaware cognitively that it's going to occur. You can say you're not having a response, but your body will know." Fear learning can look like intuition: you begin to brace when the orange square shows up, intuiting that something bad is about to go down. Sheridan's research on children aged four and five shows that those who have grown up in threatening environments acquire fear learning earlier than kids who grow up in more tranquility.

A seminal 2002 study by Seth D. Pollak and Pawan Sinha reflects this. They presented a group of physically abused children a spectrum of fourteen faces. Face 1 was completely blurred, and at regular intervals resolved to a completely clear Face 14, which revealed the visage of an angry man: furrowed brows, tightened jaw, pursed lips. Physically abused children accurately recognized angry facial expressions earlier and with less information than the control group, children who were not abused. Meaning the abused children could more rapidly detect anger on a pixelated face that was imperceptible to children who had grown up in safety.

As Sheridan explains, "If you can detect emotion in faces earlier on than anybody else, that can be experienced as intuition." Reading microexpressions on a human face is an adaptive trait developed to protect oneself. But it also looks like intuition—presaging anger before it fully erupts. As a matter of survival, the children Sheridan studies have become experts in the human face.

—

What laypeople might call intuition, some scientists call expertise. Maria Konnikova, bestselling author, Columbia psychology PhD, and late-in-life professional poker player, explains: "Intuition is basically another term for incredible domain expertise. Let's apply this to poker. I have found myself in situations where I have a gut feeling my opponent is bluffing. I can never trust that gut feeling, because I've been playing poker for all of a few years. I do not have the domain expertise. But my coach, Erik Seidel, has been playing poker since the 1980s. So if he has a gut feeling, he should actually trust that."

Because that gut feeling, she tells me, is actually something else entirely: "That's hundreds of thousands of hours of practice he has put in, hundreds of thousands of hands. If he thinks a guy is bluffing, that's not intuition. That's pattern recognition."

Truly, and yet Konnikova, more novice than Seidel, still gets intuitive feelings at the poker table all the time. So how to know if and when we should act on what feels like an intuitive impulse?

"I would try to figure out why am I making this decision, whether it's calling or folding or raising," she says. "How reliable is the information? What is my degree of confidence? Sometimes I really don't like the guy and I just want a reason to call, so I decide he's bluffing. But that's not a good reason. You have to constantly learn to go back and be attentive to your own thought process and the factors you're using to make a decision."

The utility of pattern recognition and domain expertise extends far beyond the poker table. When one has mastered their area of expertise and integrated their wisdom into their very being, drawing upon it at the critical moment can appear almost miraculous to the untrained eye. Dr. Matthew Wheatley is an attending physician at Grady Memorial Hospital, in Atlanta. He tells me a story about an older man who came to him with a bad septic infection. The patient arrived via ambulance, and by the time Wheatley and his team saw him, his blood pressure was stable. But Wheatley saw something else. "I told my residents that his heart rate was about to fall off a cliff," he recalls. "We acted quickly and got some invasive lines in so we could give him medicines to stabilize his blood pressure."

Wheatley assures me that he had this intuition not because he is a soothsayer, but because he had been there before. "Often the ambulance, the flurry of activity, getting IVs in can make a patient's cortisol levels spike," he says. "Sometimes we get reassured by those initial vitals and then a nurse will come running in to say that the blood pressure has dropped. You don't want to get behind the eight ball."

When Wheatley was a resident, a mentor taught him that a lot of ER medicine is pattern recognition: *I've seen a patient like this before—what did I do in that case?* You use your successes, but also your failures." After the years of reps he's amassed, tapping into that body of experience happens instantaneously. In his book *How Doctors Think*, Dr. Jerome Groopman concurs: "Clinical intuition is a complex sense that becomes refined over years and years of practice, listening to literally thousands of patients' stories, examining thousands of patients, and, most importantly, remembering when you were wrong."

I experienced this kind of clinical intuition firsthand in an exam with my dermatologist. I have a history of melanoma in my family, so every six months I put on a paper robe for Susanna Franks, at Washington Square Dermatology. One time, she was going over my left forearm with her dermatoscope and kept returning to a mole. She'd look at it and move on to another section, then like whiplash be drawn back to the suspicious spot a few seconds later. She did this several times, jerking back to the spot in a way that seemed almost beyond her control. "I just don't like that one," I remember her saying. Her clinical intuition was right. The cells in that mole turned out to be cancerous, and less than a month later I was in surgery to have the spot removed.

—

It's a warm September Friday evening when I meet Sheridan and her colleagues from the UNC–Chapel Hill Psychology and Neuroscience Department for dinner. I sit down with Sheridan, Kristen Lindquist,

Jessica Cohen, Keely Muscatell, and Eva Telzer. All have young children, ranging in age from six months to seven years. From this dinner table, the field of neuroscience looks like a matriarchy. (After a few more rounds of cocktails and glasses of wine, they quickly disabuse my innocence—it ain't.)

We are gathered here this evening to discuss all things intuition from a brain science perspective. For me, having failed most every math and science course I have ever attempted—in college I scored so low on a math placement exam that I had to take a remedial course about robots; not AI, more like R2-D2, literally, as one student did her final project on "famous robots from movies"—it feels like having a private audience with NASA.

We put in an order for appetizers, and I ask them for their scientific definition of intuition, and whether it might diverge from their personal definition, gleaned through lived experience.

"Gut reactions?" offers Telzer. "I actually don't think I have a single definition, because it's more of an *intuitive* thing," she says, laughing.

The professors offer explanations for the mechanisms underlying intuition: "Unconscious processing," I hear. "Memory activation!" Muscatell distills it down: "It's prediction. You enter a situation and your brain makes predictions based on what has happened before so you don't have to stop and think about it." And yet, she notes, "that's not quite intuition either, because prediction is happening all the time. But intuition usually has an emotional valence."

What our brains choose to remember, or memory bias, plays an enormous role in what we consider intuitive hits. "I think a large part of intuition is a random physiological sensation you interpret," Cohen says. "Maybe you're right, maybe you're wrong. But when you are right you remember it, and when you are wrong you forget it."

Sheridan shares a memory about a phase of life in which she felt especially intuitive: her early clinical practice, when she saw patients as a psychologist and felt almost as if she could read their minds to say the right thing, to give them what they needed in the moment. "I could enter the room and know people are upset," she recalls. Upon advancing in her training, however, "I realized I was just good at seeing microexpressions."

This is the training in which these doctors have been immersed: examining a human phenomenon by breaking it down into tinier and tinier pieces to explain the whole. Telzer breaks it down further: "There's something magical to thinking intuition is"—she pauses, searching for the precise word—"interesting," she concludes, laughing wryly. The neuroscientists chuckle in recognition. Their world is not one of magic and mysticism, the language in which intuition is often cloaked. "It feels intuitive and deep, when it is probably just knowledge and memories and what you pay attention to," Telzer says.

Humans, it turns out, are especially adept at paying attention to faces. So much so that there is an area of the brain that scientists have been fighting over for some time: the fusiform face area, or FFA.

"It's in the temporal lobe," Cohen tells me.

"Right here!" Lindquist says, touching the left side of my head above my ear, which is actually very helpful. "The whole debate is over whether this area is about faces or expertise." Meaning: Is the FFA solely for studying and storing faces, or is it a center of specialized knowledge? A 2007 MIT paper showed that shepherds with impaired facial recognition could still tell members of their herd apart from other nearby sheep, indicating that the FFA is really a center for storing expertise, whatever one's specific expertise may be.

"So which is it?" I ask.

"*Expertise!*" the table concurs.

"The people who think there's a part of our brains we are born with just to process faces?" Sheridan says, a few glasses deep. "Imagine organizing a brain. Can you imagine having one cell, or one area, for each thing? That's not a good choice! I just want to say for the record, it's an offensive idea."

"If you're blind, the FFA does totally different things," Lindquist adds.

So, expertise. Expertise that happens superfast, without our knowing—just like Maria Konnikova, who would fit in extremely well at this table, told me. Or, as cognitive neuroscientist Sarah Laszlo puts it, intuition is "practicing so much it feels like magic."

If intuition is equivalent to expertise, then we must become experts in ourselves. And if intuition is, according to science, pattern recognition, then we must begin to recognize our own patterns. This is the first step in untangling anxiety from intuition.

———

Where do you go when things become uncertain? I mean mentally. It can be really complicated. In later chapters I will talk more about trauma responses, but right now I invite you to think about your bespoke patterns of mind. Cognitive behavioral therapy (CBT) is a mode of identifying thought distortions, as described here. These include all-or-nothing thinking (seeing things in black and white), jumping to conclusions, and personalization. What is the specific flavor of *your* bad inner monologue?

For me, it's catastrophizing (see: *We're fucked*). I can imagine the worst possible outcome to any benign, or even positive, scenario. The hotel won't have my reservation. The flight will be canceled. My kid won't be able to go to preschool in the fall because he will not figure out the mechanics of his bladder and the potty in time, thus initiating him into a life of crime. And I then of course apply this apocalyptic filter to myself and my shortcomings. This is just what my brain does. In its misguided way, I think it's trying to inoculate me against any of these eventualities. If I can imagine the doomsday scenario, then I can prep for it mentally. This, of course, never works. It only puts me on edge and prevents me from experiencing life as it is when my tendency is to white-knuckle it, always on the lookout for what can and will go wrong. It sucks, but it's what many hours of therapy and reams of those CBT worksheets have revealed.

Since I know this is my habit, I have to be very skeptical of any "intuition" suggesting the worst. If a thought comes to me like *My husband will leave me*, or *everyone hates me*, or *I will live in this park-*

THOUGHT DISTORTIONS

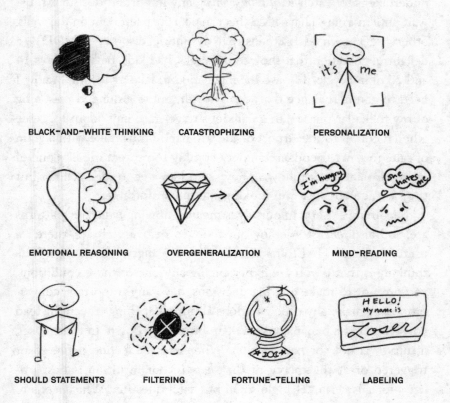

BLACK-AND-WHITE THINKING	**CATASTROPHIZING**	**PERSONALIZATION**
EMOTIONAL REASONING	**OVERGENERALIZATION**	**MIND-READING**
SHOULD STATEMENTS	**FILTERING**	**FORTUNE-TELLING** **LABELING**

ing garage forever, that thought is very unlikely to possess any useful truth, other than to alert me to my sense of unease in that moment. If the punch line is "I'm fucked," the windup is anxiety, not intuition.

But here's the tricky thing: when you stop and gaze out at the world before you, with fascism and roasting global temperatures and people being mean to one another online, then catastrophe is, indeed, real. But how can we approach it more skillfully?

Examining and naming thought distortions is one way to become an expert in our patterns. But we also face a whole other suite of circumstantial challenges that contribute to a delicate mental state. When are you an unreliable narrator? My thinking is not clear at nighttime—

I'm exhausted from the day, and the most intellectual endeavor I can undertake is to watch *Real Housewives*; any important decisions must wait until morning. I have PMS that can peel the paint right off the walls, otherwise known as premenstrual dysphoric disorder (PMDD)—a delightful condition that showed up after I had kids. Between days 14 and 28 of my cycle, if I have the inclination to fake my death, I know I need to counterbalance that idea with the more grounded reasoning of my follicular phase. I'm an anxious traveler, so any doom I foresee when it comes to the airport or the trip itself I must take with a grain of salt. You, my friend, are anxiety coming to protect me like one of those airplane neck pillows. They seem like a good idea at first, but they are actually just foul-looking and uncomfortable.

Becoming experts in ourselves means knowing *what* our patterns are, and also *when* to deploy our tools. In recovery circles, there's a useful acronym: HALT. It stands for "hungry, angry, lonely, tired." The thinking is that if you are experiencing any one of these conditions, you are not to make any big decisions, have any important conversations, or make any proclamations about what things mean. Instead you are to eat a banana, take a deep breath, lie down. In these cases, intuition is not for prescription. When we are feeling depleted or triggered or at the mercy of the *shoulds*, our intuition is best utilized for answering a single small but vital question: What needs to happen next? Literally, in this moment, the moment after that. The answer is unlikely to be to move to Portugal or get a divorce. More likely, it's to drink a glass of water. To log off. To rest. Here, intuition is for triage. What is the next, most vital, caring step I can take? Intuition can be hugely cosmic and sweeping, like getting information from spirit guides about how best to live your life. But it can also be as straightforward as guiding you to your very next action. Intuition, at its most essential, can help lead us back to equilibrium. And from that place we can make clearer, more informed decisions.

HALT is incredibly useful when it comes to the anxiety/intuition dilemma too. In addition to these four categories, what is your personal profile of circumstances that cloud your thinking? One friend says that when she hasn't exercised for a few days, she will be keyed up and on edge. Another says that when her digestion is off, everything is off.

So when we are experiencing HALT or any of its cousins, intuition is not for diagnosis. Instead, it should be for triage. Resist any invitations to big action when you are under the influence of HALT. Don't have the conversation, even if you feel a strong urge to tell your boss what you really think of her. Instead, use your intuition to answer the very simple question "What needs to happen next?" This might be as simple as realizing you've been holding it for hours and need to visit the ladies' room. You might need to close your laptop and stare into the middle distance for three minutes. You very likely need to get off your phone and have a snack. Here, in these instances, we can use our intuition to bring us back to peace, not to solve big problems. They will be waiting there for us to engage with wisely and intuitively once we have reached a more even keel.

Melissa Coss Aquino explains how this everyday intuition shows up for her. "There's definitely more pattern recognition," she says. "I notice when I'm tired and when grinding on work instead of just going to bed means I'm going to have to do the thing twice." Her intuitive practice is pretty simple: "It's part of the tool kit of every day. I feel like you have better days because you don't bully yourself into doing all the things and you intuitively do the things that are a priority. You check in with yourself: *The real priority today is* . . . and you follow that."

What if intuition is actually this pragmatic? What if honing our intuition, following the gut, rather than being an airy-fairy spiritual pursuit, is actually the most grounded, realistic strategy for life? Life happens in days. I want more better days.

—

During my time in North Carolina, Sheridan and I have a conversation one afternoon about the amygdala, which is really a conversation about our essential human conundrum: how we grasp for certainty in a very uncertain world. We are walking from the Psychology and Neuroscience Department to the medical school so I can get into the fMRI machine to see the inner workings of my brain, to confirm once and for all whether it is composed entirely of jelly beans. She's wheeling a giant electric bicycle on which she ferries her children around town.

We often hear the amygdala being called "the lizard brain." It is almond-shaped and about the size of a peanut, nestled deep inside the lower region of the brain. It accounts for less than 0.3 percent of the brain's volume but initiates much of our emotional landscape. This is the place in the brain that, when our ancestors were stalked by predators on the savanna, would inspire them to fight, flee, or freeze. But over the course of our many hundreds of millions of years on earth, the amygdala has developed to do more than just determine our response to danger: we use it in all kinds of situations when things are uncertain. Here's the bad news: things are always uncertain.

In order to sort out the difference between anxiety and intuition, we first need to better appreciate the relationship between anxiety and uncertainty. A central tension in our human predicament is that humans really don't care for uncertainty, and yet we live in an uncertain world. We like patterns and knowing what comes next. This is simply not always possible. Where information is incomplete, we tend to fill in the blanks. And so we feel anxious. Our amygdalae compensate by trying to soothe us into a sense of comfort by grasping when and where they can.

"I think that's why we love Google Maps," Sheridan says. "You know where you're going, but you can also just plug the address into your app and be sure. It's also why we love texting to tell your friend you're almost there. No one needs to know that, but we love it. We've created these tools to decrease our uncertainty."

Honoring our response to uncertainty is the first step toward developing better intuition. Neuroscientists can't quite land on a single, streamlined definition of intuition but this relationship with uncertainty is a most essential human experience. To be human is to confront uncertainty. It is the most constant force in the universe—and the most annoying to our little human brains. Uncertainty is ubiquitous.

And I don't mean the big, brooding questions about the kind of uncertainty where you wonder whether you will ever meet your match or if you're in the right career or if you will one day have kids. What I'm talking about is the urge and instinct to find solid ground in the form of checking, checking, checking.

Checking your email. Googling the average duration of the common cold. Texting your friend to see if they made it home safely. Confirming the time of the fitness class you take every week at the same time. Looking up the weather instead of looking outside. Making sure the kids are breathing at night.

The list is truly endless.

When this checking goes into overdrive, you get conditions like obsessive-compulsive disorder, in which people find uncertainty intolerable and go to great lengths to soothe themselves in the constant quake of life.

The amygdala gets reduced to "the lizard brain," but have you ever watched a lizard sun itself on a rock? They are pure presence, sucking up the heat with eyelids at half-mast.

Our sweet little amygdalae just want to keep us alive, and they do so by pushing us to go see what that rustling is or, more often, seek out some piece of information that will momentarily put us at ease. The problem is that there will only be more uncertainty in the very next moment.

The American Buddhist nun and intellectual Pema Chödrön puts it like this: "The source of our unease is the unfulfillable longing for a lasting certainty and security, for something solid to hold on to. Unconsciously we expect that if we could just get the right job, the right partner, the right *something*, our lives would run smoothly. When anything unexpected or not to our liking happens, we think something has gone wrong." But what we don't realize is that *nothing* has gone wrong; we are just unsettled by uncertainty and are always on the lookout for the thing that will ease our spirits. Because of this tendency, we miss a lot. As writer Mark Nepo notes, "We are the only creatures that seek out guarantees, and in so doing, we snuff the spark that is discovery." Author Brené Brown sees that ambiguity as an integral part of intuition, which she defines as "our ability to hold space for uncertainty and our willingness to trust the many ways we've developed knowledge and insight, including instinct, experience, faith, and reason."

Uncertainty is fact. It doesn't mean there is anything wrong. Sometimes we can be with it. Standing at the shoreline, feeling the tide suck the sand from under your soles. The sun beaming, and then gauzed over by wispy clouds. The glitter, the wind whipping and switching directions, the sandpipers zipping toward and away from the waves. It's always changing, and in those rare instances we don't mind. All the parts converge, and depart, and we feel our tiny place in nature.

But this happens, what, once a year? Twice? You, standing on the beach, not trying to change the shifting tides. The crucial reason these moments of transcendence stand out is because we are not trying to do anything about them. We accept them as perfect in their liquid movements.

Now imagine you are on the same shoreline and, instead of feeling the pleasant pull of sand underneath your feet, you start googling "sand pull accidents." With every movement of the clouds and the sun, you adjust your sunglasses and hat according to the glare. Instead of soaking in the fabulous roll of glitter across the waves, you take out your phone and try to capture it to be saved in a library of videos you'll never watch. You angle your body against the wind or try to measure the force of it with your phone every time it changes direction. You run toward and away from the sandpipers as they go, and they come to see you as a threat and take their nervy party to a more distant shore.

That may sound like you at the beach, because it sure as hell is me, a lot of the time, correcting for temperature dips and crests, the movement of the sun. The changing seascape is one of shifting, of flight, wind, tide. Of uncertainty. That's not the stressful part. The anxiety comes from the activity we layer on top of it in order to catch it, and, in doing so, we smother it.

Uncertainty feels like the problem. But really it is our short-sighted self-soothing that creates the bulk of anxiety.

I think that, to improve our intuition, we need to get better at living in and being with uncertainty. What if we didn't pathologize our discomfort with uncertainty as "anxiety," but came to see it as an organic, ancient response? What if we could cultivate some level of comfort around knowing that this is our great human inheritance, as well as our great human challenge? Maybe even as teeming with possibility? In 1844, Søren Kierkegaard characterized anxiety as the "dizziness of freedom." Anxiety, from his point of view, was our nat-ural wonder at the potential we can realize.

To train our intuition, let's first quell our anxiety to get attuned to our birthright of uncertainty. John Keats defined negative capa-bility as cultivating comfort with intellectual ambiguity. That's hard on its own. I'm talking about the uncertainty of our body, mood, and mind in this very moment. Just realizing, and deeply knowing, that uncertainty is going to happen, instead of being bombarded by it at every turn. We will never feel fully comfortable with uncertainty; we are not built for that. But we can recognize discomfort with uncer-tainty when it is happening. When I start to spiral, even just saying the word *uncertainty* brings me back.

Often when I am at the gym, in a class lifting weights or kicking a leg up into the air in yoga, I'm thinking about one thing: the next time I can get to the gym. I do complicated equations, trying to see my cal-endar in my mind—I could go to Barre on Tuesday after school drop-off if I pack all my work stuff with me and ride my bike. Or I could dress in proper clothes, work first, and do a Mirror workout at three thirty and be home in time to shower for five. I know now, after years of doing this, that the plans I lay for future workouts during current workouts almost never come to fruition. Someone is sick, something comes up—the day comes around and tells me what is possible, rather than the other way around. I know this. And yet I so desperately want to be certain about the next time I can generate some endorphins, so as not to burn the house down or yell at strangers.

I sometimes think about the raw kilocalories I burn in my brain with all this military-level strategy that never sees any battlefield. I have an inkling that if I could just stay with the uncertain, which is another way of saying *be present*, I could save myself a lot of energy and be less likely to burn the house down to begin with. If I could roll with uncertainty, I might then be better able to hear my intuition.

So what if I just try, try, try something else when I see my mental generals plotting their battle strategy? There you are, amygdala, doing your little safety dance. I can try to respect it instead of hating it or, worse yet, obeying it, and pulling out color-coded pens and systems to create a certainty that is as brittle as a toothpick castle. I can get more comfortable with uncertainty to help me better differentiate between anxiety and intuition.

Anxiety has a lot of scurrying around it. A lot of googling, checking, cross-referencing, confirming, double-checking, triple-checking. It is hard to stay present because it feels so uncertain. The future, with all its idealized better-than-now-ness, is more fixed in some ways. Because it isn't real.

I think my tendency to seek certainty is the hardest habit for me to abandon as I try to get more intuitive.

But this intersection of expertise—of knowing oneself—and how we live with uncertainty is where the rubber meets the road, and where the scientists have something to teach us about how we experience intuition, even if they might not say it as such.

—

"Brains hate uncertainty," Lindquist says at dinner.

"Is the human experience about finding different ways to cope with uncertainty?" I ask the group.

They all hard agree.

"All of religion is that," Sheridan says.

"All of science is that," I counter.

"Morality is that," Sheridan continues. *"If this happens, do that.* Uncertainty sucks!"

"But it's also the most exciting part about being human," Telzer says. "The excitement is in the not knowing, in getting to try things out. And there are different types of uncertainty—there's uncertain threat, which we don't like, and uncertain reward, which we do like, the excitement of potential reward."

Coping with uncertainty is what makes me anxious, but this dinner is making me realize that I can become an expert in my own patterns and learn to be more intuitive about what is real and what is ambient anxiety. Learning the anatomical and evolutionary reality of these feelings is incredibly helpful. It externalizes these feelings that live inside me, that sometimes feel unbearable and out of control. Instead I can thank my sweet little overactive amygdala for trying to keep me safe and certain, even though there is no such thing, really. When I feel the urge to check the gym schedule yet again, I can instead just send a shout-out of praise to my amygdala, one of the oldest parts of this bag of bones, for doing its job passionately, if overzealously.

According to the neuroscientists, intuition includes but is not limited to: confirmation and memory bias, pattern recognition, domain expertise, microexpressions, fear learning, and memory activation occurring below the level of conscious understanding. It's cool, sure, but so is everything the brain does. "I don't begrudge people for calling these processes intuition," Muscatell says. "I don't attribute it to a higher power or anything mystic. But that's the privilege of science. We know how to explain this thing."

Pattern recognition and domain expertise are one way to understand intuition. Applying those principles in cultivating expertise about our patterns is one way in. We must first become experts in ourselves to discern what anxiety feels like, in contradistinction to intuition. And that, in itself, can be a life's work. Novelist Sally Franson, who grew up in an abusive household, explains how she has learned to differentiate her *yes* from her *no*. "It's actually pretty complicated," she tells me. "A *no* in my body can mean a *no* in the present moment, or it can mean *no* to a past moment that I'm being reminded of. I'll have to take time and space to figure it out." Similarly, learning her *yes* has taken time. "Sometimes my body will say *yes*, but it's an icky *yes* where I'm repeating fucked-up patterns. That's not the kind of authentic *yes* I'm talking about." Now, after years of working on it, when she gets a *yes*, it's "a sense of joy and connection and possibility and love. It feels like a blooming, a whole-bodied, wholehearted, open-throated *yes*." It's taken years of becoming an expert in herself, and in learning her patterns, but, she says, "I can trust my *yes*es now."

That kind of personal pattern recognition and cultivating expertise in oneself—and about what we do with uncertainty—is just one facet of an incredibly complex diamond. Once we better appreciate our sweet yet misguided quest for certainty, we can begin to make better decisions.

CHAPTER 3

THE LIMITS OF RATIONALITY

I catch up with Penny Jones* two weeks after her divorce was final-ized. Her two children, ages eleven and nine, are out of the house so she can speak openly.

Jones is an academic who lives in an artsy college town. She had been married for more than a decade when she found out her hus-band had been lying to her for years about his whereabouts—an out-of-town work trip that was in fact a days-long orgy, for example. Her husband went to great lengths to cover this up. She unlocked a trove of his online activities when she happened across an alias he had been using that sounded weirdly familiar. All of this came to light in February 2020.

Jones experienced a nightmare: *The life you have been living is a lie. The person closest to you is not who you understand them to be.* The past years had been false; every feeling, every interaction, every story had to be reevaluated. She has been through hell. So where was her intuition in those decades? And where is it now?

"Of course I had suspicions," she tells me. "And once, years ear-lier, I found something." She and her husband had gone to visit his parents with their children, then one and three years old. They

---

* Name and identifying details changed.

spent a few days at her in-laws' home before going on a camping trip. During the night, her husband would disappear for hours. "He told me he was driving around, visiting old places," Jones recalls. She accepted it. She had two young kids and was feeling worn thin. She wasn't that concerned. Plus, he'd never given her a reason not to trust him.

The grandparents' house didn't have cell phone service, so after putting the baby to bed, she logged on to her husband's computer to look something up. His browser revealed directions to a porn store where people also met up for sex.

She confronted him about it and he told her she was violating his privacy. "That drove him underground for years," she says. But there would be other suspicious incidents. Once, she came home from a conference and found all the blinds drawn. He explained it away by saying the house cleaner had come on a day she wasn't scheduled because he wanted Jones to come home to a tidy house. "It didn't sit right with me, but sometimes he would do really sweet things. He bought me a package of massages once when I was stressed with work," she recalls.

The amount of evidence she stumbled upon just before the pandemic was damning and disturbing. He couldn't deny his behavior, but it still didn't square with the person she knew. "He had been in AA for years, so he's supposed to be dedicated to a life of honesty. He was trying to start a #MeToo movement in our town, and then he's over here reviewing prostitutes online," she says. They immediately separated, but it took three years for the divorce to be finalized. He comes from a rich family and fought her on everything. All of this was happening while she was working full-time and caring for her kids in a pandemic. The trauma of the revelations hijacked her concentration and her inner life. "I couldn't read a book for two years," she says. "The profound dissonance between my supposed and actual life was all I could think about. It took everything I had to focus on the text enough to read a few pages of student papers."

So how does she make sense of all of this now? "I don't," she says. I get that. Some ruptures in our reality are simply too outrageous. But what of intuition? "I had it," she says. "I knew that something was wrong. I knew it as a fact of the world. I had intuitions about him at the time. But I let my rational mind override it. I would explain to myself why what he said made sense."

We have been led to believe that intuition is fanciful, and reasoned, rational thought is solid, grounded. Jones's experience, however, shows that intuition can be the hardest of evidence: she knew in her bones that something was amiss. Embroidering rationality over that profound personal knowing? That is the ultimate form of magical thinking. In these cases, our intuition bumps up against our desires. We want everything to be okay. We meet our distaste for uncertainty with a manufactured rationality.

—

We have been conditioned to believe that rationality is superior to intuition, and to see the two faculties of mind as opposed. In 1779, Benjamin Franklin wrote a letter to his nephew offering advice about choosing between two women to be his wife. It created the mold for rational decision-making going forth:

If you doubt, set down all the Reasons, pro and con, in opposite Columns of a Sheet of Paper, and when you have considered them two or three Days, perform an Operation similar to that in some questions of Algebra; observe what Reasons or Motives in each Column are equal in weight . . . and when you have struck out from both Sides all the Equalities, you will see in which column remains the Balance. . . . This kind of *Moral Algebra* I have often practiced in important and dubious Concerns, and tho' it cannot be mathematically exact, I have found it extreamly useful. By the way, if you do not learn it, I apprehend you will never be married.

This Enlightenment celebration of rationality is what we deem moral and right—Franklin characterizes it as such. Philosophers of the era preferred laborious problem-solving to organic, aha moments of insight. Immanuel Kant wrote that "reason acquires its possessions through work" and that the truth can be found only through "herculean effort." Franklin himself, though, realized the fallacy of believing you arrived at your outcome by reason alone. In his *Autobiography* he wrote, "So convenient a thing it is to be a *reasonable Creature*, since it enables one to find or make a Reason for everything one has a mind to do." In other words, you can tell yourself a story that you applied rationality, when really you chose what you wanted and then gave a post hoc explanation.

There is something to the pro-and-con list, no doubt. That exercise can inform a great many straightforward decisions: which dog leash to buy, whether one should spend a long weekend in Paris or Mexico City. But what about when the columns are equal in length? Or when we are trying to make a decision of the heart? A friend of Penny Jones's later told me that many times over the years, she would get together with Jones to make a pro-con list about her marriage. Was he a good father? Check. A good provider? Check. Together they rationalized away many red flags. How can we predict from a purely rational perspective the person with whom we spend our lives, or the best-suited career? How can we predict what will fulfill our future selves? Economist Russ Roberts writes in *Wild Problems*:

> To beat the traffic or develop a vaccine . . . we rely on data, algorithms that can be tested, and experiments that can be replicated. For certain problems—I call them tame problems—the relentless application of science, engineering, and rational thought leads to steady progress.

> But the big decisions we face in life, the wild problems—whether to marry, who to marry, whether to have children, what career

path to follow, how much time to devote to friends and family, how to resolve daily ethical dilemmas—these big decisions can't be made with data, or science, or the usual rational approaches . . .

But rationality is hard to define if you don't know what it's like to experience one of the choices you're facing.

Roberts emphasizes that we apply Franklinian comparisons at our own peril. For so many decisions we make, rational frameworks just don't apply. We need to better differentiate between tame problems and wild problems and use the framework that makes the most sense for the situation. And yet, as Franklin espoused, relying on the rational has a moral supremacy to it, even when it is not the appropriate lens through which to evaluate merits. When Jones attempted to apply the rational lens to her husband's behavior, she missed something major. Intuition is not irrational; it's extra-rational. It goes above and beyond what the certainty-seeking amygdala can see.

—

One of the most influential theories of thinking and decision-making in the twenty-first century comes from Nobel Prize–winning organizational psychologist Daniel Kahneman. Kahneman's dual-processing model of cognition argues that intuition and reason are two distinct modes of processing information. System 1, intuition, is reflexive, fast, automatic, nonconscious, effortless, holistic, nonverbal, affect-laden (meaning we have feelings about *it*, whatever *it* is), self-evident, inferential, experimental, and imagistic. It is "a neural process that can 'cut through' details and quickly arrive at a conclusion in a socially complex setting." (I imagine those VEN neurons firing away here.)

System 2, on the other hand, is rational, reasoned thought. It is slow, conscious, effortful, detail-oriented, mentally taxing, verbal and declarative, affectively neutral, hypothetical, diagnostic, and limited in scope. System 2 is the linear, step-by-step processing that Franklin advocated.

The problem with the rational System 2, as Kahneman lays it out, is that it gets tired very easily and defers often to the intuitive System 1. Kahneman and his collaborator Amos Tversky encapsulated this glitch in "the Linda problem."

The researchers outlined a caricature of a feminist in 1983: that she was "31 years old, single, outspoken, and very bright." She majored in philosophy, was active in social justice causes, attended anti-nuke protests. An independent woman, Linda worked as a bank teller. Kahneman and Tversky then presented the following statements, and asked them "to which degree does Linda resemble the typical member of each of the following classes?"

1. Linda is a teacher in elementary school.
2. Linda works in a bookstore and takes yoga classes.
3. Linda is active in the feminist movement.
4. Linda is a psychiatric social worker.
5. Linda is a member of the League of Women Voters.
6. Linda is a bank teller.
7. Linda is an insurance salesperson.
8. Linda is a bank teller and is active in the feminist movement.

In *The Undoing Project*, the writer Michael Lewis summarized the problem Kahneman and Tversky found:

Danny [Kahneman] passed out the Linda vignette to students at the University of British Columbia. In this first experiment, two different groups of students were given four of the eight descriptions and asked to judge the odds that they were true. One of the groups had "Linda is a bank teller" on its list; the other got "Linda is a bank teller and is active in the feminist movement." Those were the only two descriptions that mattered, though of course the students didn't know that.

The group given "Linda is a bank teller and is active in the feminist movement" judged it more likely than the group assigned "Linda is a bank teller." That result was all that Danny and Amos [Tversky] needed to make their big point: The rules of thumb people used to evaluate probability led to misjudgments. "Linda is a bank teller and is active in the feminist movement" could never be more probable than "Linda is a bank teller." "Linda is a bank teller and active in the feminist movement" was just a special case of "Linda is a bank teller."

In other words, we decide something intuitively, and then reason signs off on it. Jones wanted her husband not to be cheating, so she deployed S2 to approve that thought. Other psychologists have theorized about different types of dual-processing models, but Kahneman's is the best known, perhaps because it is the most cut-and-dried; rationality and intuition are easy to pit against each other. For the sake of scientific experimentation, these different faculties of the mind become a binary—you are either rational or intuitive, fact-based or feelings-based. Living in the messy, uncategorizable world, we know that these categories are more theoretical than practical. Most of us, I'd wager, are a bit of both.

In an interview with organizational psychologist Adam Grant, Kahneman delineated his terms: "You really have to distinguish judgment from decision-making. And most of the intuitions that we've studied were fallacies of judgment rather than decision-making." Along with Tversky, the pair ran famous experiments looking at "cognitive biases," or unconscious reasoning errors that distort and cloud our judgment. One such example is what Kahneman and Tversky deemed "the anchoring effect," meaning that if you are exposed to random numbers, you will have them at the fore of your mind. In one seminal experiment, experienced judges were inclined to give a shoplifter a longer sentence after rolling dice loaded to show high numbers.

Kahneman speaks specifically about the importance of "delaying intuition" in "formal decisions" like hiring an employee or taking a job. In these cases, he urges people "not to decide prematurely and not to have intuitions very early"—to remain open. Gather unbiased data. Particularly in instances when the potential hire looks different from you. In *Before You Know It: The Unconscious Reasons We Do What We Do*, Yale psychology professor John Bargh writes, "We should not trust our appraisals of others based on their faces alone, or on photographs, before we've had any interaction with them. . . . Our unconscious reactions to people *after* we have had some experience with them, have seen them in action for even a little while, is a surprisingly *valid* predictor." He believes that we can and should trust our intuitions about other people, but only after we have seen them in action. In other words, once we have gathered data.

"When you have formed an intuition, you are no longer taking in information," Kahneman said. Allowing time for that intuition to resonate is important. Kahneman urges people to delay rushing to action. Sleep on it, in other words. See how you feel in the morning. On the flip side, though, he believes, "I don't think you can make decisions without their being endorsed by your intuitions." We should have the best, most open-minded data at our hands, and have given ourselves time with the decision. By then we should be able to tell how our judgments are impacting our decision-making. Only then should we proceed with the courage of our convictions.

—

Since intuition is so "nonconscious, effortless, holistic," as Kahneman writes, it seems difficult to study. But Laura A. King, a University of Missouri psychologist, has dedicated her career to ascertaining what makes life meaningful, and intuition is a big part of it. Intuition is a key component in experiencing a meaningful life. In a 2016 paper co-authored by King, she writes, "Meaning in life [MIL] shares a positive relationship with reliance on gut feelings, and high MIL may facilitate reliance on those feelings." What King found is that there is a virtuous cycle of meaning in life and intuition. More intuition, more meaning in life.

I ask her what her research has concluded gives people a sense of a life well lived. "It feels meaningful to have goals," she says, "when you feel like you matter to other people, and when life makes sense, which is where intuition comes in, big time." Following one's intuition, piecing together the breadcrumbs, solving the puzzle of one's own life, and paying attention makes it feel meaningful.

But where does this thing that makes life make sense reside? Curiously, when we speak of intuition, it is as if it is outside of us. Intuition is like a pet: with us, by our side, but not us. We say "my intuition" like we say "my Apple Watch" or "my cat Marbles." And I can't think of an analogous faculty of the mind. When was the last time you said, "My rational faculties told me to apply for that job"? Since intuition seems to pop up out of nowhere, its origin point feels mysterious. This is why some people speak of intuition almost as external guidance—signs, nudges, symbols. Is the universe or some mystical intelligence propelling us in a direction, or is it the highest part of ourselves that notices the signposts to begin with?

This paradoxical location of intuition is perhaps the true both/and of it all. When I feel my intuition, it does feel like it is coming from the deepest part of me, the smallest doll at the center of a *matryoshka*. And it also feels like gentle guidance from a place beyond me. Sometimes that guidance takes the form of how the day shakes out—a canceled appointment, which then allows me to be available to pick up an important phone call I would've otherwise missed. Other times, that guidance feels like a magnetic pull, like the time I entered an overpriced gift store as if in a trance to buy a candle with Frida Kahlo on it so I could give it to my friend Brooke. It wasn't Brooke's birthday, and as far as I knew she didn't have a Kahlo fetish. But when I gave it to her she gasped: Frida Kahlo was her friend Becky's fave. Becky had recently died from cancer at age thirty-six and Brooke feels a deep connection with her. I knew about Becky, of course, but not about Frida, and how Becky's friends consider the image of Frida Kahlo to be a sign from Becky on the other side. "My intuition," like my children, is both me and not me at all.

Some scholars contend that people envision their intuition as their "true self." A 2019 study published in the journal *Emotion* found that the true self is "the essence of the individual, unwavering in its character and values. It is contrasted with how the actual self might outwardly, waveringly think or act depending on different situations." This is the idea of a self within you that knows best, that acts right. It is the goodness at your core, which is often obscured by moods, psychic garbage, worries, and neuroses, the *sturm und drang* of daily life. "The true self reliably points in the same direction regardless of which way the wind blows," the authors write.* Going with one's gut, or making a "feelings-based choice, more than a deliberative choice, evokes the true self."

So when we say "intuition," maybe we are talking about our truest self?

Connecting with intuition—feeling guided, piecing together signs from the universe, going with one's gut—does indeed contribute to what William James called "the feeling of right direction." He described this feeling as "a sort of wraith . . . beckoning us in a given direction, making us at moments tingle with the sense of our closeness." This, perhaps, is the intuitive meaning-making King highlights as making our lives worthwhile.

---

* Okay, not to be a total philistine, but isn't it amazing that people get grants and lines on CVs for publishing academic articles that systematize very essential ideas about human life to which our least educated and most ancient human ancestor would be like, "No shit, Sherlock"? Yet because this idea has the imprimatur of institutions and the data of a sample of humans who got a Starbucks gift card or whatever, we find it more credible. And if I can just go a step further down what is surely a regrettably broad characterization, I just want to note that this facet of my research has introduced me to what I'll call "MBA psychology" (organizational psychology—see Grant, Kahneman, et al.), which, at its most nefarious, seems to concern itself with understanding human motivation and behavior so as to better control/exploit/sell us things. It's gross, and wildly popular for the aforementioned evil reasons, and I'm now attempting to extract these findings and apply them to a less evil framework—you and your own intuition—independent of the marketplace and the workplace, if such a place exists. Send help.

A 2019 study out of Switzerland's University of Basel asked participants to reflect on daily decisions they had made. They found that people reported having felt better both *before and after* making intuitive decisions than they did when making analytical ones. Whether we opt for intuitive or rational thinking in the first place seems to be determined by mood. The authors of the paper write that "laboratory studies have repeatedly shown that analytical processing is more likely to occur in a negative mood state whereas positive mood fosters intuitive processing." They found that making everyday life decisions makes people feel good. The authors say, "Kahneman and his associates did their experiments . . . with objective criteria for correctness. . . . However in everyday life, there is often no objective criterion for the correctness of a decision. One way to evaluate whether the choice that one made has satisfied personal needs and goals is to ask oneself 'how do I feel?'" What would feel good to my body to eat? When I walk to work, should I walk on this side of the street or that? What is the perfect pair of pants to put on today? There is no objective answer. So why not mess around and follow the wraith of right direction?

We must become our own laboratories. This study suggests that a most accessible, cheap, and easy way to do that is to start by noting what kind of mood we are in to begin with. Noting our mood reveals what kind of decision-making process we are inclined toward in that moment. As King explains to me, "When you're in a good mood, you must be in a safe environment. That's a perfectly good time to go with your gut. And when we are in a good mood, we have broader association, and therefore we can see connections more readily." Being in a good mood perhaps helps us access our truest self. In a bad mood, when we feel unsafe, our judgments come to the fore, clouding our decision-making ability. So trust intuition when you are in a good mood. In a bad mood, it's harder to discern. This is another way of applying HALT, from chapter 2.

But mood itself is an important criterion we often take into account. In social psychology, that tendency is called affect-as-information

(AAI). In *How We Change*, Ross Ellenhorn writes, "Research on AAI shows that emotions help you with more creative and flexible planning (the result of emotional intelligence), distinguishing things as good or bad, and deciding on the attitude to take and how quickly to respond in the face of a significant event. A lot of what we do when we make decisions, in other words, depends on a gut response."

———

And yet we often reserve our intuition for when the stakes are at their very highest. My friend Fatima* recently had one of those nightmare situations where she scolded herself for "not listening to her intuition" because the bad outcome she feared would occur indeed did occur.

Fatima, a single woman in her forties in New York, makes her living as a writer. Seeking health insurance and security (thank you, amygdala/common sense), she applied to a job that would tap her skill set as a reporter for a worthy cause. When she interviewed for the position, she got a big intuitive no—the person who would be her boss was inexperienced and didn't appreciate the intricacies of the work. From her first Zoom meeting, she had a bad feeling. But when she got an offer to make more money than she ever had, doing something not entirely soul-crushing, she accepted the position.

Just as her intuition had counseled, the problems she foresaw materialized. Her boss asked for projects to be completed on superhuman timetables. We were stretched out on a picnic blanket in the park on a summer evening, talking about the problems she faced—not only with her job, but with her intuition. The problem: she heard her intuition, loud and clear. But how to act on it? "My intuition is telling me my boss is kind of an idiot," Fatima says. But counter that with the promise of a hefty paycheck when one is solo in a cruelly expensive city? What does "following your intuition" look like then?

---

* Name changed.

Which self is the master: the true self, which knows this job is not the one, or the self that has rent due?

I turned this problem over in my head. What courage, or gall, would it take to reject a cush job on the premise of bad vibes? What kind of wizard (or scion of independent wealth) would one have to be to say no? After our evening picnic, in the middle of the night, I scrawled out "Fatima job is level 10 intuition" and went back to sleep. Unlike most of my midnight scribbles, this actually made sense.

Recruiting our intuition for a level 10 problem makes acting on it almost impossible. The curve is just too high. You wouldn't attempt to learn German by trying to translate *Der Zauberberg*. You'd start with baby vocabulary. Intuition is the same as learning a language: the language of ourselves. We need to begin at level zero: Which socks should I wear? Intuition is a muscle and a practice, and so many of us enlist it at moments when our System 2 Kahneman rational thinking has us tied up in knots: jobs, real estate, relationships. The pros and the cons come out equal, so we call on a gut feeling. And if we are true intuitive geniuses, perhaps we are brave enough not only to listen but to employ our insights. To say no to the job.

But that is not most of us. We need to start small. That is what the research tells us. By developing our intuition around decisions where there is no right or wrong answer—*My feet and my fate on earth will likely be fine whether I wear crew socks or fuzzy socks*—we build confidence in trusting ourselves. Instead of just going on autopilot, we can start to listen to what we actually want in low-stakes places. We cannot start the race at the edge of a high dive. The kiddie pool is where it's at. From there we can progress into deeper waters.

From the kiddie pool, we can begin to take baby steps. Like Fatima's realization about her job, not every intuition we have can be acted upon in its fullest expression. We still have bills to pay. Once you have the big intuition, how can you plant seeds toward realizing it? Maybe it's having coffee once a month with people in fields that interest you. Maybe it's carving out a few minutes a week just to dream. Peloton instructor Robin Arzón tells a story about how she took small steps when she realized she wanted to change careers: "When I was a lawyer, I set a calendar appointment for 10 minutes a day for myself, and I was ruthless with that time. And in those 10 minutes, maybe I sent one email or made one call for myself, but I moved the needle little by little."

There are lots of ways to move the needle, however minuscule. Julius Kuhl, a German psychologist, studied intuition throughout his career. On the day I interview him, ResearchGate says he's been cited 15,299 times. He underscores the importance of being with uncertainty to develop intuition: "Today people like to spend time in bubbles, in social networks. They don't want to be confronted with anything that doesn't fit right away. But exposing yourself to contradictions and learning to tolerate them is the recipe for developing creative intuition. Don't try to control the solution right away. You don't have to decide between black and white." Here he refers to Keats's negative capability, or intellectual uncertainty. So maybe when you have the intuition to change careers, getting out of your context is crucial. Perhaps reaching for the more elevated cognitive uncertainty of the mind can train a more basic tolerance for uncertainty in the brain, in our sweet, freaking-out amygdalae. This is where our minds can help us.

Kuhl continues: "The Gestalt psychologists more than 100 years ago showed that before people reached an intuitive solution, they stopped analytical thinking. They gave themselves a break. They slept on it." When stumped, both Kahneman and Kuhl urge us to go back to bed. Research has shown that when our attention isn't focused on a specific task, we can make unexpected connections that can result in answers and epiphanies. It's the same reason you don't sit down at your desk to have intuitions; more likely you get them out in the world, going through life. So when you find yourself at an impasse, there's no need to push through. A maxim popular in recovery circles echoes this: "When you don't know what to do, don't do anything."

—

There are a great number of books about rationality, and why you shouldn't trust your intuition. But broken clocks are right twice a day. In Harvard psychology professor Steven Pinker's 2021 book *Rationality: What It Is, Why It Seems Scarce, Why It Matters* (why do I feel like the title wants to fight me?) he describes humans as "intuitive dualists, sensing that our minds can exist apart from bodies."

He continues:

> Many of our experiences really do suggest that the mind is not tethered to the body, including dreams, trances, out-of-body experiences, and death. It's not a leap for people to conclude that minds can commune with reality and with each other without needing a physical medium. And so we have telepathy, clairvoyance, souls, ghosts, reincarnation, and messages from the great beyond.

Research suggests that an inclination toward intuitive thinking makes people more open not only to the paranormal, but also to conspiracy theories. Psychologists have developed a number of questionnaires to assess one's thinking style. The most iterated upon is the Rational Experiential Inventory (REI), developed largely by Seymour Epstein. The University of Massachusetts psychologist studied another dual-processing model called the cognitive-experiential self-theory, or CEST. This theory also puts the analytical and rational on one side of the ledger and adds the dimensions of experience and feelings to the intuitive. This makes a lot of sense to me. If our intuitions are pattern recognition, as neuroscientists believe, then we call up that store of information and experience when we have an intuition—we remember how it felt. Kahneman's model doesn't include much in the way of experience or feelings.

The REI is a forty-question survey that pits rationality against intuition. A respondent rates statements like "I have a logical mind," "I enjoy intellectual challenges," "I believe in trusting my hunches," and "I like to rely on my intuitive impressions" to determine whether they are more intuitive or more rational.*

Researchers ask their subjects to complete the REI survey and then do a task that measures their affinity toward conspiracy theories. Conspiracy theories abound. One study from 2020 found that 63 percent of the American public believed at least one political conspiracy theory and half of Americans believed at least one medical conspiracy. Another 2020 study found that people who are more intuitive also jump to conclusions more readily. They presented subjects with two jars of differently colored beads. In one jar, 85 percent of the beads would be blue and 15 percent orange. In the second jar, the proportion was reversed. The jars were then hidden from view, and subjects were consecutively presented with beads from one jar or the other. After each round, researchers asked the subject if they would like to make a guess as to which jar the beads came from. Next, the researchers presented subjects with twenty different conspiracy theories, from chemtrails to the JFK assassination to the Illuminati. The study concluded that "participants who displayed the jumping-to-conclusions bias were more likely to endorse conspiracy theories than subjects who did not jump to conclusions." So does being an intuitive thinker mean you also jump to conclusions?

Laura King doesn't think so. She was the lead researcher on a team that published a paper in the *Journal of Personality and Social Psychology* in 2007 called "Ghosts, UFOs, and Magic: Positive Affect and the Experiential System." While researchers have long found that people who hold paranormal beliefs have high faith in intuition and lower reflective thinking, King's team found that highly intuitive people could get behind paranormal beliefs and magic only

---

* If you enjoy taking personality quizzes like the Myers-Briggs, head on over to www.psytoolkit.org to find out how intuitive a psychologist would deem you to be.

when they were in a good mood. So perhaps be cautious about reading a chupacabra Reddit thread when you are feeling jolly. Or at least revisit the thread in a bad mood to see what kind of credence you give it. When you are tracking your own intuitive development, note what kind of mood you were in when you got an intuition. From there, you might be able to decide for yourself if what you are experiencing is anxiety or intuition, or something else entirely. You can be analytical about your intuition!

"Within the experiential system, seeing is believing," King writes. Therefore, the belief in the paranormal or conspiracy theories "derives from an independent system that is not likely to be influenced by [rational argument]." I think we know this from experience. Your aunt who believes in Pizzagate is unlikely to have her mind changed when you send her a *New York Times* article debunking it. The beliefs quite literally exist on a different plane from rationality. King, though, sees the merits of studying the mechanisms underlying seemingly outlandish ideas. Psychologists, she says, should "explore the ways these beliefs contribute to a sense of meaning and purpose for those who hold them."

We shouldn't underestimate the power of purpose. I've seen many an acquaintance from high school sharing their new knowledge on Facebook, hoping to red-pill others. They feel empowered. But these conspiracy theories have real social repercussions: fewer people getting vaccinated and the downfall of democracy, for two.

What "feels true" can be dangerous. We see this in the scapegoating of groups who have nothing to do with society's ills. We see it in racism and bias. Hugo Mercier, a cognitive scientist and author of *Not Born Yesterday: The Science of Who We Trust and What We Believe*, has an interesting take on conspiracy theories. He points out that most conspiracy theories do have intuitive underpinnings (meaning they make a kind of sense, if you squint). Segments of the population have historically found vaccines repulsive, for example, because of the contagion effect. How can we infect our healthy bodies with the very virus we are trying to avoid? If you don't know anything about immunology or basic human biology, that makes sense. Same with flat-earthers. "Imagine you have no knowledge of astronomy," Mercier writes. "Someone tells you that the stuff you're standing on, the stuff you see, is called earth. So far so good. Now they either tell you that the earth is flat, which fits what you perceive, or that it is spherical, which doesn't. The first alternative is more intuitively compelling."

But Mercier goes further, building off the work of Dan Sperber, to argue that belief in conspiracy theories is a reflective cognitive process rather than an intuitive one. Conspirators are cherry-picking what they are paying attention to:

> Even though many misconceptions have an intuitive dimension, most remain cut off from the rest of our cognition: they are reflective beliefs with little consequences for our other thoughts, and limited effects on our actions. The 9/11 truthers might believe the CIA is powerful enough to take down the World Trade Center, but they aren't afraid it could easily silence a blabbing blogger. Most of those who accused Hillary Clinton's aides of pedophilia were content with leaving one-star reviews of the restaurant in which the children were supposedly abused.

We tend to think of conspiracy theorists as intellectually lazy. But if anything, Mercier tells me when I speak with him, a conspiracy theorist's MO is "certainly not lack of cognition. If anything, it's too much cognition. They do a lot of time-consuming research. So clearly they are not lazy." Identity and a sense of autonomy seem to make one more predisposed to conspiracy belief than to intuitive thinking, he says. "A strong determinant to conspiracy theories is narcissism," he says. "You want to see yourself as somebody who makes up their own mind, someone who has their own ideas, someone who isn't told what to think by the media, the government, the authorities. Someone who does their own research." He pauses and laughs. "Scientists tend to be a bit narcissistic too, but they happen to do their research in a sound institutional environment," he concedes.

But just trusting our hunches in lieu of facts has an even darker side when it comes to racism and profiling. Intuition, then, should be situational. What feels right when it comes to what we eat for lunch is one thing, but what about when it comes to who we deem hirable or electable? These are big choices with huge consequences, where intuition should not be the first line of decision-making. Here's where Kahneman's delineation between judgment and decision-making is important. We often think we are making a decision, when actually we have made a judgment.

"People's guts can be biased," King tells me. "Everyone's surprised that it turns out AI can be biased. Our intuition is the same way. Garbage in, garbage out. If we have these kinds of associations, they can lead to biased decision-making." We live in white supremacy and we have internalized its messages, no matter how woke we fancy ourselves. Living in New York City, in the close quarters and diversity on the subway, I often have to make a quick calculation about who is acting crazy enough on the train car to warrant my getting up and moving. At rush hour, that is no easy feat. Train cars are jam-packed and people are breathing up on each other. Lately I've been trying hard to investigate my biases around who I deem threatening enough that I'll push my way out of the car and into a new one.

The history of the United States shows that young white men are the greatest threat we face in terms of random acts of violence. Yet it is so drilled into us that men of color want to hurt us. So who do I move for? Here's what I've found:

If someone is moving erratically—fast-moving hands, rocking, invading the few centimeters of personal space nearby—I will move. But I was recently next to a man on the subway who fit an eerie profile. He was wearing a camo jacket and playing a violent video game on his phone. He had big Travis Bickle energy. He checked the boxes for what I've determined to be a threat: young, angry, aggressive white man. But I didn't move away from him. I realized I possess a bias that—even though in my rational mind I believe this type, broadly, poses a threat—probably made him feel less scary to me

because he was white and because of the shitty cultural conditioning I've been subject to. If I hadn't been trying to monitor this sort
of thing, I don't think I would have noticed. So what does it mean?
These are the types of low-level privilege we assign even when we
don't think we are doing it. And it has big ramifications for our intuition.

I speak with Carlos Alós-Ferrer, a professor of economics at Lan-
caster University Management School, about these faulty biases. As
an economist, Alós-Ferrer prefers harder data to intuition. He agrees
with Kahneman that intuitive decisions can often feel like an easier
lift than the rational. "There's something very attractive about not
having to put in the work," he tells me. "Some people will make
sweeping predictions about the direction of the stock market, for example, and sometimes they will be right. But it is a bit of a mirage."

The mirage, in part, can come down to availability bias. "I ask
students which is bigger: Berlin or Busan? Everyone except the Ko-
rean students says Berlin, because they've heard of it," he says. "The
problem is intuition gives you these feelings on the basis of nothing.
When we start applying intuition to more complex problems, it is
much more likely that we make mistakes." So, as Fatima experienced,
it is difficult, and maybe not even advisable, to apply intuition to a
high-stakes decision. If you're buying a car, he says, you shouldn't
select the one that simply gives you a good feeling. Read *Consumer
Reports* and reviews. (Although I just want to state for the record
that the worst coffeemaker I have ever owned was *Wirecutter*'s top
choice, so riddle me that. Everything under the sun is subjective.)
When it comes to buying a car or a coffeemaker, enlisting quantifiable data points to help arrive at your decision makes sense. In a
Psychology Today article, Alós-Ferrer writes, "If you are not an expert
in a field, your intuition is untrained, and it will serve you poorly. It
is best to stop, think, and gather data."

But I think of Russ Roberts's distinction between the tame problem of buying a car and the more vexing life choices we confront.
"I feel funny asking an economist this question," I say to Alós-Ferrer,

always a good start, "but what about when it comes to big life decisions that don't have easily accessible data, like selecting a romantic partner or deciding to have kids? What then?"

"We all have blind spots," he says. "Get data from people who know you well about big decisions, like relationships and kids."

Our blind spots are terrifying. And we need to investigate them. This is another way of inviting ourselves into making the unconscious conscious. Why not survey your friends? My best friend, Brooke, and I are committed Bravoholics. One of our favorite shows is *Southern Charm*, a reality show about heavy-drinking socialites in Charleston running amok. One of the cast lotharios, Austen, recently revealed that Craig, my fave, will often leave a vacation in the middle of the night, simply because he is over it. Upon learning this, Brooke said to me, "That is so you! No wonder you love Craig."

Now, this character revelation was surprising to me. I would never describe myself as one who slinks away from a group trip under the cover of night. Mostly for logistical reasons: I'm not a confident driver and the rental car is rarely in my name. But upon further reflection, I realize she has a point. I do tire easily of forced camaraderie, especially when one is trapped in a cabin in the woods, and if I had my own transportation I would absolutely ditch my friends come Sunday morning, in favor of open roads and getting a jump on the week's chores. This is a silly example, but familiarizing ourselves with our blind spots, while daunting, provides vital information for decision-making.

—

So let's train it. And we begin to train it just by noticing. And then by keeping track. And then by overlaying more contextual information: What kind of mood was I in? Does this touch on one of my blind spots? Hey, friends, what kind of partner do you think I need, anyway? Intuition in our minds comes in recognizing our patterns, becoming experts in ourselves to sort anxiety from intuition.

Brooklyn-based artist and designer Derya Altan has something similar to say about intuition. She has developed her own intuitive lexicon. "Intuition is always just a statement that has a period at the end. Anxiety for me comes in the form of questions that lead to more questions, and a spiral develops. Anxiety is a question. Intuition is a comment," she says.

In a recent relationship, her intuition told her the guy she was dating was not the one. This was not the answer she wanted. And it came to her not in a moment of serenity, but when she was "scream-singing on the BQE," she says. If you can hear an intuition on the Brooklyn-Queens Expressway, then it is certainly one worth listening to. "Just very clearly, I got the phrase 'He is not it.' That's intuition. As opposed to anxiety, which is like, 'Well, maybe he's not great, but we could make it work?'" Noting the distinction between the statement and the question is her heuristic for discerning her own intuition. Similarly, the morning of the 2022 shooting in Uvalde, Texas, she got the sentence "Something bad will happen today." Anxiety, on the other hand, comes with a tizzy of questions, like "What do you think is the bad thing that will happen today? Should I stay home? What will I do when the bad thing happens?" Altan has become an expert in the field of herself. She has learned the language of herself.

The option behind door number three, which I so rarely even think to take with my conscious mind, is waiting. Doing nothing. My conscious mind tells me I have to act; my amygdala wants certainty. I want a yes or a no so I can orient myself toward coping. Hanging out in the murky middle of uncertainty is deeply uncomfortable. Doing nothing—resisting the temptation to send the email—is perhaps the hardest of all.

This moment, I think, is where meditation comes in. Some of us need to get quiet in order to hear our intuitive voice, and meditation is a place to cultivate that quiet. Quiet is cool, and a great many books on meditation will tell you that this is the key to hearing your intuitive voice. But quiet is hard to come by, and not always possible. (See: my children busting down the door while I am merely trying to pee in peace.) Not everyone needs quiet for everyday intuition. For those like Altan, intuition can come in the noisiest moments, literally and emotionally. Or, as the experts I interviewed suggested, intuition more often comes when one is not actively noodling on the problem, and in interstitial times, too.

But meditation also trains us in how to stay, in how to notice what is going on and not act on it. When I sit in meditation, I am constantly shifting left and right, trying to find the least uncomfortable angle of my coccyx on the cushion. I'm sweeping loose hairs from my face, itching wherever on my body is calling to me. But once I settle, the point of meditation can be to simply feel that itchy sensation and not to scratch it. To feel its pleading texture without trying to fix it. To watch it crest and recede and be replaced by another sensory stimulus begging for my attention. To be in that middle moment between stimulus and response is to carve a space for intuition to get in. Not everything needs to be acted upon. But you have to learn to allow your mind to hang out, suspended between feeling and action, long enough to decide.

This is where the conclusions of the economists and the organizational psychologists have a lot to teach us, in spite of their sometimes dubious intent and methods. Kahneman said: *Sleep on it. Go back to bed.* Even though intuition comes hard and fast, we needn't necessarily act upon its instructions immediately.

One part is developing that expertise and systematizing it. As the chief expert in Liz Greenwood, I now have a vocabulary to differentiate my anxious thoughts from my intuitive ones. Anxiety for me, as with Altan, is verbal, interrogative, and laden with *shoulds*. It wants certainty and will demur to a rational framework to get it, by any means necessary. It very much feels like the province of a busy mind. But the mind is only half the story. We have much to learn from the body.

CHAPTER 4

INTUITION OF THE BODY

Kayvon Pourazar has made his body his life's work. He is an award-winning dancer and has taught as a guest artist at festivals domestic and international, as well as at Eugene Lang College of Liberal Arts, in New York City. But arriving at peace and freedom in his body was a journey.

Pourazar was born in Iran at the time of the Islamic revolution. His first years of life were during wartime, and he lost close family members and friends. He was a refugee at six and lived in Turkey before moving to England. He had much older siblings living in the United States, and they were able to secure visas for their parents. But not for him. "When I was fourteen, my parents decided to leave me with my brother, who lived in London. And he promptly left for China, and left me in his apartment," he tells me. "I went hungry for nights. They didn't send me enough money." He was in council housing, where the electricity got turned on via a coin-operated slot. Pourazar could not afford even electricity. "So I was in the dark, eating out of cans, so many nights." He was eventually evicted but not before receiving letters from the Home Office informing him his deportation to Iran was imminent. "I was doing drugs to escape the nightmare," he says.

What Pourazar experienced is unimaginable for most of us—the trauma of war, coupled with abandonment. He managed to find one buoy. "I went to a performing arts school and studied dance at this time. And that was my lifeline," he says. Had his parents been in England, they never would have let him attend such a school. At eighteen, he reunited with his family in the United States and attended the State University of New York at Purchase to continue training as a dancer. He found little comfort in his family. "The message I got from them was to stop complaining. Their attitude was *We've all gone through hell and you should be grateful to get out of Iran.*"

He continued to dance, but a year out of college, he sustained a debilitating injury: tendinitis of the groin. As part of his recovery, he saw a craniosacral therapist. Craniosacral therapy is a form of massage that uses gentle pressure to relieve tension. He describes a turning point after one session: "I was sitting on the ground, having lunch before rehearsal. And my left leg just started to move on its own. It was twitching with these involuntary tremors. When I got home, I got in bed, and whatever that energy was started coursing through my whole body and my spine started convulsing. I was literally off the bed with these undulating spasms."

Pourazar now understands what was going on: "It was clear to me that there was some great unwinding happening. All of those years of trauma, everything that had pent up, was finding a way out." He stopped dancing and dedicated himself to releasing the trauma his body carried. "I would wake up at 6 a.m. and spend three hours with my body, letting it do what it needed to do. I'd go to work, and at my lunch break I would go into the bathroom and do more of it. Then I would come home and make dinner, and until midnight I would do more of it. I felt the release happening." That lasted for one year. He was twenty-four at the time.

Today, Pourazar is forty-eight years old and has a corona of silver-streaked hair. From the intuition of his body and the hard-won wisdom of his experience, he has developed a practice called Guided Bodily Reverie. It is an hour-long experience that is unlike anything you might find at a gym or a spa, and it seems to be suffused with his very DNA. The practice is the culmination of his life's and his body's experiences.

We meet in an airy loft with hardwood floors and big windows looking out at Tribeca. He's set up an altar of crystals and healing stones in the middle of the floor. I lie down on my back, and he starts with some gentle hands-on work, jiggling every joint in my body in the smallest, tenderest way. He massages even my tiny pinkie knuckle, which no one has ever done before. He leads me through a guided meditation and says I can put my hands on a place where I am carrying pain. I place my palms on my forehead: the pain I'm carrying on this day is in my mind. Then I move ever so slowly from the floor to standing, and we vocalize primary vowel sounds. This is the closest I have ever come to singing in front of another person when not drunk at karaoke. He puts on music and we dance. Then I'm lying on my back again and we clap at the same time and join palms, feeling the clap reverberate through each other's bodies.

When I arrived at our session, I was grumpy and nursing a migraine. After our session, I sit by the Hudson River. The foul mood and headache have dissipated, replaced by a thrum of wonder. As I let the sparkle of the sun on the water dance over my eyeballs, I feel compelled to grab passersby by the lapels. *Are you seeing this? This miracle of light and motion, right before us? Why are we walking on like nothing is happening?!* Pourazar's work has left me energized and inspired.

Describing the experience doesn't do it justice; words fail what the body can experience. While rationality is tied up in language, intuition often expresses itself in physical sensations. This is one reason why our bodies are a most profound site of intuition.

—

Descartes severed the brain from the body ("I think, therefore I am"—ring any bells?), and it wasn't until the pioneering work of Dr. Antonio Damasio in the 1990s that people began to be put back together again. In his work as a neurologist, he treated hundreds of patients with brain damage and became intrigued with "consciousness and with identifying the parts of the brain necessary for knowing what you feel." He consolidated his findings into the landmark Somatic Marker Hypothesis. "My idea," he wrote in 1994, "is that somatic markers assist in the process of sifting through such a wealth of detail." In other words, you feel emotions and memories in the body. Bodily sensations are tied to emotion. And these aid in decision-making. Damasio researched subjects who had suffered injuries to the emotional centers of the brain, like our friend the amygdala, and found that they were paralyzed to pull any kind of decisive trigger. They could come up with endless reasons why they should or should not go with an option, and could never ultimately make a decision. People who relied on somatic markers, like sweaty palms and an elevated heart rate, were able to make better decisions for themselves, and more quickly. Damasio triangulated thought, emotion, and the body to show how this ensemble of elements influences decision-making, which can be responsible for a lot of our intuitive downloads. The body and emotions are more closely linked with the right hemisphere of the brain, which some argue governs our more intuitive powers. This idea was revolutionary when it debuted.

So what is a somatic marker, anyway? Essentially it is a feeling in the body associated with an emotion. It's the pricks of sweat in your armpits when you realize you left your cell phone in the Uber. It's the flood of warmth when you wrap yourself into a hug from a friend. It's the queasiness in your stomach when you watch footage of surgery on a TV show. Your body state changes in these different scenarios, and these shifts, to Damasio, are emotions. With time and experience, the emotions become linked to the scenario, even at levels way below consciousness. I may have a bad feeling walking into a brand-new restaurant, perhaps because the shade of paint is the same as that of the wall an ex sat in front of when he broke up with me. My thinking mind won't know that, but the feedback in my body is doing the work of remembering for me, and sending feelings of disgust (because how dare he) as soon as I enter the room. My accessible brain might not remember, but my body and its somatic markers will.

The field of study within neuroscience that Damasio's findings helped create is called interoception, or how people feel and understand what is happening inside their bodies. Interoception has three main categories. The first is body urges based on need: feeling hungry, needing to pee, feeling one's heart race after a scare. The second is the unconscious communication happening between our bodies and our brains. As Jessica Wapner describes it in *The New Yorker*, "our brains detect high glucose levels in our livers, for example, then release hormones that trigger our metabolisms, and we are unaware of the process. A vast number of these silent interoceptive processes are going on within us all the time."

And the third is putting the whole of your current emotional state and how your body feels together. "Close your eyes at any given moment, and you can gauge your over-all mood—good, bad, excited, tired, a bit down, or generally pleased," Wapner writes. "This mood combines what's going on in your mind with how your organs, muscles, and nerves are embodying the moment." In other words, interoception refers to our ability to read signals from our bodies consciously, and also unconsciously—yet being able to take into account those signals in the decisions we make and the behaviors we perform. Understanding our bodies' signals can create a feeling of autonomy. In *The Body Keeps the Score*, Dr. Bessel van der Kolk writes, "If you have a comfortable connection with your inner sensations—if you can trust them to give you accurate information—you will feel in charge of your body, your feelings, and yourself."

There is a distinct correlation between interoceptive aptitude and harnessing intuition. Your body is constantly giving you a running news ticker of feelings based on immediate circumstances. And, similar to how we must be able to differentiate the stories of our minds (like my tendency to catastrophize) with true intuition, so too must we be able to sort out deeply rooted bodily responses with the best intuitive information. Getting in our bodies and becoming intimately familiar with their quirks and tendencies can make us more intuitive.

And bodies provide profound information. Joyce Pope, a retired elementary school teacher, tells me a story about one day in 2008 when she was shopping in a grocery store and all of a sudden she was felled with terrible abdominal pains. When the cashier asked her what was wrong, she said, "I don't know, but I need to go home right now." Pulling into her driveway, she saw her neighbor standing there. "The nursing home has been trying to reach you," the neighbor said. Pope's husband, Nick, who had late-stage Alzheimer's and was in a memory care facility, had been rushed to the hospital. Nick died three days later. "My body reacted to what was going on," she says. "Was it intuition?" she wonders. "As a Christian, I think it was the Holy Spirit screaming at me. Whatever it was, my body recognized the emergency."

If you are an embodied person, this will come as no surprise. Outside of grave emergencies, your body likely gives you a great deal of data about any room you enter, choice you are confronted with, or person you meet. It also comes as no surprise that people's interoceptive abilities vary greatly. Some people feel every little constriction of their blood vessels, can tell you the precise moment at which ovulation is occurring, and equate feeling peckish with impending meltdown (me). Others are taken aback when they begin to feel headachy and grumpy around 6 p.m., only to realize they forgot to eat lunch (my husband).

Scientists have come up with metrics for gauging people's interoceptive abilities, and the most famous among them is the Iowa Gambling Task. This experiment was established by Damasio and colleagues in 1994 and first performed on people who had a damaged ventromedial prefrontal cortex, the area of the brain responsible for processing risk, fear, emotion, and decision-making. It has since been adapted a zillion times over to measure interoception and intuitive learning.

Participants are presented with four different decks of cards.

Some decks pay money, and some deduct winnings. There is a system for which deck pays and which takes away, but it is difficult to deduce. The participant learns the system intuitively. Tim Dalgleish, a psychology professor at the University of Cambridge, explains to me how the Iowa task measures interoceptive and intuitive ability: "People running the experiment record signals from participants' bodies and measure when people are considering bad choices versus good choices; the bodily signals are different. They are completely unaware of those signals, but in the end they learn to make the good choices. And they really can't tell you why. They just say, 'Well, it seemed like the right card to choose.'" People who are more interoceptive are drawn to the profitable decks and repelled by the low-paying cards.

The players who figure out the well-paying decks earlier also experience low-level physical feedback pointing them in the right direction: after about ten pulls, on average, participants' palms start to sweat near the bad decks. This physical response occurs far sooner than participants are able to articulate, yet that subtle bodily cue points them to the better decks. By being able to pick up on these cues and appreciate feedback below the level of consciousness, these people choose the profitable decks. Being aware of those early gut sensations helps them make a good conclusion. They allow their bodies to lead them to the best possible outcome.

—

While in Chapel Hill, I meet with Kristen Lindquist again over coffee. She's a leading researcher on interoception and gives me some excellent tips on how to enhance our interoception. For children, she recommends what is known as "heavy work," which basically involves any kind of pushing or pulling physical activity. Have a child push a laundry basket loaded with objects across the room, to feel their body engaging with the task. For adults, just do anything physical—go for a run, go to yoga—and spend a few moments placing the attention of your brain on the sensations of your body. How do your legs feel? Can you sense the flow of blood coursing through your veins? Be aware of your gut reactions, "but be aware of the context," Lindquist suggests. "If I'm feeling anxious about something, I want to stop and ask myself, *What is this really about? Have I had a ton of caffeine today? Am I really tired or getting sick?* Those factors can contribute to feelings of anxiety," she says. "But if I'm feeling an anxiety level of 7 on something that would usually be a 4 for me, then perhaps that anxiety is telling me something about how I feel about the situation."

In other words, consider where you are with HALT. Know your patterns.

Meeting with Lindquist on this warm fall morning, however, what intrigues me most is engaging in a task that measures interoception. Lindquist has been using this metric as part of a study she is running. She graciously allows me to try it for myself.

We walk through UNC's lush campus to a most hideous specimen of architecture: Davie Hall, the Neuroscience and Psychology Department building. Many psychology departments sprang up in the 1960s, when blocky brutalist architecture was all the rage, so go to any college campus and you can find the psychology offices simply by identifying the ugliest buildings.

We trudge up the stairs to her lab, which consists of several small, carpeted rooms and students helping study participants with electrodes that measure their heartbeats. A PhD student, Mallory Feldman, sets me up with the heartbeat discrimination task. Mallory puts me in a room with a computer monitor and headphones and attaches a finger sensor to my left index finger, which tracks my pulse. A series of tones plays through the headphones, and my job is to decide whether those tones are playing faster or slower than my pulse. (The tones sound kind of like the worst techno music you've ever heard.) "Sometimes it's going to be really different, so it will be obvious whether the tones are faster or slower than your heartbeat," Mallory explains. "Sometimes the difference will be really small. Maybe your heart is beating at seventy-four beats per minute and the tones will be seventy-six beats per minute. So judging faster or slower will require a bit more sensitivity."

Mallory fires up the program and shuts the door. The beats play, and I have what feels like a split second to select Faster or Slower on the computer. If I hesitate and think too hard and for too long, that round is struck and we move on to the next. You really have to go with your gut. Most of the time, I make a snap judgment between faster and slower. I think I am good on the edges, when the tones feel perceptibly faster or slower. When it's harder to tell, that's when the bell rings before I can answer. As the experiment progresses, I try harder to just go with my intuition on faster or slower. In this case, it seems counterproductive to overthink. Perhaps that's applicable to a lot of life.

When the program concludes, I put down my headphones and meet up with Mallory for my results.

"You actually did very well," she reports. "Only a few incorrect." I summon all my power to keep from jumping up on the table and doing an end-zone victory dance. "You had 80 percent accuracy." Most people score around 50 percent. I offer Mallory the chance to ask me, an interoceptive genius, any questions. She laughs politely and declines.

Why do I relish this scientific validation of what I already know intuitively: that me and my body are tight, and I am aware of what's going on inside? I suppose because someone in a lab coat with a printout of percentages feels more real than me just shouting about it to anyone who will listen. And, I think, because this shows that my understanding of my body is, in fact, a kind of data. Seeing that validated in the lab is empowering. Tim Dalgleish concurs: "What we've learned from research on intuition is that your emotional system, which is essentially bodily sensations, is actually telling you something really, really important based on what's happened in the past," he says. "It's not irrational stuff we should ignore. It's just a different form of information. And it's just as rational, because it's based on prior experience. It's just a different form of rationality."

I had a situation recently in which I could not find my intuition. Or, rather, I had intuition but didn't trust it, not immediately, at least. Indeed, my interoceptive signals were all firing, but I wasn't immediately willing to trust it as a form of data. It was a version of a situation we are put in often: sacrificing my comfort and sanity for the sake of appearances. It involved someone who makes me profoundly uncomfortable, where the fallout from our interactions haunts me for days after. It was a situation where there was no right answer, just degrees of bad. "I have no intuition on this," I said in a voice memo to my sister. "I just feel physically sick."

She responded in a text, "It actually sounds like you have a ton of intuition on this." Indeed, I did: my throat had constricted, a pit had formed in my stomach, and my speaking voice had dropped several octaves to a whisper. I was diminished. These physical cues were so present, and yet they were easily drowned out by the voices in my head: the *shoulds*, the potential regrets, the fear of making a mistake, of hurting someone else, my ego wanting to cling to a story of the type of person I am—one who is caring—and how doing what is in my gut could potentially contradict that story. For days I was hijacked like this, unable to sustain any concentration, edgy and short with my family, my mind on a loop of pros and cons. And my mind, I think, was going through these mental gymnastics to protect me, in its imperfect way. Because when I stopped, I just felt a well of pain.

My body was screaming and sounding an alarm that said only one thing: *Stay away!* But it was so easy to ignore. How often do we ignore the signals of our bodies—when we are tired, sick, burntout—and keep pushing through? We are conditioned to tune out our bodies' pleas because there is work to be done, people to take care of, jobs to show up to.

Moreover, I saw how I considered my body's data unreliable. From the neck down, my body knew exactly what was going on, but from the neck up I was spinning out to compute a "rational" decision I could live with. Ultimately, with my sister's wise counsel, I realized that I was just pro-conning to catch up to what my body already knew. I let my amygdala search for certainty where there is none, where there is no right answer. Only the answer that is best for me. It was a no for me. I came to it intuitively, but not lightly, which is not the same thing, despite what some might have you believe. The intuitive decision, the intuitive insight, is not always effortless. But it is always worth the effort. The next time my body is screaming, I hope I can save myself some grief and abide its voice sooner.

———

Intuitive ability is synonymous with going with your gut. (The third chakra, the energetic center of intuition, is located in the solar plexus, in the region of the stomach.) Dr. Emeran Mayer, a world-renowned UCLA gastroenterologist and author of *The Mind-Gut Connection*, explains it to me this way: "Gut reactions are your brain responding to something it perceives as a disturbance of the homeostatic state. You can feel butterflies in your stomach, and the valence of those butterflies can be positive or negative. You can feel positive butterflies falling in love, or more negative ones if you have to give a speech," he says.

It makes sense that we feel so much in this organ system. Our gut—the set of organs comprising our gastrointestinal tract—can be thought of as our largest sensory organ, much bigger and more complicated than the skin. The gut is the only organ that can work somewhat independently of the brain, so it quite literally has a mind of its own. The enteric nervous system (ENS)—a network that wraps "around the intestine from the esophagus to the rectum"—contains between fifty million and a hundred million nerve cells, equal to the number contained in the spinal cord. More than 95 percent of serotonin—the hormone that makes life worth living—is produced and stored in the gut, with a mere 2 to 3 percent found in the brain. The small intestine measures twenty-two feet, and if you were to spread the organs of the ENS out, it would cover the floor of a basketball court. When our ancestors were colonies of single-celled microbiota in the sea, before they wriggled themselves onto land hundreds of millions of years ago, they were enteric nervous systems first. The central nervous system developed much later. If you've ever hung out with a newborn, you can see the predominance of the enteric nervous system right away. Babies are primarily digestive systems with eyes for a startlingly long time.

The gut connects to memory, and therefore to intuition. We access our somatic markers and the attendant feelings Damasio proposed when we have meaningful sensations in our tummies. Mayer explains, "Over a lifetime, our brain receives all sorts of sensory information from the gut. So every emotional moment creates both the feeling and also the gut sensation that came with it. From infancy, our brain collects these emotional moments, like a massive supercomputer of video clips." The gut is gathering information 24/7, even in our sleep. We can later draw on these sensations for making decisions. Mayer elaborates on the metaphor in *The Mind-Gut Connection*, writing, "Billions of these clips, or 'somatic markers,' are held in the biological equivalent of miniaturized servers in our brain and 'annotated' (linked) with motivational states. . . . When faced with the need for action, your brain predicts how a given response will make you feel, based on its emotional memories of what took place when you were confronted with other, similar situations throughout your life." A better question than whether we can trust our gut feelings, Mayer says, is whether we can accurately identify what they are. This is where interoception and connecting with our bodies is crucial.

This data is vast and interesting, but the gut, like all our other organs and capabilities, is enabled by the brain, Dr. Michael Gershon tells me. Gershon is a Columbia University professor of pathology and cell biology and has been referred to as "the father of neurogastroentonology." In other words, he says, the brain makes our body and its extraordinary memory storage and feelings possible. When we talk about gut feelings as a location of intuition, this is the language of metaphor, he says. "What people are really feeling is something very basic. They don't believe they are thinking it; they feel it. They refer it to the bowel," he says. "When the feeling you are experiencing feels basic, you assign it to your innards. And some people do get feelings in their guts. Whenever I call the National Institutes of Health to find out how one of my grants has done, I become painfully aware of the kind of effect the brain can have on the gut."

Gershon wants us to know that it is our brains creating intuitive feelings, which many experience in the body as a gut feeling. But the role of the serotonin in our guts is indeed profound. The level and quality of the hormone influence our moods, which color our intuitions. "Intuition is a spontaneous thought," Gershon believes. "So if you're depressed or anxious, that will affect the types of intuition that you have." This makes so much sense. If anxiety is the water in which your thoughts are steeped, then naturally that will impact your outlook. "If you know you're anxious," Gershon says, "you shouldn't trust your intuition." (I'd say you should trust your intuition, but you should know how it is a distinct experience from anxiety.) Same with depression: upping serotonin levels, whether naturally, by eating a balanced diet full of omega-3s, or synthetically, via SSRIs, can change the background mood. Extrapolating this out, you could therefore alter the kinds of intuitions you have.

Our relationship with food and eating is a place where it is difficult for many of us to hear our body's intuition. Elyse Resch, a registered dietitian and the co-author of *Intuitive Eating: A Revolutionary Anti-Diet Approach*, now in its fourth edition, tells me why. "Your average person who has been on one diet after another has been fully taken away from their intuition, in an instinctual sense," she says. While the drive to fuel oneself is among the most essential, value-laden cultural noise around how bodies should look and which foods are "clean" interferes with this mechanism.

Resch developed the principles of the Intuitive Eating framework to get people back to their original programming, eating the way we did when we were toddlers—what we want, when we want. She had suffered from an eating disorder when she was younger and sought to take the morality and drama out of eating. She and her co-founder have been anti–diet culture crusaders since the mid-1990s, before such terminology existed. The guidelines for Intuitive Eating are simple but not easy: Eat when you are hungry; monitor and feel your satiety; savor and experience pleasure from food. Weight loss may or may not occur, but that isn't the objective. Hundreds of academic studies have examined Intuitive Eating, including a 2021 meta-analysis that found positive links to body image, self-esteem, and psychological well-being.

Intuitive Eating uses our relationship with food as a way to develop interoceptive awareness. But our body's signals are not static, Resch explains. "Sometimes you lose touch with hunger. I've had so many clients who are so anxious that they rarely feel hungry at all. We might be good at interoceptive awareness when everything is clear, but not when we are sick," she says. Learning to listen to our bodies is a skill, and a daily practice. It almost seems quaint and old-fashioned when there are a plethora of semaglutides on the market to help people quell so-called food noise. So why bother learning the language of your body?

"You become free to just trust yourself," Resch tells me. "When you learn how to give your body what it wants, you awaken to a whole new way of trusting your body. It gives you the freedom to be able to trust that inner wisdom that you were born with." And stemming from that belief in oneself, Resch has noted a cascading effect in other areas of people's lives. "This whole new world opens up, and people begin to look at relationships and professional experiences," she says. When you've developed a trusting intimacy with your body, new possibilities emerge.

We can train our interoceptive awareness. But our early experiences inform our intuitive responses from the jump. Mayer explains, "If someone has a strongly negative-bias salient system from their early life experiences, they are going to make a lot of wrong intuitive decisions." In other words, they experienced trauma; their brains have been wired to expect the worst. That's when we see PTSD conditions like hypervigilance—the state of increased sensitivity to threat, even if it is not there. And that can look and feel a lot like intuition.

—

The most intuitive people I know, people like Melissa Coss Aquino, who obtain intuitive information fast, all share one trait: they experienced trauma in their early lives. One woman was sexually abused by her father for years, and now her body is like an instant-read thermometer that can sense a person's lack of boundaries immediately. One friend whose mother grew up with alcoholic parents says she "can clock an addict in thirty seconds." RuPaul shares a similar instinctive sense he developed in early life as "an ability to read the room." In an interview on *Fresh Air*, he said, "I grew up in a house with my mother and father, who were at war the whole time I was growing up. And I learned how to be a diplomat. I learned how to read the room, figure out what people wanted from me, and be able to do that. Because ultimately I needed to get through the situation, or I needed to get something from the situation."

The disruption of Melissa's early life was textbook trauma, one that you can see reflected in the Adverse Childhood Experiences survey, a metric to quantify potentially harmful and dangerous circumstances. The ten questions include whether, before their eighteenth birthday, the child didn't have enough to eat; experienced physical, verbal, or sexual abuse; lived in a home where a parent was incarcerated; lost a parent due to abandonment or death; or lived with an adult who was mentally ill. Undoubtedly, these are horrific experiences, which some people, like Melissa, learn to cope with. Others don't. Have they internalized the "fear learning" Sheridan studies in children? Has their PTSD frozen them into hypervigilance? How can one transmute awful experiences into sharper intuitive ability?

Melissa turned her experiences into art. In her exquisite novel *Carmen and Grace*, about a gang of lost girls in the Bronx, she uses the phrase "instinct injured." In the opening scene, a teacher says to a group of incarcerated women, "At some point you confused raw survival instincts with self-protective instincts. They are not the same. . . . When the little voice inside told you to run the other way, you ran fast in the direction of the very trouble waiting for you."

As a result of the chaos in which Melissa was immersed, she says, "my instinct as a person in this world veers toward the chaotic. It doesn't matter how crazy something is, I'll figure it out. That's what I grew up doing." So that instinct for survival, which in others who grew up in more tranquil circumstances leads them to turn away from chaos, got misdirected somewhere along the way and does the opposite of what it is supposed to do. Or, as Bessel van der Kolk explains, "Traumatized people chronically feel unsafe in their bodies. The past is alive in the form of gnawing discomfort. . . . They become expert at ignoring their gut feelings and in numbing awareness of what is played out inside. They learn to hide from their selves."

Melissa's circumstances are both extreme and all too common. But she thinks residing in the modern world has us all separated from our true instincts. "I feel like 90 percent of us are instinct injured from capitalism alone," she says. "I don't need to be happy and at peace—I need a new car!" And we are further separated from our instincts, from our intuition, by technology, by the million layers of packaging we engineer between ourselves and the world around us. "The modern world wants to take your intuition," she continues. "Think about your phone. There's an app for everything: when to eat, when to stand up. It tells you when you've been sitting down too long and to get up and move around. It's trying to obliterate our instincts *and* our intuition." We all feel this when we reject the urge to rest and replenish but keep chugging along toward the productivity and prosperity capitalism says we must achieve. Rather than adding another thing to the regimen of productivity and optimizing, intuition might be a process of stripping away. It's cutting through chatter to hear something new. It's not something you can buy, but something you already own.

—

I catch up with my friend Sarah Perry to get her take on the connection between trauma and intuition. I met Sarah in graduate school, when she was working on a draft of what would become her stunning, award-winning memoir about her mother's murder, *After the Eclipse*. I've always felt that Sarah is particularly intuitive with people.

We meet at a wine bar on a sultry summer afternoon. Sarah is sweet and androgynous on the outside, with the tensile strength of working-class Maine and roller derby on the inside. When Sarah was twelve, her mother, Crystal Perry, was murdered in their home in the room next door. Sarah ran miles to town in a nightgown and bare feet to try to find help. She was the only daughter of a single mother, and spent the rest of her adolescence being shuttled between family members who were less empathetic than they could have been. She was interviewed by police for years, as the case remained unsolved. Sarah was working an office job in North Carolina after graduation when she got a call that the killer had been found through DNA matching.

Sarah defines intuition as "knowledge that is nonlinear that you have to be very still to pay attention to. I receive my intuition in a really cheesy manner, because I actually have a small, quiet voice inside." She has experienced hypervigilance born of trauma. "If you've been in a traumatic situation, you are motivated to find out who is safe and who isn't. And then, if that trauma initiates further destabilizing events"—like bouncing around and moving a lot as a kid, as it did for her—"that strengthens your ability to quickly read this situation: *What do people want from me? Who is good, who is bad?*" There is a downside, though. "It can lead to trying to pull too much data. It's like when you're reading a textbook and you highlight everything," she explains.

Sarah is aware of how her early life experiences have colored her worldview, and the distinct before and after of who she was prior to Crystal's murder and in the aftermath. And because of that, she sometimes tries to access a version of herself from the *before* time. "For me, I feel like there is an essential self inside of me, and I try to choose the thing that would make ten-year-old me proud and happy."

Journalist Stephanie Foo is the author of *What My Bones Know: A Memoir of Healing from Complex Trauma*. She set out to understand her history within the context of her family and Asian American culture and experimented with a wide variety of healing and therapeutic styles. She explains how her particular shade of trauma shows up: "Because of how I was raised and having my life endangered when I was a child," she tells me, "I have a tendency to think people are angry with me." This was an adaptive skill when she was growing up. "PTSD is not a mental illness when you're in danger," she says. "It was a skill that kept me alive. The only reason it isn't a skill now is because I am no longer in danger." And yet the brain wants only to protect us. Because of the imprinting Foo experienced as a child, her brain still has her on the lookout for anger. Her experience of navigating threat and violence set her filter, as it does for all of us. As she puts it, "You touch the stove and you learn that it's hot. So what stoves have you touched in your lifetime?"

As a result of her filter, Foo says she doesn't always trust her intuition: "I think one of the scary things about intuition is that it's guesswork. And I don't want to guess. I want to be really clear and specific on things that can allay my fears." Foo invested in healing her complex PTSD through a variety of modalities, and getting to know her body's signals was a big step. She found restorative yoga particularly helpful, as well as wearing a Fitbit, which monitored her heart rate and helped her gauge whether she was triggered when she was disassociated. "Intuition is not one-size-fits-all," she says, "and for people with trauma it becomes a double-edged sword that can be very effective in times of actual danger and really constraining in times of peace."

Differentiating between actual and perceived danger is challenging for all of us. And it is the difference between fear and anxiety, as the writer and security expert Gavin de Becker notes in *The Gift of Fear*. "Real fear occurs in the presence of danger and will always easily link to pain or death," he writes. Fear is in the present moment. (*The snake is biting me, oh no!*) Anxiety is almost always about the future (*I'm afraid I'm going to be bitten by a snake*) or the past (*I'm such an idiot for getting bitten by a snake*). I call that past-tinted anxiety douche chills, personally—a familiar feeling the morning after drinking too much at a party and being unsure of how one's jokes landed. But when your hackles go up about something in the present moment—the vibe you get from a person, or feeling afraid walking on a certain street—that is intuitive fear that should be listened to. Fear is right now. Anxiety and worry, on the other hand, according to de Becker, are "the fear we manufacture. . . . Anxiety, unlike real fear, is always caused by uncertainty." The word *anxiety* comes from the Latin root *anxius*, "to choke." Anxieties make us feel like we are choking, a sensation in the body. To wit, my throat constricts when I'm at my most anxious.

Dr. Julie Holland, a psychiatrist and author, notes that anxiety is almost always future-oriented. "You're borrowing pain from the future," she tells her patients when they are obsessing over how things may turn out. "If you're worried about a bad thing happening two weeks from now, I tell them, 'Why don't you wait two weeks instead of having the bad feeling twice?'" Anxiety does not hold up under this kind of interrogation. Fear, on the other hand, and an immediate threat in the *right now*, and your body responding to what you may not be able to see—that is worth your attention.

Similar to recognizing the misplaced gifts of our amygdalae and their quest for certainty, it may be helpful to check in with our intuition by asking: Is it fear or anxiety? If something is squarely in the category of a clear and present danger—you're about to be hit by a truck, for example—you likely will not have time to broach that query at all. So that's one way to know. But in a more nuanced situation where interpretation is necessary, it can be useful to slow down your racing mind to ask: Is what I'm feeling fear, with an intuitive yes, or anxiety, with a wordy, verbal narrative?

Because things can make us afraid but still be right. Big life events, like going to graduate school and getting pregnant, terrified me. But I knew intuitively that these were meant for me. A friend told me about the messiness she had to sort through in the early part of her relationship with her now husband. It was scary, but she knew he would be worth the work. Fear and intuition can go hand in hand sometimes.

Another way to sort fear from anxiety is by noticing the kinds of jokes you make. My humor compass is oriented to dark comedy in the first place, but it is worth paying attention to. Holland tells me that the only time she ever got assaulted when working at Bellevue, the New York City psychiatric hospital, was ten minutes after she'd made a joke to a colleague about getting punched in the face by a particular patient. "A part of me knew this patient was danger- ous and that he was going to hurt me. And I'd never joked about that any other time. And I really didn't listen," she recalls. De Becker names humor, particularly dark humor, as "a messenger of intuition," so when you find yourself making onyx-hued jokes out of the blue, pay attention.

Our bodies always exist in the present moment; they cannot spi- ral into the future the way our minds can. I meet up with Laurie Dawson to learn more about the knowledge our bodies hold. Daw- son is a somatic therapist who practices on the Upper West Side of Manhattan. She has a warm, friendly manner that I imagine puts the people she works with at ease. Before this phase of her career, she worked as a massage therapist. When she put her hands on people's bodies, she could physically feel the holding patterns of people's trauma, where they were storing their pain. Her work now entails helping people to get in touch with their bodies, release pent-up trauma, and understand the stories of their lives. Most of her clients come from psychotherapy referrals. When we go through trauma, certain stimuli and stories become "overcoupled." She explains it like this: "Say I fell off my skateboard in front of a blue house. Now I can't take my skateboard down that street, because there's that blue house. And then I noticed that you're wearing a blue shirt; I started to have a panic attack. And then I can't go outside during the day, because the sky is blue. Now blue is dangerous." She provides this simplified example to convey a profound truth.

These subconscious fears end up running the show, Dawson tells me. When trauma is unprocessed, it can show up as fear. "Some people only have the experience of noticing their body when it is in a state of discomfort and that informs their experience, so if they listen to their body and they find fear, that can get mistaken for intuition," she tells me. "Or if it's happening in my body that I'm listening to, it's going to put me back to a traumatic event that I don't want to feel—and then I feel shame. And that takes us away from our intuitive knowingness. So I help people feel into safely knowing that a blue house is just a blue house, it isn't actually dangerous now. And we need to help the body know that. I empower people to be the experts in their bodies," she says.

She does this in a number of ways. Some of it looks like talking and guided meditation, and other strategies to activate the vagus nerve, to get into the parasympathetic nervous system. Some strategies you can do at home include breathing so that your exhale is longer than your inhale, and harnessing the power of cold temperatures—from holding ice cubes to cold plunges. Some of it looks like putting her hands on a patient's kidneys while they lie on a massage table. She will narrate what she feels—a spreading, a releasing, warmth—and always ask what a patient is feeling. "It's a bottom-up approach to healing," she explains.

Connecting with our bodies should be simple. But because of how our lives are mediated by more and more technology that distances us from feeling our bodies, and because of the trauma that some (like Dawson's patients) have experienced, understanding what our bodies are trying to convey to us is increasingly difficult for people today. Because we live in a moment in time suffused with misinformation, many gravitate toward data-driven practices as a result. Tracking our own bodily experience doesn't feel like enough. Perhaps in an effort to separate themselves from less rigorous sources, people cling to what feels like a harder science.

This makes sense, and accounts for the popularity of the Andrew Hubermans of the world. Andrew Huberman is a Stanford neuroscientist and the host of the wildly popular *Huberman Lab* podcast, which is often on the list of Apple's top ten most popular podcasts. He offers listeners biohacks "proven" to help you sleep better, be more focused, and generally live a healthier and more productive life. Episodes regularly go longer than three hours. At the center of his protocols are what he calls the five pillars of health and performance: sleep, sunlight, movement, nutrients, and water. These pillars need to be replenished every twenty-four hours.

I listen to Huberman's podcast and even bought the electrolyte supplements he endorses, but I've noticed how the authority of his lab can disempower listeners from their own lived experience, our personal labs of life. Most of us have probably noticed that "every 24 hours we need to re-up" on sleep. I don't think we need someone with a PhD to prescribe going for a walk with a friend in the fresh air to feel good. He espouses the benefits of training your "no-go function" for better impulse control. But the characters Frog and Toad figured that out in the children's story "Cookies" too. (They eat too many cookies and get tummy aches.) These are things we know, biological necessities that are our inheritance as human beings. So when we hear Huberman (or any number of influencers) endorse essential human experience, packaged and systematized with the backing of a lab, we feel validated. We are doing it right. What we knew to be true has the badge of data.

The ascension of Andrew Huberman reflects our cultural disconnection—from ourselves, from one another. We willingly disempower ourselves and consign our inner authority. We surrender the messages of our body to the protocols of a podcast. We fit our intuitive body knowledge into a mold of Western male rational systems. After a while we come to rely on a Huberman to tell us when to eat, when to sleep. Instead of being our own best authority, we are looking for a dad to tell us what to do. Instead of learning to trust ourselves, we overlay more layers of distance with podcasts, data, study. We stand out in the rain, confused: *The weather app says it's not raining, so how can it be raining?* We want answers, and a man with a lab steps in to deliver them.

Maybe we can learn to be with our bodies better, to hear their messages and cravings and desires. No doubt Huberman helps people feel better. And, as with Foo's Fitbit, data can reflect back to us what is going on internally and be a bridge to enhancing our interoceptive abilities. But you can help yourself feel better, too. It's why I haven't given up caffeine or alcohol but definitely regret the second cup of coffee or glass of wine. I've noticed that if I do not get enough movement, whether walking or dancing or pumping iron, I will be a ball of nerves. It's why, when I wake up at 4 a.m., I just get up and read or watch crappy TV instead of thinking about how much the next day will suck on such little sleep. It's why, when I feel my heart constrict and my stomach tighten when logging into my email, I can recognize that this is a habit of stress I have taught myself, rather than a premonition of doom to come. I can log off. Touch grass, as the kids say. I can help my body feel better. If you can better learn what your body is telling you, you can hear what your intuition is trying to say.

You can sort what physically feels intuitive from what feels anxious. "Intuition has less cortisol," Laurie Dawson says. Anxiety, for me, is keyed up and *fast fast fast*; it wants whatever decision I need made to have been made five minutes ago. It feels speedy, like bad cocaine. Intuition, I am learning, may come fast—the hit while in line at Trader Joe's that I need to text a friend, for example, or the sudden hunch that my kid will come home sick from school today. But the quickness of those thoughts' arrival does not come suffused with a vibrating thrum of forced momentum. They come quickly, but just as "facts of the world," as Penny Jones said.

Disentangling and decoupling is a lot of work, no doubt, especially if your body has been violated. This kind of bodily awareness takes a lot of effort, and there are so many ways for us to leave our bodies behind these days, via screens and technologies. So why is it worth it? I pose this question to Dawson. "Because bad shit stops happening," she says. "Because you start to feel more like yourself."

There are a million ways to come into your body. You can do your own version of the "heavy work" Lindquist recommends for children. You can garden, you can rearrange the living room. You can check in with your body's signals, while considering the context. I often wonder why I am ravenous at 10 a.m., when I ate breakfast a few hours before. I am hungry then, but more for human connection, like a phone call with a friend. My body telling me to eat as its most accessible metaphor for a different kind of nourishment.

—

Developing an understanding of our bodies' innate interoception is a critical step toward developing everyday intuition. But laser-focusing on our individuality misses something. This is what Kayvon Pourazar showed me in his Guided Bodily Reverie. Our bodies are miracles and have so much to teach us. But these meat machines are only part of the picture. They are but a single part of the greater living organism of life on earth. And we are suffering from a grave myopia to believe our selves to be the alpha and the omega. Toward the end of our session, Pourazar led me back to the floor to lie down and read a passage by the philosopher Evan Thompson that brought tears to my eyes: "A bird needs wings to fly, but flight isn't in the wings, and the wings don't generate flight. Flying is an action of the whole animal in its environment."

The intuition of our bodies is the intuition of our bodies in space. We are not just us, but our connection to the world. When I later asked Pourazar how he decides what to do in his sessions, he paused for a moment and then returned my question with a question: "What does the moment need?" The moment is not just us, nor our bodies, nor our brains and minds, but the ensemble of elements that create the here and now. You. Me. Nature. Circumstances. Asking this question is the quickest way back to sanity—in parenting, in relationships, in work, in most anything. It decenters the individual and takes the larger context into account. A moment in time includes so much more than just our demands. *What does the moment need?* Pourazar put me inside my body, but he also made it the right size, the way you feel when you look up into the stars on an inky night and feel small. When we begin to appreciate the majesty of our bodies, in their grandeur, in their insignificance, we can begin to feel real intuition.

CHAPTER 5

WOMEN'S INTUITION?

On the evening of March 1, 2023, Ariana Madix was watching her boyfriend's band play a show at an L.A. bar. She and Tom Sandoval had been in a relationship for nearly a decade, and they owned a home together in the San Fernando Valley. That night, like so many nights before, she held on to Sandoval's phone as he vamped onstage, performing cover songs. The band has fans, ostensibly, because he and Madix star on the long-running reality TV show *Vanderpump Rules*. But that night, Madix felt compelled to do something she didn't normally do: she went through her boyfriend's phone. And, lo, caught-red-handed evidence revealed itself. Sandoval and Rachel Leviss, a co-star and close friend of Madix's, were embroiled in an affair. Some scenes on this show are fabricated. This drama was not, and became a media event in and of itself, making its way to the pages of *The New York Times* and the White House Correspondents' Dinner, immortalized forevermore as #Scandoval.

"For reasons I still do not know," Madix said in her legal declaration on April 30, 2024, "call it a woman's intuition, when the set ended, I felt the need to check Mr. Sandoval's phone." For better, for worse, her intuition was validated.

Somewhere along the way, intuition got feminine-coded. We've all heard of the notion of women's intuition. To connect the dots back to figure out why, you don't have to look too hard, but you do have to go pretty far back.

—

The beginning of time is a good place to start. Through the lenses of religion and medicine, women have always been seen as *other*. Go to the Bible and you'll read stories of woman being crafted from man's rib, then being blamed for original sin for her curiosity about a piece of fruit. Fast-forward a few thousand years to ancient Greece and Aristotle: "We should look upon the female state as being as it were a deformity." Religion and philosophy saw women as less than men, and the field of medicine solidified those notions through the lens of science. As Dr. Elizabeth Comen writes in *All in Her Head: The Truth and Lies Early Medicine Taught Us About Women's Bodies and Why It Matters Today*, "medicine had been captive to the idea of the male default: men's bodies were the healthy standard. Women's bodies, in their differences, represented deviations from the ideal." The legacy of that notion persists today, as most medical studies are conducted on male participants and the findings then extrapolated upon theoretically to be applied to women. Humorism, the diagnostic practice that dominated medicine from the time of Hippocrates until the mid-nineteenth century, determined that women were "phlegmatic"—leaky, liquidy, slow. "Menstrual blood, breast milk, vaginal discharge, urine; to be a woman, it seemed, was to be constantly discharging fluid, particularly from one's genitals," Comen writes. Women were always considered icky, and men used (pseudo) science to prove it.

The Middle Ages are synonymous with the condemnation of women for their proclivity toward the supernatural, culminating with the witch hunts. (*Witch* is the word in northern European cultures, but the witch and witchcraft exist in most every place. African American folk magic is known as conjure or hoodoo, in Mandarin

Chinese a witch is a *wupo*, in Italy a witch is a *strega*.) Women were understood to be inherently more corruptible: "From at least the late Medieval period onwards, a pervasive stereotype existed that women were thought to be both impressionable and lacked rationality," Tabitha Stanmore tells me. Stanmore is a professor of history at the University of Exeter and the author of *Cunning Folk: Life in the Era of Practical Magic*. "Medical texts from the sixteenth century and earlier drew on Aristotelian models of biology, which dictated that a person's sex was determined by the level of heat a fetus was exposed to in the womb. In this model, women are described as being the necessary opposite of men: they're half-baked, half-formed, they're soft, doughy, and very easily manipulated." Stanmore's research into magical practices of the late medieval to early modern period in England reveals the contemporary conception of women as akin to children, innocent and impulsive.

In the eyes of the law at the time, women were essentially seen as minors, less than full adults, and didn't often have legal personhood. They were forbidden to own property unless they were widowed. And the underlying belief of women's essential spineless nature warranted the witch hunts from fourteenth-century Europe to seventeenth-century America. "One reason women were more likely to be witches was because they were less likely to have the necessary level of rational thought to overcome their emotions and reject the devil's advances," Stanmore says. "The belief of the time was that women don't have that kind of rational thought." Ironically (or perhaps not), the words *wit* and *witch* derive from a common root: "to know, to understand, to be a person of intelligence."

As one of the most infamous misogynists of the time, Heinrich Kramer—author of *Malleus Maleficarum*, a witch-hunting manual so off the rails that even Pope Innocent VIII declared it rather extreme— put it in 1487, "When a woman thinks alone she is evil." But the scientific philosophies in the years preceding the witch hunts set the stage. Barbara Ehrenreich and Deirdre English echo Comen in their seminal treatise *Witches, Nurses, and Midwives*, writing, "European medicine became firmly established as a secular science and a *profession*. The medical profession was actively engaged in the elimination of female healers—their exclusion from universities, for example—long before the witch-hunts began." Kramer declared midwives to be the worst witches of all. Midwives knew how to use herbs and plant medicine to bring forth or end pregnancies, to commence labor or delay it. Comen explains:

> The midwives, who had long been the primary custodians of knowledge about the medical issues that impact women specifically, found themselves relegated to the fringes. Medicine began to fracture into the system of specialization that still exists today, as doctors began to conceive of patients less as whole people than as an amalgamation of systems and body parts. As medicine became professionalized, it also became specialized.

Historians now estimate that around 200,000 people across western Europe were accused of witchcraft, and about half were killed as a result, 75 to 85 percent of them women.

People of the period looked to the "wrong" way to be, in order to better understand themselves. The world in which the witch hunts took place was extremely hierarchical—feudalism and monarchy were the governing principles. But at holidays and in art, playing with those roles was all the rage. Nobility would reverse roles with servants around Yuletide. Shakespeare expressed this contemporary worldview of inversion in *Macbeth* with the famous line "Fair is foul, and foul is fair." (Some scholars believe Shakespeare included witches in the play to please King James, an ardent witch-hunter.) Witches were always a symbol of opposition and challenging orthodoxies. And women, generally, were understood to be the opposite of men, like a photo negative revealing all the dark parts. Historian Stuart Clark explains the medieval/early Renaissance obsession with witches as a social utility, writing, "Establishing in exact detail

what occurred at a witches' sabbat was not arid pedantry or intellectual voyeurism but a (logically) necessary way of validating each
corresponding contrary aspect of the orthodox world."

Enlightenment philosophy severed the brain from the body with
Descartes's famous maxim "I think, therefore I am." The reigning
mindset championed objective rationality over all other kinds of
knowledge. Women historically had been seen more for their bodies
than for their minds. And where there is sexism, racism is not far
behind. As Charles Darwin saw it, "Women's physiology appeared
characteristic of the lower races, and therefore of a past and lower
state of civilization." With medicine now being a professional endeavor, women were shut out of formal education. Ehrenreich and
English write, "Another myth, fostered by conventional medical histories, is that male professionals won out on the strength of their superior technology. According to these accounts, (male) science more
or less automatically replaced (female) superstition—which from
then on was called 'old wives' tales.'" Here we have an origin point of
the "woo-woo": healing practices to which science does not lend its
imprimatur. The authors note how the cultural mood of the day determined the reasons given for shutting women out: "Witches were
attacked for being pragmatic, empirical and immoral. But in the
19th century the rhetoric reversed: Women became too unscientific,
delicate and sentimental. The *stereotypes* change to suit male convenience." And these ideas were codified into scientific education.
A well-known 1848 obstetrical text stated that "she [woman] has
a head almost too small for intellect but just big enough for love."
Rationality took on a male valence, and irrationality, along with intuition, thy name is woman.

As writer, artist, and professional witch Amanda Yates Garcia
writes, "When we're encouraged to be rational, often we're really
being encouraged to see ourselves as separate and in competition
with others." These inheritances are visible today. Comen writes,
"When controversies arise within medicine, they still break down
along gendered lines in a way that invariably elevates a rational,

traditional, masculine-coded approach over the squishy, feminine, woo-woo: 'Eastern vs. Western,' 'natural vs. science-based,' 'alternative vs. conventional.'" The breakdown can be subjective and biased. As Julia Moskin of *The New York Times* writes, "One man's woo-woo, of course, is another's deeply held belief system."

If women's intuition exists at all, this insistence on intuition as a subpar form of data makes it hard for women to trust their intuition in the first place. Women have been told they are inherently wrong, not the norm, "a deformity," by none less than Aristotle, whose name was emblazoned upon the library of the university I attended. The most widely read book on intuition, Malcolm Gladwell's *Blink*, self-consciously resists using the word. Instead he calls this process of knowing without knowing why "rapid cognition." Does Gladwell avoid the term *intuition* because it smacks too much of the feminine, something that lacks the rigor of the rational?

From the neuroscientific perspective, intuition is pattern recognition born of expertise, occurring at a subconscious level. And from the somatic perspective, the body dials up stored memories to explain current stimuli in nanoseconds—your body will know before your brain does. Women are perhaps required to utilize these incredible evolutionary tools because we live under threat. Brandi Auset, a psychic in Southern California, tells me, "Every girl has that experience of feeling a gaze on her and knowing it's not okay, and feeling unsafe, but maybe not even understanding why. Dangerous situations are sometimes the first opportunity women feel like they have to use their intuition."

Women are forced to be more aware of our surroundings and of potential predators. Go to a local gym and you will likely encounter "women's self-defense" training. You would be unlikely to encounter "men's self-defense"—that would be called boxing. That kind of intuition—protection—is socially sanctioned. De Becker's *The Gift of Fear* focuses almost exclusively on arming women with confidence in their instincts, to save their lives from predators. A MasterClass by FBI profiler Joe Navarro teaches people to listen to themselves, not to enhance their creativity or better their lives, but to save their lives. De Becker and Navarro come from backgrounds in law enforcement where all too often they saw the grisly ends female victims met at the hands of abusive husbands and random psychos. And yet it is this kind of intuition as self-defense that we are taught to believe is real. It exists to protect us.

And even this locus of intuition is rife with contradictions. While on the one hand we have self-defense classes that teach women to be vigilant against predators, women are also socialized to be good, quiet, not make a scene. In her landmark tome *Women Who Run with the Wolves*, Clarissa Pinkola Estés puts it this way: "Early training to 'be nice' causes women to override their intuitions. In that sense, they are actually purposefully taught to submit to the predator." For women of color, that pressure is manifold. When she was nineteen, the actress Gabrielle Union was raped at gunpoint at her job at a Payless shoe store. She recounts the assault in her memoir, writing, "When the man first walked in, I was straightening a display of fake Timberlands. He came up behind me and asked about the boots. I took one look at him and wanted to run, but I didn't. I was aware of how my coworkers and the people in our mostly white community viewed black people, so my racial solidarity and 'good home training' as a 'polite' woman kicked in."

Some evolutionary science suggests that this imperative toward safety—not just for the individual from predators, but to ensure the survival of their offspring—forced our female ancestors to develop keener intuition to read the environment. "[Women's] brains were trained with peak awareness because they were protecting a heart outside of their own bodies. Female brains therefore evolved to have a larger composition and ability to organize chunks of environmental information at a time, giving them an edge to read people," says an article from *Medical Daily*. Jo Anne Kelly Richards, an herbalist at Brooklyn's Remedies Herb Shop, puts it this way: "Women are the invisible healers, the invisible caretakers, going back generations. We cook for our families, and the first line of medicine is being nourished. We are the first to see when something is wrong."

As a socially subordinate group, women have been "forced to acquire certain nonverbal skills," writes Audrey Nelson, an expert in gender communication for *Psychology Today*. "Women needed to pay attention to the moods, likes, dislikes, emotions, and reactions of the dominant group almost as a survival instinct." This results in a "politics of empathy," as Daniel Goleman, author of *Emotional Intelligence*, calls it. This tendency doesn't just extend along gender lines—all socially oppressed groups and classes are sensitized to the feelings and whims of the ruling classes and races. It is an empathy to ensure survival.

Rose Hackman, the author of *Emotional Labor*, echoes these findings. She argues that intuition is a skill that not only women possess. "Subordinate's intuition," she tells me over breakfast in a café, "is someone with less power trying to figure out what's going on with someone that has more power, for basic survival."

In an interview on *BBC Woman's Hour*, Hackman said, "So much of the feedback I got as a journalist when I began looking into emotional labor is *women are just better at emotions, women are just better at intuition*. I set about trying to figure out if this is actually true. The research is pretty damning. It shows if women are indeed 'better' at intuition, it's not because of biology. It's because of subordinate's positionality. It's because we are in society still expected to cater to the feelings and experiences of other people, often men." She describes a seminal study from 1985 that randomly paired women and men, assigning one person as the leader and the other as a subordinate. Leaders, the study found, did not possess any intuitive awareness of their subordinate. But subordinates were expected to be extremely perceptive about the expressions of the leader, regardless of gender. The study found no connection between gender and intuition; it was all about the position of dominance within the pairing.

"It's the compensating guesswork of emotions, of predictive intuitiveness, of perceptiveness, that anyone who is in a subordinate position—in this case women in the patriarchy—are expected to do, not just to survive but to figure out ways to survive and not ruffle the feathers of the person who has power," Hackman explains. "Women's intuition is one version of emotional labor," she says, and that work is offloaded not just onto women, but onto any marginalized community. Intuition is "a defensive emotional labor," as she puts it. And it is situational. People growing up in a home with a parent who has a temper, for example, learn to perceive and react to the emotional tenor. As RuPaul recalled in his memoir, he learned how to read the room as a child. So intuition, from a sociological perspective, is not fixed and essential; it's learned and adaptive.

—

Is it anxiety or intuition? When I pose this question to most women, they instantly get it. Perhaps that is because we live under threat and we've learned to be a little paranoid at every dark alley, whether in the literal streets or the passageways of the mind. Sometimes when I pose the question, people (usually men) don't know what I'm talking about, and I envy their placidity. But there is one scenario in which this tension becomes instantly recognizable to all: the urge to check on a newborn baby. Is this impulse a mother's intuition to swoop in at just the right moment when the tiny creature might be imperiled? Or is it worry gone haywire?

The so-called maternal instinct comes from the mistaken belief that women are hardwired to know how to care for the screaming naked strangers who emerge from their bodies. This is "a crock of *scheisse*," Paige Bellenbaum, LCSW, founding director of the Motherhood Center of New York, tells me. "Becoming a mother is a learned behavior, and we all learn how to do it differently and on our own trajectories." Chelsea Conaboy, author of *Mother Brain: How Neuroscience Is Rewriting the Story of Parenthood*, writes in *The New York Times*, "The notion that the selflessness and tenderness babies require is uniquely ingrained in the biology of women, ready to go at the flip of a switch, is a relatively modern—and pernicious—one.

It was constructed over decades by men selling an image of what a mother should be, diverting our attention from what she actually is and calling it science." Women who become mothers do not automatically know how to take care of babies; I sure didn't when I had mine.

I outright reject the idea of a maternal instinct—but a mother's intuition? Maybe. Around the same time I had my first kid, I felt my intuition kick in in a big way. For me, that intuition wasn't knowing exactly what my baby needed, when, and how to do it. With a newborn and the attendant birth recovery, sleep deprivation, and hormonal melee, intuition helped prioritize what needed to happen next, for me: Put the baby down in his crib for a nap. Take a shower. Attempt a jagged nap on the couch. Eat? Yes, we should all try to eat. These notions came to me quick and complete. At the same time, when I was supposed to be resting, I would have the overwhelming urge to check on my sleeping child. These feelings came from the same place—they felt urgent, and solid. So if I feel directed to check on my sleeping baby and protect him from sudden infant death syndrome, or SIDs, a terrifying condition—which really needs to be rebranded, by the way, as it is exceedingly rare if you take the right precautions, so perhaps it could be renamed Scary Thing That Doesn't Happen Very Often So Go Back to Bed—is that intuition, or is that anxiety? It's hard to tell when the stakes are so high.

I meet Dr. Philippa Gordon at her home in Brooklyn to get her take. After practicing pediatrics for twenty-seven years and founding her own practice, she has seen it all. Her soothing manner and expertise have made her something of a celebrity among Brooklyn parents, the neurotic ones you read trend pieces about. Gordon is slight and warm, wearing a scarf knotted around her neck like a French mariner. I take off my boots in her foyer and she places them by the radiator so they will be warm and dry for my departure. Over a pot of green tea ("good for cholesterol," she says, and adds with a mischievous grin, "so they say"), I ask her the mother of all questions: anxiety or intuition?

"I had a mother once who kept imagining that she would drop her baby and a bus would run it over," Gordon tells me. "I walked her to the psychiatrist." That ruminative, invasive quality is a symptom of postpartum anxiety. This cortisol-infused, spiraling flavor harked back to other definitions of anxiety (as distinct from intuition) I'd heard. It's the perseveration that keeps you up at three in the morning. Throw a new baby in the mix and the feeling gets injected with steroids.

"But worry is important," Gordon continues. "I don't like anybody who dismisses a parent and tells them there's nothing wrong. The term 'women's intuition' can be an insult to say you're illogical and to pat you on the head. No one should ever brush your concerns away. If a parent comes in and is worried that their baby has cancer, even if there's a 99 percent chance it isn't cancer, I'm going to offer the parents a blood test. This gives you a ladder out of the well of fear." So what Gordon is saying is that if you have a suspicion, take your kid to the doctor. A good doctor won't dismiss you. "And if we investigate and find nothing is wrong, that's not a waste of resources. That's a good outcome," she says.

In twenty-seven years of practice, Gordon says, it's always been the mothers who are most worried. She's encountered only one father who was more anxious than the mother—she remembers him to this day. That anecdote is striking.

Barbara and Allan Pease, a married Australian author duo who describe themselves as "body language experts," ran an experiment where a group of people were asked to watch a ten-second video clip of crying babies. There was no sound on the video, only visual cues. Women, most of whom were mothers, could detect a wide range of emotions and experiences, from pain to hunger to sleepiness to gas. When men viewed the same videos, fewer than 10 percent could identify more than two emotions, and those male participants copped to guessing. The study also tested grandparents. Grandmothers' identification scores were analogous to those of the mothers, and many grandfathers could not even successfully identify their own grandchild.

Yet a 2013 peer-reviewed controlled experiment published in *Nature Communications* found just the opposite: "Both fathers and mothers can reliably and equally recognize their own baby from their cries, and . . . the only crucial factor affecting this ability is the amount of time spent by the parent with their own baby." The results underscore the importance of "exposure and learning in the development of this ability . . . rather than sex-specific innate predispositions."

Other studies have revealed the same plasticity in the brains of primary care–giving fathers. A highly cited Israeli study from 2014 used brain imaging to examine differences in cerebral structures and levels of oxytocin between first-time primary care–giving mothers, primary care–giving fathers, and primary care–giving gay fathers without maternal involvement. The authors of the study note that, because of the progress of social norms, this was the first time in human history that it has even been possible to measurably interrogate centuries-old beliefs about gender and parenting. The results showed that the circuitry of the brain that lights up when raising children—structures related to vigilance, salience, reward, motivation, social understanding, and cognitive empathy—were similar in fathers and mothers. These findings demonstrate the malleability of brains and child-rearing ability based on time and experience, regardless of gender.

We've seen the impact of expertise on intuition. So it would make sense that the parent experiencing intuitions about a baby is the person with more time in the field. In heterosexual couples, that is still overwhelmingly the mother. Even though fathers are just as competent at taking care of children, mothers are often the food source and therefore more tethered to a baby. Throw the trauma of pregnancy and childbirth, along with sleep deprivation, into the mix and you have a recipe for anxiety. (And not everyone feels intuitive in the first place. As writer Jen Glantz recalled of her postpartum days, "I don't have a gut. I literally don't know.")

But it is also, perhaps, a recipe for intuition. Dr. Harvey Karp, pediatrician, inventor of the Snoo bassinet, and author of the blockbuster

Happiest Baby on the Block, puts it to me this way: "Women go through pregnancy and delivery, which is a totally animalistic, non-cognitive experience. That may open you up to greater anxiety, on the one hand, but also greater openness to non-cognitive flows of information." This can result in heightened environmental and sensory awareness, which can look a lot like intuition. A study showed that women in late pregnancy were able to decode angry or threatening faces with more accuracy and precision than women in early pregnancy. Another study reported that a sample of German policewomen who returned to work after maternity leave were more vigilant on the job, and better at spotting crimes.

So the takeaway is that there is indeed a distinction between anxiety and intuition. The experience of new motherhood is an excellent place to disentangle the knots. The experts agree that anxiety has a looping quality that hijacks the nervous system and won't always subside in the face of facts. Paige Bellenbaum walks me through a scenario of postpartum anxiety:

> Say my baby has a rash and I'm worried. I take the baby to the pediatrician, and the doctor says it's no big deal and gives me some cream. But I still don't feel reassured. I'm ruminating, I'm catastrophizing, I'm jumping to conclusions. I'm worried my baby is going to die, I've been online for hours and hours and have found that the rash is connected to diabetes and heart failure and all these things. Now I'm convinced something bigger is happening and I go to a different pediatrician, and I call again and again because I need to be continually told everything is okay. I can't manage my stress around the condition, and now it's interrupting my ability to take care of myself or my baby. I can't remember the last time I took a shower, and sometimes I'm forgetting to feed my baby because I'm fixated on trying to figure out what this rash is.

That feeling of being swept away by the problem is a good indicator of anxiety, not intuition. And, fortunately for moms and birthing people today, we have some vocabulary for this condition. Bellen-baum runs an inpatient day program and support groups for moms who are struggling with mental health in the perinatal and postpartum periods. Women who have preexisting mental health conditions are more at risk of experiencing this kind of intense anxiety or depression. Talking to a doctor is never a bad idea when a new mom is being snowed under by ruminative thoughts.

A mother's intuition might not always have a negative charge. I speak with Talia Kovacs, a mom to a three-year-old in Brooklyn, who describes a very different intuitive experience in her pregnancy: her intuition told her that everything was fine. This was while doctors kept insisting that everything was not fine, that it was, in fact, dire. She had intrauterine growth restriction (IUGR), in addition to gestational diabetes and a two-vessel cord. Her doctors were closely monitoring her and the baby. "It's not that I didn't agree I had IUGR; I did. I just didn't think it was as bad as they were making it out to be. They wanted me to come in every week for measurements, and I asked to come in every other week. The measurements made things more stressful and didn't actually contribute to the health of the baby," she says. She resisted medical interventions that to her felt superfluous. Her daughter was born perfectly healthy and did not spend any time in the neonatal intensive care unit.

I am bowled over by how Kovacs maintained her inner authority in her first pregnancy, in the face of doctors' precautions. She contends that her own intuition was another piece of the puzzle, no better or worse than experts' opinions. "The ultrasounds and measurements were good information," she says, "but my intuition is also good information." This is pretty amazing to me. She points out that one reason we're willing to consign our agency to experts may be that "a benefit of listening to doctors over our own intuition would be that there's somebody to blame." Kovacs now coaches families on raising resilient, capable kids. On the prevalence of anxiety, she says, "It's not just about not knowing what's going to happen. Anxiety is also not trusting your own ability to handle it." A hallmark of anxiety is mistrust, whereas intuition is about trust. The more Kovacs trusted herself and her ability to handle the hard things, the more she was able to keep her anxiety at bay.

Mother's intuition, like any intuition, is a muscle that is developed. It comes with time, experience, and getting to know your children, watching them develop into an individual with whom you have a relationship. "We earn intuition," Bellenbaum says. "It comes with practice, mastery, and experience."

Echoing the wisdom of neuroscientists and psychologists, Gordon says she always listens to grandmothers, as they are repositories of hard-earned expertise. "If a grandmother is concerned," she explains, "this is someone who has been around a lot of children and has impressions I should listen to." A grandmother's sense might be truer intuition—she has a larger sample size of data and can spot an issue with clearer eyes.

Abigail Tucker, a science journalist, author of *Mom Genes: Inside the New Science of Our Ancient Maternal Instinct*, and mother of five, explains it this way: "I don't think intuition is intrusive. It's expansive. It has a slightly more inspired quality. One way to differentiate is to tell yourself your body has changed, your mind has changed, and it's doing what it's supposed to do. You can try to remind yourself, *I've been profoundly changed and I'm going to learn how to be kind to me.*"

Looking back at those foggied early days, I wonder whether I had postpartum something. I think I had a complex emotional reaction to a complex human experience. I felt anxious about the eight-pound people I brought home from hospitals because how could I not? I felt anxious about whether I would ever be able to walk or sleep or think normally again. The new normal is scary indeed. But when I drill down on what I really experienced, it felt like something more akin to grief. A grief that had nothing to do with my kids themselves, because they are great and I love them beyond measure. The grief I felt was more about the job title and role of mother. It felt like an inheritance, feeling the weight of what women have sacrificed and tamped down, the work they made in snatches of moments at kitchen tables. My mom's mom writing poetry at night. My dad's mom packing up the household to move to another army base, to make a home anew. The creativity that was denigrated as "women's work," the dreams that were given up. There were ideas about inequality I understood only intellectually until a person emerged from my person. I felt my friends' sadness at their husbands' insensitivities and the careers that had been curtailed and promotions denied because of maternity leaves. My insides had been rearranged.

This fact is both common as dirt and monumental when it happens to you. It's the same as death. When you lose someone, you can't believe we are all just sitting here in the café, paying bills, texting in the group chat. Why aren't we running down the street shouting at the top of our lungs that people die? That we will die? That someone was born? And in that birth, a birth into a line of ancestry?

What I had been born into was a connection to generations, multitudes whom I would never know personally but to whom I now had a blood bond. Some people probably feel this deep in their bones without having to give birth—perhaps I'm just very literal. Now, a few years out, I see that what I was feeling was a postpartum transformation where a part of me came alive in a very visceral way—ancient knowledge that isn't instinct, not exactly. More like a realization. *Oh, that's the heaviness my mom carried.* Those are the scars we create from our own bodies. The histories of women and mothers that had been diminished were now so vivid. When we hear about how many children used to die in infancy and think that's just how it was—no. That is a world of loss. That's history that has been expunged from the record.

In those early days it was grief, but now I see it as something else: a thread that connects me to the strength that's so mighty and also so minimized. A power that makes the world go round. Our very existence. That paradox rhymes with intuition, the power that is denied and belittled and what has also kept us alive.

—

Whether or not you are someone who has reproduced, there can be something maternal about intuition. Intuition comforts and provides wise counsel. When we develop our intuition, it can become the voice of an elder who only wants the very best for us. Intuition can hold us as if we are a sweet youngster. I am loath to invoke "the inner child"; I was born twenty-seven years old and have no gauzy fondness for childhood. And yet I think of the question Sarah Perry asks herself before making important decisions: What would make the younger version of me happy? The one who ran barefoot in the grass (in my case, imagining she was running in stilettos on her way to a cocktail party), before she was leveled with shame and told to shut up?

If summoning your younger self is just too cringe, thinking about the advice we would offer a friend can be helpful, too. Women mother each other in beautiful ways. Some of my most powerful friendships are marked by a care and comfort we offer each other: anticipating needs, nursing heartbreak, sending soup when one of us is sick. We can sometimes mother our friends better than ourselves, or accept care from our friends in a straightforward, sweet way. So the next time you are up against a wall with a tough decision, think about what advice you might give a friend. I wager it is more pure, simple, and loving than the punishing prescriptions you foist upon yourself.

Community among women is integral not only to fostering intuition but to living a happy life. And yet, as wise and nurturing as our peers can be, sometimes they simply have not lived long enough to help us deepen our intuitions. Our perspectives are too narrow, our words heartfelt but lacking the gravitas of a life lived. This is why we need elders: to stretch our purview, to present evidence of survival through cycles of grief and confusion, to dispense wisdom gained through experience. Like Gordon said, a grandmother's concerns are important information. We also need to be elders to younger women. Both sides are incredibly healing and broaden our point of view.

Because of historical realities—from women being othered in medicine and religion to exclusion from education and formal institutions for centuries—women's knowledge and healing practices were passed down from mother to daughter, neighbor to neighbor, midwife to new mom. But we live in a culture that celebrates older women only when they look young. "Antiaging" products (the greatest trick the capitalist devil ever played) are a multibillion-dollar industry, and the Pyrrhic victory given to older women is for Martha Stewart to appear on the cover of *Sports Illustrated* at eighty-four, looking decades younger than her years. Our culture would prefer older women to be invisible, or to erase their age. But any older woman will tell you—with invisibility comes freedom. The most confident, self-possessed women I know are women in their fifties, sixties, seventies, eighties, nineties. Life lived through them, and they ran out of shits to give. So if you really want to develop intuition, whatever shade on the gender spectrum that you identify as—find your elders.

Humans are one of only a handful of mammals, along with orcas, whales, and chimpanzees, to go through menopause. "The grandmother hypothesis" explains why: grandmothers possess such a wealth of acquired knowledge and skills for the group as a whole—how to raise young, how to care for mothers as they become mothers—that it is more evolutionarily advantageous for them to stop reproducing and instead pass on their knowledge. Grandmothers, then, are a key to the survival of our species. As Gordon said, when a grandmother has a concern about a child, she pays extra-close attention. As Sharon Blackie, the author of *Hagitude: Reimagining the Second Half of Life*, explains in an interview, "Back in the day, the wisdom of elder women was very important. Older women were mentors to the young. We had women who were truth tellers when the culture needed to hear some difficult truths about itself." Elder women are critical to our survival and can teach us a lot about developing our intuition.

Elders are everywhere, once you start looking around. And they need not be limited to your family. No matter how loving your relationship with your own mother is, that relationship is complex, and her advice hard to hear because she is *your mom*. So I encourage you to look beyond your immediate family, widen the scope of your web of connections. In *Women Who Run with the Wolves*, Estés refers to these intuitive teachers as "little mothers." My elders include Sindy Grappy, my children's nanny, who has raised dozens of kids and can clock immediately when something is wrong. She knows when an illness or behavior is something mild and when it is something more concerning. That's pattern recognition of the highest order. That's Gladwell's ten-thousand-hour rule at play.

Melissa Coss Aquino is my friend and inspiration, and also my elder. She is a model of what an intuitively led life can look like. And then I have elders who may not even know they are my elders. I devour the Substack magazine *Oldster*, where people over forty answer questionnaires about the aging process, and listen to Julia Louis-Dreyfus's podcast *Wiser Than Me*, where women of a certain age dispense gems of hard-earned knowledge.

—

We are bombarded by so much imagery, so much messaging, that it can feel impossible to hear yourself think. For young women today, the noise has never been louder. Toccarra Cash, an actress and activist, started the organization the Image Monster to help young women sift through the cacophony. "When we were younger, the messages we received were coming from our family, our peers at school, celebrities you saw on TV," Cash tells me. It's the same today, with one key difference: "With the onslaught of social media, in one scroll session you can encounter all of that at the same time—a peer posting a picture of herself with a filter, a celebrity, an ad for Ozempic, a family member commenting on a picture of you. The acceleration of all that messaging has been magnified times a million." Women have always received a lifetime of contradictory messages, but now it has reached a fever pitch. "It gets so loud," Cash says. "You can't hear your own voice, you can't feel your own intuition, and you can't feel your own self-perception. How you perceive yourself is informed by so much, and that's what I'm trying to help young women unpack."

Cash's workshops are aimed primarily at young women of color, because "the epitome of beauty is something you are not. In the case of Black women in particular, the messages we receive are that our hair is wrong, our skin is wrong, our bodies are wrong. And then you have messages in your community that tell you you shouldn't feel the way you feel. If I would state that I felt badly about my body, it was like, 'Black girls don't do that. Black girls don't get anorexia. Black girls love their curves.'" While all women are forced to navigate so much, women of color contend with extra layers of complexity.

It's so much. I ask Cash how we can begin to untie it all. "One of the major ways to address it is through connection," she says. Meeting in person is a vital component of the workshops. One revealing exercise that gets participants talking is when the women are asked whom they consider beauty role models, and are then instructed to stand in one of the four corresponding corners: family, peers, celebrities and influencers, and your own self-perception. "That last corner always has the least amount of women," Cash says, "which I find fascinating."

Through other writing and creative exercises, young women dissect their experiences and connect with one another. Leading these workshops has been incredibly healing for Cash: "There's so much wisdom to be gained from elders, and it's a feature of the African American community. While I'm not at an age that's considered 'an elder,' I'm coming to embrace my role as a woman who is able to guide my younger sisters. It's actually a little selfish, because I heal the childhood and adolescent parts of myself being able to be something like an elder for the younger women." Participants often remark that they wish they'd had the program when they were even younger—the college women wish they'd had it in high school, the high school girls wish they'd had it in junior high. Their desire to apply Cash's tools shows that you can be an elder at any age.

Women connecting with one another to hear themselves think is vital for intuition. It's also an act of resistance. "I think because we live in such a capitalist society we're never encouraged to get quiet and just stop and be still," Cash says. When you're not consuming, posting, working, you might be doing something different. Listening. Resting. Connecting. And from there? Who knows what is possible.

You can be an elder through professional mentoring organizations. I've been working with Mei Ting Xie, a sophomore at Hunter College, through Girls Write Now for three years now, and helping Mei with her writing and the other inevitable challenges of transitioning into young womanhood has been a joy of my life. Spiritual communities often have similar opportunities to pair up, or you can lead your local Brownie troop, like my friend Caty did.

Since we are always changing, our intuition is always changing too. Intuition is not a static quality that remains the same over the course of your life. When you have elders, they will infuse your perspectives with wisdom and fresh ideas. When you act as an elder, you distill your lessons into what you wish you had known. True mastery comes from being able to teach another. We need to continually stretch our perspective, both forward into the people we are becoming and backward to the people we were. This dynamic flow of knowledge keeps our intuition fresh and alive.

—

Before pivoting to full-time work as "a pragmatic witch," Rebecca Auman was president of a large academic medical foundation. Now she describes herself as "the Walmart greeter of the underworld." She's always been able to see what people are going to say before they say it, and this ability made her an excellent fundraiser—she led teams that raised more than $2 billion over the course of her career. She was a people pleaser, going through the motions of what was expected of her as a southern woman: getting married to a man when she knew she was queer, taking on additional emotional labor at her job. It all led to burnout. She began spending more time with her tarot deck, which she'd been practicing for thirty years. She eventually left her job and today coaches women who are high on the corporate ladder on how to honor their intuition.

Auman has a honeyed North Carolina accent and gray, witchy hair. We FaceTime on a Monday afternoon, and she takes my call as she's sitting in the sun by a river in the woods. Being in nature helps her connect with her intuition. "When I think about women's intuition," she tells me, "I think more in terms of what we're trying *not* to listen to." She gives the example of getting on an elevator with a person who gives you a bad vibe and, instead of stepping off, you ride all the way up. You don't want to be rude.

Auman may be one of the few witches who has experience both in corporate America and in the magical, or what some might call the "woo-woo," a dismissive term laced with misogyny. On her podcast, *Voices in the River,* Auman interviewed Emi Kolawole, an executive at Google X who gives TED Talks, and said calling tarot and the like "woo-woo" sequesters these ideas in the occult. But those tools "give women the ability to see ourselves in equitable power and in equitable self-knowing, and that empowerment is highly, highly disruptive," she said. "That's why the woo-woo label comes out so quickly. That's dangerous to people who want to harness your intent for their own ends. Knowing what you want and putting your intention in the world is highly disruptive." Many of Auman's clients share a challenge: "I work with some powerhouses, and it all comes down to worth. *Do I belong at the table? Am I enough? Am I worthy? Do I deserve this?* Believing in our worth as women is the work of a lifetime."

For all women, and especially the high-octane women Auman works with, it is hard for us to be still. There is always something we could be doing—for our families, for our careers, for our friends and neighbors. "We think there's something wrong in quiet," Auman says. "The enemy of our intuition is the feeling that productivity equals value. When we are producing, we're definitely not intuiting. How do we understand that just being with ourselves, even if it's for five minutes, is enough?" Auman used to be a single mom who worked full-time. She managed to carve out time by "making it really simple. When my son was little we'd just light a candle and put on special music for five minutes when I got home from work. That for me was a time of transition, and it taught him to listen to himself, too." She also works with men, and notes a key difference: "Men are so open to receiving because they have been conditioned to trust themselves. They tend to question less. They don't have to constantly be on guard."

—

What about when your intuition is just plain wrong? What about when it overlaps too closely with delusion? This really hit me when I got rejected for a fellowship that I was certain, in my bones, I was going to get. In hindsight, I think I just really wanted it to work out. I called my mom to get her take. "Maybe intuition is like batting averages," she analogized. "If you hit one ball out of three pitches, you're doing really well," she said. I don't love baseball and understand nothing about batting averages. Getting a hit one-third of the time doesn't sound great, honestly. We live in a world where three out of three balls is the goal. But what the greatest professional athletes know, what my mom knows, is that achieving 100 percent is not humanly possible.

Maybe the goal, then, is to swing at every ball like it will be your career-defining grand slam. And at the same time to realize that one out of three ain't bad.

I imagine that a New York Liberty player stepping up to the foul line, who gathers her breath, shoots the ball, and misses, probably should not throw a fit and spiral into self-doubt after every miss. Instead, the player has to approach each new opportunity with the confidence that she is going to make a basket. The better she can become at utilizing the time between shots—to move past the sad realization that the ball didn't sink into the basket and know there is another chance coming her way—the more likely she is to hit it next time.

We somehow got the message that our intuition is always right, and I think this is a damaging idea. It raises the stakes so high that when it doesn't pan out, you are suddenly questioning your most essential self. We can fail better with intuition, and this writing business is rife with rejection. Memory is not infallible, nor is our factual recall or so many other cognitive processes. Even our physicality isn't perfect: sometimes you don't see the black ice and you slip. It doesn't mean you need to amputate your feet. Intuition is the same: it can be wrong without it meaning *you* are wrong.

—

Amber Tamblyn, the writer, activist, actress, and editor of the essay collection *Listening in the Dark: Women Reclaiming the Power of Intuition*, echoes the idea of how difficult silence can be. "The patriarchal world wants women to shut up and be quiet," she tells me. "But that's not the kind of silence I think women should adhere to. We owe it to ourselves to have a relationship with introspective silence—one that allows information to come in and nourish us. It's opening a space for ourselves internally, instead of what the outside world is demanding of us." Just carving out the silence and sitting in the discomfort of not *doing* anything is hard enough. And on top of that, the information you get might be difficult. The silence required to hear your own voice might tell you something different from the social conditioning you've been going through, and the yardsticks of success you've been working to meet. Intuition, when you begin to listen to it, can actually make your life more difficult. It might tell you your job or relationship isn't right for you anymore, or that your group of friends might not be healthy. "That's when your rational mind takes over," Tamblyn says, "and gives you the million reasons not to listen to your intuition—it'll destroy your marriage, we need job safety, we're afraid of what people might think about us. Your rational mind will try to cut intuition off at the pass."

And for a simple reason: listening in the dark can be scary. Your intuition might show you things you'd rather not see, truths you'd rather not confront. But Tamblyn urges that it needn't be a zero-sum game. "I think intuition is like turning the teakettle on," she says. "Maybe you don't pour the tea, but you boil the water. You get the pot going. And if you decide you're going to have a cup of tea, then you can have it." As Talia Kovacs said, her intuition during her pregnancy was another piece of data in addition to sonograms and ultrasounds. It was another part of the puzzle. And when you learn to trust yourself, you undo the message that you are wrong. Actually, you are right. And from there, anything is possible.

CHAPTER 6

DIPPING INTO UNCONSCIOUS
WATERS

One Friday afternoon in early spring, I ride an uptown train to Harlem to ingest a cocktail of MDMA and psilocybin and lie on the floor blindfolded while two musicians play instruments inches from my head for five hours.

Earlier that day, I was attempting to write about the unconscious—what it is, how it relates to intuition. You know who else has attempted to pin down this slippery concept? Freud and Jung, to name a few. There I was at the kitchen table, yogurt fossilized at its edges, giving it my best shot. The memory of this endeavor comes to me as I lie on the mat with gongs and singing bowls vibrating my cranium. "What was I talking about?!" I think (or say out loud, who knows), which strikes me as ridiculous, ironic, hilarious. My response to this thought is to heave laughter from the depths of my belly. It's the kind of laugh that clears out years of gunk and leaves you feeling spent, postcoital. What strikes me as so funny is that hours ago, I was fumbling to theorize, to verbalize these inner recesses. The mode and mediums—the conscious mind and language—were the problems, I now realize. Now I'm spelunking into the very cave of the unconscious.

Occasionally, intuition emerges from its subterranean labyrinth, like a prairie dog popping its tiny head out of the rocky soil, delivering a packet of information in the form of a bodily sensation or a dream or a simple truth. When we allow ourselves to stop and recognize these moments, they can feel transcendent. Maybe they feel so profound because we often can't quite pinpoint their origin; all of a sudden, we know something without knowing why. Or leave transcendence out of it altogether and take the scientific definition of intuition: pattern recognition based on expertise that occurs rapidly, below the level of conscious awareness. We lug around lifetimes' worth of memories in the unconscious, and those memories get unlocked and activated based on stimuli in our present environment. And, as someone once said, it happens in the blink of an eye. Digging around in the sandbox of the unconscious—through therapy, through psychedelics, through hypnosis, through dreams—can bring intuition closer to the surface.

But what even is this shadowy no-man's-land of the unconscious? Having spoken to dozens of experts—from evolutionary psychologists to manifesting gurus to Harvard professors to shapersons to dream analysts to a retired narcotics cop turned psychedelics evangelist to therapists who have their own TV shows—I've come to see that the unconscious means different things to different professionals, and they all use their own metaphors to describe it.

One popular image is the iceberg, with conscious thought as the very tip, the snowy cap peeking out of the icy sea. Just below, we have the much more sizable level of the subconscious. Here we store memories, associations, the names of bands we once listened to, the scent of the janitor mowing the lawn outside your elementary school window in June and the restlessness it inspired. The subconscious lugs around the trove of information you've accumulated throughout your life that you can tap into, if compelled, but that you are not actively thinking about as you go through the motions of your day. "Like footprints on the beach" is how my therapist described memories in the subconscious. I picture it as the back seat of a family minivan. We're driving to Grandma's, our eyes focused on the road. But if the kids start fighting (or their iPads go on the fritz, or the baby has thrown his juice box at your head in a fit of pugnacious boredom), we might Stop This Car. And when we pull over and start digging around, lo, here is the shriveled string cheese of generational trauma; here is the lone sock that is the shame of getting your period and not knowing what the hell was going on; here is the wilted sandwich lettuce of the absentee parent; here's the lint-covered lollipop of the mean girls on the bus. The crap in the back seat isn't impeding your voyage, exactly. But if you are so inclined, you can wade through the detritus and see what's there. And if you clean it out, the trip itself might get clearer—lighter too. It's not even that there's less junk back there. But the noises and odors emanating from the back seat are no longer as mysterious. You have more focus for the road ahead.

For Freud, to whom we owe a great deal of our lay understanding of the unconscious, it's the least accessible layer of our experience, filled with memories, drives, desires, and evolutionary impulses that keep us alive. Writing in the early twentieth century, Freud thought the unconscious was mostly filled with repressed urges for sex and violence, penis envy and Oedipal complexes. The Freudian conception of the unconscious has been summarized as "hot and wet; it seethes with lust and anger; it was hallucinatory, primitive, irrational." The Freudian understanding of the unconscious was supernatural, a bit infantile, and deeply unpleasant, "a dump for moral refuse." Carl Jung, Freud's student, built upon his mentor's idea of the unconscious, envisioning it as more positive and expansive, "a rich source of creativity." Jung believed "the unconscious will express its ideas by means of dreams, fantasies, spontaneous imagery, slips of the tongue. If the unconscious message is ignored, then neurosis or even physical disease may result." Jung was very into intuition, dream analysis, and coincidences, believing them to be vital pieces of data for understanding human life.

The New Psychology movement of the late nineteenth century, based in the United States, conceived that "two distinct trains of Mental action are carried on simultaneously, one consciously, the other unconsciously . . . that not only an automatic, but an unconscious action enters largely into all its processes," William Carpenter wrote in 1874. More than 130 years later, Leonard Mlodinow commented in his book *Subliminal*, "It's a profound insight, one we continue to build on to this day." Mlodinow holds a PhD in theoretical physics, wrote a book with Stephen Hawking, and has lent his pen to the TV shows *MacGyver* and *Star Trek: The Next Generation*. He explains the necessity for these two tracks of processing:

> Evolution has provided us with an unconscious mind because our unconscious is what allows us to survive in a world requiring such massive information intake and processing. Our sensory perception, our memory recall, our everyday decisions, judgments, and activities all seem effortless—but that is only because the effort they demand is expended mainly in parts of the brain that function outside awareness.

Instead of the unconscious being a repository for our base impulses, contemporary neuroscience and psychology understand the unconscious as an evolutionarily adaptive mechanism, and "kinder, gentler . . . more reality bound."

The unconscious is one of our most ancient and valuable gifts. John Bargh, the Susan Nolen-Hoeksema Chair in Psychology at Yale and author of *Before You Know It: The Unconscious Reasons We Do What We Do*, looks at unconscious processes through the lens of adaptation and drills down on the way intuitions in their most essential state serve to keep us alive. He writes, "While our conscious attention is often elsewhere, this unconscious monitoring process helps us decide what to embrace and reject, when to stay and when to go. . . . Good or bad, stay or go is the original animal reaction to the world. Eons of evolutionary time have made 'stay or go' the fastest and most basic psychological reaction of the human brain to what is going on outside of it." What he is talking about is a kind of visceral protection mechanism. And yet this feeling of being pulled toward or away from something or someone is perhaps the most fundamental manifestation of intuition. Yum or yuck, yes or no, stay or go. Bargh and other scholars argue that this is "a very old and primitive effect that existed long before we developed conscious and deliberate modes of thought." Even single-cell paramecia have approach and avoidance reactions: when scientists put an electrical current into a petri dish, the paramecia will move away from it. When a little sugar gets dissolved into the dish, they swim toward it. That toward/away is the most essential function in even the most basic of living things, as it assists in their sole imperative, which is to survive.

I've been excited to ask Bargh more about his findings. When I launch in with my first question about the unconscious, he quickly offers a generous but definitive correction, the way you would a child picking their nose in public: "My first quibble is that there's no *the unconscious*. The problem is the word *the*, mainly because it implies a separate kind of mind." He contextualizes what he means, going back to the work of Antonio Damasio, who linked the mind and body inextricably. No matter how much we'd like to be able to sort mind and body into distinct buckets, they are one and the same. So even the iceberg metaphor, which therapists the world over still reference (and which is useful in theorizing what memories and emotions we tamp down and what is closer to the surface), Bargh rejects as too stratified.

Instead of invoking the static, hierarchical (and oh so cold) iceberg, Bargh likens unconscious processes to dolphins. They can swim in the waters of unconscious processing, but they need to come up for air, into consciousness. "There's this dynamic interplay from conscious to unconscious, and they are influencing each other in a mutual way. Unconscious processes create consciousness, and conscious processes create subsequent unconscious ones," he says. And experiences in early life, which we have no conscious awareness of, no memory we can readily access, affect us for the rest of our lives. While we think we may have freedom and free will, so much has already been determined unconsciously. Unconscious processes are the puppeteers, and we are the marionettes, to add another metaphor into the mix. Or, as philosopher Daniel Dennett conceived, consciousness is more the press secretary than the president. The press secretary can observe and report on the workings of the mind but is not privy to many of the decisions made behind the closed doors of the Oval Office.

So what does all of this have to do with intuition? Like the constant dynamic interplay of our mental dolphins emerging and diving back into the water without our having to do anything about it, intuition comes to us easily. "We believe intuitions the way we believe sensory information, because it is so immediate," Bargh says. "I look out my window, I see the lake, the trees. I don't question it. Thought, effort, and figuring out reduces your certainty." As Daniel Kahneman characterized intuitive thinking, it requires little effort. Like gazing out at the landscape before us, intuition just is.

Bargh believes we can harness unconscious processing for better intuitions, and better problem solving. He tells me the story behind creating his book *Before You Know It*. He'd gotten the contract in 2014, and by 2016 he had not yet written a word. His publisher gave him six months to turn it in, in its entirety.* Bargh still had a full slate of teaching and administrative responsibilities at Yale. He drafted his manuscript by invoking a trick from Norman Mailer (and not the stabbing-his-wife part): he gave his unconscious assignments. Mailer would write, and then go off drinking and carousing, but not before telling himself that by the time he sat down at his desk the next morning, he wanted the next bit of material ready for him.

---

* To those of you thinking *Six months is a lot!*: in book-writing time, I assure you it is not. Grandparents with Storyworth subscriptions notwithstanding, in six months you could certainly write the number of words (75,000 to 100,000) that would compose a book. The difference, though, is that the words major presses like to publish need to be words strangers would want to read. And Bargh, as a writer of nonfiction (and, worse yet, an academic who is burdened with both a day job and translating jargon and esoterica into frothy prose the average business traveler might peruse at Hudson News), cannot make things up from his imagination. It is a dirty, inefficient business.

Bargh wrote in the mornings, and before breaking to teach in the afternoon, he told his mind he wanted the next part of his book figured out. "You're the CEO, and you delegate to the brain company what you want accomplished," he says. By working this way, he had dreams that structured chapters, and flashes of insight that stitched ideas together. "That's the only way I got it done," he says. He beat his deadline by three days.

We can all do this. Before going to sleep at night, give your unconscious processes some homework. The more complex, the better. Conscious thinking is great for simple rule-based tasks. But difficulty is where the back office of the brain thrives. So perhaps you ask for help in how to approach a difficult conversation, or how to better parent a child. You can ask for ways to make more money, or what your one-woman show is really all about. Whatever stumps you in your waking life, whatever you cannot think your way out of, delegate to unconscious processing. (Spiritual people might call this prayer.)

Bargh's perspective on unconscious processing as an essential adaptive tool in our human survival, and one you can hack for better results, makes a lot of sense. And yet we know from experience that we don't always pull toward what is good for us and push away the bad. Dimitri Mugianis, my ceremonial guide who dosed and sang over me, and ultimately performed what can only be described as an exorcism, lends a most revealing insight about intuition: "At one point in my life, my intuition told me to shoot as much heroin into my arm as was possible." Intuition: it's not always good for us. What *feels* intuitive, synonymous with natural, organic, and possessing a gravitational pull, can, in fact, be very bad for us. Here is where intuition and delusion, intuition and addiction, swirl together. And this is why we must venture into the unconscious to better understand whether an intuition is worth listening to or just a maladaptive urge.

Perhaps intravenous opiates aren't your drug of choice, but if you are a human living on planet Earth, you probably engage in some behavior that isn't the most beneficial. Be it scrolling your phone in a trance state, spending your hard-earned money on fill-in-the-blank-thing-you-don't-really-need-but-want-for-the-dopamine-hit, or saying you want one thing and doing the very opposite, we are all subject to unconscious drives, formed by nature and by nurture, by society's imperatives, by evolution and by our familial and genetic inheritances. Relationships, perhaps, are the stage upon which unconscious impulses get played out. As Freud noted, in a couple there are six people present, because each person brings their two parents into the relationship. And relationships are indeed a most difficult place to hear our intuition.

From adolescence to my early thirties, I pretty much exclusively favored romantic partners who were emotionally unavailable, professional dilettantes, and who would drop me quicker than a full-time job. They frequented Zeitgeist and Max Fish, rode skateboards, had no money, lived with roommates or their mothers, had cracked phone screens and stick-and-poke tattoos, didn't always know what month it was, had the romantic attention span of fruit flies. Yes, we were young. Yes, we were all finding ourselves. But if I was pursued by a more stable, conventional, "nice" potential romantic partner—Charlie who worked for a hedge fund, Toby who ran half-marathons, various one-date wonders like kind teachers, marketing execs, dentists—I ran the other way. I was like a self-sabotaging Emma Lazarus: Give me your married, your ghosting, your substance-addicted fuck boys yearning to be free! My mouth said one thing—"I want to have an authentic, honest relationship with a benevolent and respectful man who one day wants to have a family"—and my behavior said quite another: "Meet me in the bathroom!" So where was my intuition? I was doing what felt intuitive, going for the type of guy I had always pursued. Yet they were bad for me. Shouldn't my inner alarm system have been tripped?

Looking back, I think alarm bells *were* ringing, and, like Penny Jones, whose husband's marital transgressions all became clear eventually, I did my best to embroider a rational story over the intuitive truth. *(Fill-in-the-blank dude) is really going to leave his wife, isn't he? He really did lose his phone for two weeks, right?* My desire to be loved often overrode the facts of the people I was trying to make do the loving. Relationships are a mess of a place to hear our intuition, because they contain the mess of life. Straight women contend with the retrograde, persistent social messaging that suggests we are worthy only if we are in a relationship, if we have a man to validate our existence. We have familial expectations, and the scripts we saw played out in childhood. I was raised by a single mom. What I came to believe (on an unconscious level, to be sure, because neither my father nor my mother was advocating this position) was that relationships are impossible, and what felt familiar was to love a man who did not show up consistently. More than a decade in therapy later, I recognize that this was the message I internalized. This is the story that I tell myself, at the very least. If I wanted to break the habit of being attracted to guys who were ultimately no good for me, guys upon whom I was acting out the pas-de-deux of wanting to be seen and proving I could be loved, I had to dig deep into this unconscious muck and mire. This revelation, simple but not easy, was life-altering for me.

These drives are almost always easier to see in others than in ourselves. This is what accounts for the wild success and deeply satisfying viewing experience of the TV show *Couples Therapy*, with its magnetic protagonist, Orna Guralnik. Guralnik listens with her whole body—she scrunches, she tilts, she furrows in response to her patients. Her kinesthetics themselves are worthy of books on the topic. In thirty-minute episodes, we get a voyeuristic glimpse into the dynamics of real-life couples, how the experiences of their early lives and families shaped their responses to conflict today. Watching real people investigate their patterns is incredibly illustrative for anyone hoping to do the same themselves.

Speaking with Guralnik feels akin to having an audience with a major celebrity. (The text messages I got from friends and acquaintances when I posted a picture of this fortuitous meeting were like what I'd expect after meeting Beyoncé.) I ask Guralnik why it is so difficult to hear ourselves in relationships.

When a couple lands on Guralnik's couch, the question of whether or not they are "right" for each other, or even whether they should stay together, is not the principal question. Rather, what Guralnik helps her patients navigate is "the unconscious," she says. Her brows knit, and she unpacks what her conception of that shadowy place is: "things that provoke desire, that provoke longing, that provoke a kind of draw that the person is not aware of what is motivating them. They just feel this draw. This is often because of some question that remains unsolved from earlier in life. A trauma that is unresolved, a question, a mystery, an intergenerational errand that draws a person to someone else that they feel like they have some key to that question," she says. When she says "intergenerational errand" I almost fall off my chair in ecstasy. "When people are drawn to someone else, strongly, it's often related to these unconscious questions or errands that a person carries within them." In one episode of *Couples Therapy*, Guralnik describes the unconscious as the voice of the collective—your community, family, culture, society, friends.

In other words, your unconscious is asking a question of the person you have chosen. For me, the question I was asking in the young adult relationships was "Can I make you love me?" That was the intergenerational errand I was on. In committing to my husband, the question became "Can I trust you to love me?" That has not been an easy question to navigate, but it has been far more satisfying. Guralnik doesn't think you necessarily need a therapist to interrogate these patterns. "A good time to engage in therapy," she says, "is when you see yourself doing something again and again and can't figure it out, when you are blocked from understanding what that intuition or unconscious drive is." When we have good intuition in one area of life (great career instincts, for example) but poor intuition in another (always choosing the wrong partner), digging into the unconscious can provide answers for what's going on. And once you have a bit more clarity and narrative understanding around your unconscious motivations, then you can begin to trust yourself a bit more. Because it all comes out, one way or another. Investigating your intergenerational errand in therapy allows it to come out on your own terms, in a contained space. Or, as James Hollis, a Jungian psychoanalyst, puts it in his absolute banger *Finding Meaning in the Second Half of Life*, "What is not faced inwardly will play out in our external world; whatever burdens within will, sooner or later, burden without."

This framework for interrogating our romantic choices—*What is the question I am asking?*—can be applied to any area of life. *What am I asking by choosing to live in New York City? What am I asking by choosing to become a mother? What am I asking in choosing this career?* See what questions come up. Even attempting this kind of reflection requires a lot of courage and, better yet, a sense of humor.

Those questions can't always be accessed through verbal processing. The unconscious doesn't yield to directives, badgering, or five-year plans. In psychodynamic therapy, the patient associates, remembers, and riffs, piecing together connections invisible to the rational mind. Therapy is a great way of getting at the questions, but it still remains trapped in the amber of language. The unconscious and its drives and motivations can't always be worded or explored with another person. Psychedelic experience is another way in.

Writing in *Time*, Ross Ellenhorn, therapist and founder of Cardea, a ketamine-assisted therapy organization, notes how psychedelics have been medicalized:

> "Neuroplasticity" is the word many mental health professionals are now using to describe the positive effect of psychedelics; a process in which the brain sort of loosens up, becoming flexible and open to learning. . . . Plasticity is why researchers believe psychedelics show promise in helping individuals who are suffering from psychological complaints related to obsessiveness, ruminations, and habits—what professionals diagnose as "depression," "anxiety," and "addiction."

Psychedelic research has focused mainly on helping people with intractable depression, veterans with PTSD, and patients with terminal cancer. The results have been promising. A 2016 New York University study of cancer patients found that a single dose of psilocybin yielded "significant improvements in emotional and existential distress in people with cancer," with 71 to 100 percent of patients reporting positive life changes after the dose. A five-year follow-up study showed prolonged positive impact. A Johns Hopkins study from 2022 found that psilocybin along with supportive psychotherapy can relieve major depressive episodes for at least a year in some patients.

Hallucinogens have been used as spiritual tools in non-Western cultures for millennia. Science is the secular religion of the West, and has placed these substances in a medical environment. When we view the benefits of psychedelic experience through the lens of neuroplasticity, which is awesome in itself, we actually overlook a crucial aspect of these drugs. "The idea of a more flexible brain misses the most interesting and most *human* element in psychedelics: When we 'open the doors of perception,' we're encountering the world in a new or altered way through our thoughts, yes, but just as importantly, through our feelings, perceptions, intuition and gut instinct," writes Ellenhorn.

Which is all to say: you needn't be processing serious trauma or diagnoses to benefit from accessing your unconscious through psychedelics. And beyond the neuroplasticity effects, the dampening of amygdalic responses, and the lighting up of pleasure centers—all evidenced by MRI scans—deciding to go on the journey itself is empowering. Because psychedelics are scary. I'd had some bad trips in my youth—when my unconscious was all awash with messages from peers, my family, school, and the culture, unsorted and unexamined—and wasn't super excited to go back into the fray. Heck, I can't even touch marijuana in any form without having a minor panic attack. For several hours to several days (depending on what you take), you must give up control. The drugs take over.* Opting to surrender the illusion of control, deciding to go dig around in the recesses of one's

---

* A note on language: It seems increasingly popular in many psychedelic circles to refer, a bit cloyingly, to substances as "medicine." I prefer calling psychedelics drugs rather than medicine, based on something Dimitri Mugianis said before my ceremony: "After the trip, you can decide if it's medicine. Till then, we'll call it drugs."

mind and spirit, and, in my experience, pretty much signing up to feel like shit the next day isn't the most attractive proposition to most people. If psychedelics are "non-specific amplifiers," as early psychedelic researcher Dr. Stan Grof said, it's scary to imagine what might be amplified.

But the cool thing about psychedelics (and something I have not seen a lot written about in the books on them, mostly by white men who are searching for heroic experiences) is that it is very possible to titrate dosing and experience. A few years back I read Michael Pollan's 2018 book *How to Change Your Mind* and got excited by the research coming out about psychedelics. The effects he described sounded healing—people made peace with their pasts, terminal cancer patients were no longer afraid to die, people with intractable addictions were relieved—unlike the terrifying acid trips of my youth. Pollan's book so catalyzed interest in the healing properties of the drugs that there is now a term in psychedelic research called "the Pollan effect": subjects' expectations that psychedelics are a magic bullet for all that ails. Still, I was not super eager to mortgage my limited child- and work-free hours to a very high-risk/undetermined reward venture. And mostly, I was just plain scared. But then a friend from my co-working space, a mom of two with a job (in cannabis marketing, but still), told me she'd bought some microdose psilocybin chocolate from a bougie boutique in SoHo. She told me how she had eaten a chocolate the previous weekend before setting out for the beach with her kids, and how vivid and present she felt from the whole experience. She felt dandy the next day. This I could get behind.

And so began my foray into microdosing, which I did for a year and still dabble in occasionally—on a morning when I need inspiration, or to ward off sleepiness before seeing a play in the evening. Unlike MDMA or other psychedelics, which require having been off SSRIs for some time before you can enjoy the effects, a little mushroom chocolate in the morning required very little of me, and bestowed some lovely benefits. When I ate a square of Azul, which contains one-fifth of a gram of active psilocybin—about one-fifteenth of a psychedelic dose—I felt locked into whatever I was doing, whether it was writing, looking at the shimmering leaves of a tree, or walking the dog. In my writing and in conversation I felt less censored and self-conscious. Microdosing to me felt like drinking a fine cup of coffee but replacing the caffeine jitters with glitter. As long as my time is my own, it is a very pleasant experience. A counterfactual would be the time I microdosed on Thanksgiving and, under time and family pressure, I picked up the same hot handle of a pan twice and then got so overwhelmed I tapped out of cooking entirely, leaving my husband and my sister in the kitchen, half laughing at me, half frustrated, half relieved, half shrugging. So my only tip is to reserve the experience for times when you can really enjoy it.

Most research on microdosing suggests that the effects users report are mostly placebo. That's fine with me. Much of what we take—from vitamins to antidepressants—is placebo. Above all, getting comfortable with smaller doses gave me the confidence and inclination to build up. After a few months of microdosing, I took two or three squares of Azul and felt more silly joy. With those bigger (but still gentle) doses I felt able to trust my instincts, whether that meant going for a walk without listening to a podcast, just basking in the beauty around me, or pretending I was Paul Revere's horse in a pool on vacation with my husband. A little bit at a time, I built the confidence to go bigger.

Kalina Christoff is a psychology professor at the University of British Columbia who studies spontaneous thought—introspection, metacognition, boredom, and psychedelics, particularly the ways in which those drugs interrupt our usual ways of relating. They explain to me how psychedelics work on the brain. "Psychedelics increase serotonin transmission," they say. "As serotonin is released, it probably counteracts some of the effects of noradrenaline and dopamine." Both chemicals are linked to addictive behaviors and anxiety. When these chemicals are downregulated, serotonin can flow more freely in the brain, and serotonin is known to increase neuroplasticity.

"I think that you can actually open up intuition by getting out of the ruts," Christoff says. "And when you are out of those ruts, there are additional benefits: it increases the ability of the neurons and the brain to rebuild themselves. You can actually build new pathways." They also note that psychedelics, while potent, are far from the only way to increase serotonin: "You can just get more sunshine, or have a nice meal with friends, or hug your kid. All of these ways of increasing serotonin are going to be beneficial." So if psychedelics don't appeal to you, there are other ways to get the serotonin pumping to disrupt canalized ways of thinking.

On that mat on the floor in Harlem, I was deep in my unconscious mind. I'll spare you the content of my psychedelic experience (mostly), but I'll say this: I felt a beautiful neutrality, an earnest curiosity toward whatever came up, whether that was the dissonant sounds of ceremonial instruments or thorny relationships or snapshots of my life. Those deep grooves in the record skipped a bit. I could offer myself another perspective. After about an hour on the floor, after sound came to me in five dimensions, when I could move my elbow a few inches and feel waves of wonder course through my body, Mugianis asked if I wanted to take more mushrooms. I declined. I liked my experience as it was. Had I been in my conscious mind, I would have considered the price tag of this experience* and said yes—I would've wanted my money's worth! I would have wanted to do this right, impress the shaman, excel. That satisfaction with the status quo, where I resisted optimization and instead said "I'm good," was one of the biggest takeaways from the experience. My unconscious, it turns out, wasn't trying to wring the last drop. Instead it said, *I am just fine as I am.*

---

* Mugianis quoted me a scale between $500 and $1,500, and I paid him $1,000, smack-dab in the middle. Before the ceremony, I bemoaned spending this much money when I could procure the substances for a fraction of the cost. What I could not procure on my own, though, was his wisdom, expertise, and musical accompaniment. When I was on the mat I realized I had not paid him nearly enough.

Spend some time in the world of psychedelics and you will encounter the idea of ego death, or being one with the universe. I did experience that. At one point, a man walked by the open window of the apartment and laughed. I laughed with him, feeling his joy as my own. But diving into the unknown actually built up my ego in an important way: it gave me confidence. It gave me the confidence to trust myself. As I wandered the corridors of my unconscious, I felt emboldened to open any door. I didn't always like what I saw there, but I wasn't afraid. I could get on the ride.

A few weeks later I caught up with Julie, a special education teacher by day and ceremonial space holder in her off-hours, who had been with me in Harlem, kindly sitting a few feet away from me. I told her how brave I felt opting into what was an intimidating experience. "Was it bad that I had more of an ego birth, instead of an ego death?" I asked her. "As women, I think we need a bit of an ego," Julie said. She related a maxim from her work with special ed students. "One thing we talk about a lot at work is what we call the dignity of risk. We want to be able to have uncertain experiences. Even if it is a total failure, I can handle it. That's important for soul development," she says. The dignity of risk—that's what I got out of that day.

I ask Andy Mitchell, a neuropsychologist, therapist, and author of the excellent *Ten Trips: The New Reality of Psychedelics* (in which he recounts taking more than two dozen trips on various substances in less than two months—do not try that at home!), where the interested but uninitiated might begin. "Take a small amount of mushrooms and go into the forest on your own," he recommends. "Rather than adding in something new, it will teach you more about what you've been missing all along."

—

Chuck Richards served for thirty-three and a half years in the New York City Police Department. His service spanned across departments, from transit to organized crime to narcotics. He was a lieutenant when he retired in 2020, when the Black Lives Matter protests found him in the crosshairs of his lived experience and departmental politics. Richards is Black and grew up in Harlem and the Bronx in the 1970s and '80s, at the height of the crack epidemic, when the Bronx was literally ablaze. After high school, he attended college in Texas and played on the football team. "I really wanted to get out of the city. I just wanted something different," he says. After a few semesters down south, his mom got sick and he needed to help his family financially. He returned and took several city jobs exams. "I got on the police department," he says, "and the rest was history."

Richards tells me this story in the warm afternoon light of a booth in a café in Chelsea. He is about to turn sixty and looks a good two decades younger. He wears beaded bracelets and neck-laces, with diamond studs in his ears glinting in the sunshine. He is warm and blessed with storytelling dexterity; his mug of black coffee grows cold as he relates tales from his years as an investigator and undercover officer. Richards says he was drawn to the narcotics beat because he had "a personal vendetta" against drug dealers. "In my neighborhood where I grew up, drug dealers were superstars. They had nice cars and looked down on people who weren't in that world. My family was affected by narcotics," he says, referencing members whose lives were destroyed by addiction. "And these guys were sell-ing in their own community. Why not take that shit downtown?" So how does a former cop with a grudge against drug dealers become an advocate and ceremonial space holder for psychedelics?

Intuition guided him. The peril Richards grew up in trained what he calls his "spidey senses" early on. "Where I grew up in the Bronx, there was a lot of crime. You always had to have your head on a swivel. That foundation stays with you," he says. "We all have dif-ferent rites of passage that we have been exposed to—biases, prej-udices, stereotypes, dramatic experiences. I think those experiences put us in a position to form our own fortress of intuition." Recogniz-ing the patterns of the street made him excellent at his job. When he was working undercover he could sense the moment before things were about to pop off. He also learned from "traumatic experiences of making the wrong call, or jumping the gun."

Toward the end of his career, he was known for practicing meditation, earning him the nickname "the Buddhist Lieutenant." When his wife started getting into sound baths and ayahuasca, he saw the tremendous benefit it had for her. Richards played trumpet as a kid and had always been interested in music. He and his wife started performing sound baths at a local community center. But he had to wait until he was off the force for good to dabble himself, lest he come up with a positive drug test.

He has since participated in ceremonies involving MDMA, psilocybin, and ketamine. (Although he has his preferences: "I'd rather knock on a door [as a cop] than go down the dark alley of ketamine again," he says with a laugh.) Psychedelics have given him a space to process the hypervigilance inculcated into him in childhood. "It's not normal to be a kid constantly looking over your shoulder," he says. He has also confronted trauma he endured in three decades as a NYPD officer. Psychedelics, he says, "would be a profound thing for all municipal employees with high-stress jobs—EMTs, firefighters. It would be a profound thing."

———

A few weeks after my ceremony, I speak with Michael Pollan. As with Orna Guralnik, it feels like meeting a niche celebrity for the middle-aged. Talking from his book-strewn office in Berkeley, Pollan confesses that he doesn't much use psychedelics these days: "I wish I had more time, but I've got to work, I've got to clean up the garden. Maybe in retirement," he says.

I ask him what to me feels like a perennial chicken-or-egg question when it comes to psychedelics: Do they put something into our brains, or do they unlock something that is already there? "I think they release certain constraints that we have on thinking," he responds. "They break habits of thought, which could manifest as anything from an addiction to depression or anxiety. There's this freedom to rewrite the narrative. If they put something in our heads, the experience would be a lot more consistent across more people."

Pollan introduces me to a theory of mind that adds on to Daniel Kahneman's System 1 (intuitive) and System 2 (rational) framework in a more expansive way. "We have two broad ways of thinking," he says. "One is constrained and the other is unconstrained. We can constrain our thought to logic and rational argument. We constrain our thoughts when we ruminate and get stuck in loops. But on the other side, you have unconstrained thought. Psychedelics lift the constraint on our thoughts and make the unconscious, whatever that is, more available. If you think of consciousness as a stream, psychedelics allow things to bubble up into that stream that might be submerged otherwise." And being under the influence of psychedelics, or even dreaming, allows those two streams of thought—conscious and unconscious—to cross, and you can meet them in the middle. Here, perhaps, is where intuition emerges.

———

You can find the place where these two streams meet every night, without drugs and for free. Emily Dickinson captured this experience—whether on the mushrooms of Amherst or just in her bed—writing:

> And then a Plank in Reason, broke,
> And I dropped down, and down –
> And hit a World, at every plunge,
> And Finished knowing – then –

To drop down into our dreams is to meet the unconscious every night, and it's an accessible way to take inventory of its contents. Freud called dreaming "the royal road to the unconscious." And there we might hear our intuition, without having to pay a therapist or venture into the unknown on psychedelics.

"Dreams are the language of your intuition," Lauri Loewenberg, certified dream analyst, tells me. Loewenberg is a recurring guest on the *Today* show, has a side hustle painting clients as pinup girls, and has a FAQ section on her website that would make any Freudian salivate: "I dream I have sex with my mom! HELP!!" Unwanted sex dreams and all, when our conscious, censorious mind is turned off, our unconscious mind can roam freely. Loewenberg explains it like this: "The little voice that speaks to you all day long, the one that says, 'Liz, you know better than this, Liz, don't do that,' is the same one that speaks to you in your dreams. But you don't have the conscious mind to tell you to shut up. So that little voice can speak to you more loudly and clearly. And instead of speaking in just words, it also speaks to you in emotions and metaphors." Indeed, the language of intuition manifests itself in many different forms.

Sometimes dreams can be the midwife of creativity. Dreams can help us work through existing problems, or provide a spark of inspiration. John Steinbeck said, "It is a common experience that a problem difficult at night is resolved in the morning after the committee of sleep has worked on it." In *The Committee of Sleep*, Harvard psychology professor Deirdre Barrett writes, "The dream's power lies in the fact that it is so *different* a mode of thought—that it supplements and enriches what we've already done while awake." Barrett gives numerous examples of works of genius that came to people in their dreams—from Paul McCartney coming up with the tune for "Yesterday" to General George Patton coming up with the plan for the surprise Christmas Day attack in the Battle of the Bulge. When I speak with Barrett,* she explains that in sleep "we tamp down some of our usual ways of thinking. Intuition gets heard in a way it might not

---

* I complain to her that in my dreams I am often doing something frustratingly mundane, like laundry or signing my kids up for camp. "I'm telling you probably Paul McCartney's single most interesting dream he ever had in his life," Barrett counters. "And it's not like all of waking thought is profound." Touché.

otherwise be." She echoes something Loewenberg had said: "Where intuition is the strongest is in the subconscious, because it's untethered, it's unblocked by all our conscious thoughts that distract us, or the ways we deny intuition. Your intuition is speaking very strongly and very freely in the dream state."

Barrett cites the "vigilance hypothesis," which explains why, in part, these extraordinary ideas are able to manifest in slumber: "Sleepers need to monitor their environment—smell smoke, hear intruders, sense temperature changes, and feel pain. It would be maladaptive to hallucinate vividly in most sensory modes. . . . Eyes closed, we do not need to monitor our visual environments, and paralyzed we don't need to move—in fact, we shouldn't move until we awaken. So we're free to hallucinate in these modes." This feels like a real gift of evolution, in so many ways.

When my dreams aren't totally boring, they can be laced with worry, which makes dream life a rich site for disentangling anxiety from intuition. When I interview Loewenberg, I'm twenty-one weeks pregnant. The night before, I had a terrifying dream about the baby not making it. (Again, I will spare you the details. Mostly.) I woke up shaken. Was this dream prophetic, an intuitive download that all was not right? "These sorts of dreams, I hate to tell you, pick up in the third trimester," Loewenberg says, which offers some consolation. "It's normal, because that is your biggest fear throughout the entire pregnancy." She then asks me to think back on the day before: Was there anything in particular that would have triggered these fears? I remember that I had watched a documentary before bed that had some violent imagery, and I was going to the doctor for an anatomy scan in a few days. Sandwiched between, I had this disturbing dream. Loewenberg diagnoses the dream not as intuition but squarely as anxiety: "This dream is a good example of how through the dreaming state we express our fears. They don't mean that this is what is going to happen. Once the conscious mind went dormant and the subconscious came to the surface, it needed to get this fear out, and to urge you to explore it. It's unpleasant, but it's healthy.

Dreams allow us to purge, to express what we are not expressing when we are awake. They are like a pressure gauge; they just release the pressure."

After speaking with Loewenberg, I begin scribbling my dreams down in the morning. This is not so much to go back and analyze the messages my dreams relay (although there are about a zillion books out there to help you do this if you are so inclined). Instead I find that jotting down the dreams of the night has several benefits. Writing down my dreams enhances my dreaming life, so that I experience them more vividly. When I begin, I can muster only an image or two. Eventually I'll be able to go back over the dreams in cinematic detail. As a lifelong insomniac, cultivating my dream life has been one of the most effective strategies I've tried for getting to and staying asleep, and I've tried everything: drugs, CBT, judgily named "sleep hygiene" practices, you name it. I think writing down my dreams has been training my unconscious to look forward to sleep rather than dread it.

But the greatest benefit of this scribbling has been to clear the gunk of the night for the day ahead. I can leave any ambient anxiety on the page and begin the day with a clean slate. This feels like cleansing my unconscious mind to go forth with greater clarity, and from that clearer state I can better hear my intuition. I used to try to do morning pages, where you let your hand take over and dump for three pages. Even though I would be newly out of bed, I found myself just listing what I was worried about for the day ahead, which ratcheted up my anxiety rather than defusing it. Now, in the dark, in words I cannot even make out, I can leave my unconscious mutterings behind and begin the day with a clear freedom.

—

Hypnagogia, the trancelike state between waking and sleeping, is called "the rhythm of genius."

Shauna Cummins, the founder of the Divine Feminine School of

Hypnosis and the author of *WishCraft: A Guide to Manifesting a Positive Future*, guides people into that fertile place. Cummins has long, dark hair and a voice like liquid Klonopin; just hearing her speak, about pretty much anything, immediately makes one pleasantly drowsy. Given her preternatural calm, it's surprising to hear that this is not her natural state. Raised in a large Irish Catholic family, she is recovering from a healthy dose of shame. She is prone to rumination, anxiety, and spikes of complex PTSD. Hypnosis gave her the tools to harness the power of imagination, turning her mind into an ally instead of an adversary. "Hypnosis brings people into their own relationship with their intuition and their imagination, where they can build self-trust and start listening to their own inner voice," she says. Far from the spiral-eyed zombies depicted in cartoons, the hypnosis Cummins teaches helps people step into their own authority.

Hypnosis bypasses the rational, conscious mind to access a deeper layer. (Cummins specifically uses the word *subconscious* to refer to this "intuitive, resourceful place," instead of *unconscious*, which she thinks has a negative connotation, smacks too much of just being out of it. Most hypnotists I've encountered seem to prefer *subconscious* as well.) And in that subconscious layer, we carry a lot of beliefs about ourselves and the world. Toronto-based hypnotherapist Pablo Milandu explains it this way: "The subconscious mind stores fundamental beliefs about self-worth and self-esteem. Sometimes our intuition will scream something. And based on how open or closed off we are to our self-esteem and self-belief, we will block that intuition." So the theory is that if you can get inside the inner script you carry around, ubiquitous and unchallenged as the very air we breathe, and stanch those limiting beliefs in favor of trust in yourself, you can better observe and even honor your intuitions. Hypnosis, then, harnesses the subconscious as a tool toward cultivating belief in oneself. "To be intuitive is to be settled into yourself," Milandu says.

The trance state is a hallmark of modern life—we fall into trances when scrolling social media or watching a movie. In this relaxed state, we are open to suggestion. It's the reason we cry at a film even though we know the actors are faking it and there's a camera crew just out of frame. "We use that natural ability of going into trance for the purposes of healing and relaxation and suggestion," Cummins explains. "When you are in the parasympathetic state, you're able to receive more deeply." One finds oneself in trance states of fear and anxiety, too (think: rumination, catastrophizing all the undesirable outcomes). "This is why hypnosis has worked so well for me, because I go into all the negative possibilities in such a visceral way. To be able to harness that and make it work for me is very powerful," she says. Hypnosis can transform those anxious thoughts into positive support, a mental alchemy available to us all.

I book a session with Cummins and we meet over Zoom on the afternoon of the full solar eclipse, which feels extra potent. Before our meeting, Cummins sent me a questionnaire asking what I am seeking to achieve (the ability to trust myself), how I would like to feel (centered, energized), and a place that is relaxing to me (a sunny meadow where I can lie down in the grass without being itchy or afraid of ticks). Having tailored a guided meditation to my specifics, she leads me into a hypnogogic dream state where I half-hear her words and half-dream images projected onto the screen of my eyelids. Her voice is transporting, and I come to as she counts down. I surface with a feeling a warm fuzziness, as though my brain has been at a spa and is now wrapped in a warm terry cloth robe. In a state of deep relaxation, she helps me plant seeds in my subconscious mind.

Working with a certified guide like Cummins is awesome, but we can all do this on our own and for free. She invokes the words of Thomas Edison, echoing Bargh and Mailer, to "never go to sleep without making a request to your subconscious." Ask for help with a perplexing problem. Cummins also thinks it's important as you are falling asleep to "thank yourself for a few things you did well that day. That works as a fertilizer for your mind to show you are deserving." In the morning, just after waking, one can "wish yourself a good day and affirm that you'll be OK no matter what happens."

It's so simple. But these little seeds planted when we are in our most receptive brain state can subtly, over time, flourish into new ideas about ourselves. Those positive messages then carry over to our conscious lives.

———

Go a few clicks past hypnosis on social media and you'll arrive at manifesting. Here gurus peddle their thirty-day courses and retreats to help you "rewire your unconscious script" and "achieve the life you've always dreamt." They cite twentieth-century prosperity gospel figures like Napoleon Hill and Joseph Murphy. In his 1937 book *Think and Grow Rich* (one of the bestselling self-help books of all time), Hill describes how he was down to a few dollars yet turned his luck around by affirming to himself that he was actually rich. Reader, can you guess what happened next? (Hill also earned several fraud charges in his life for failed business ventures, and made unsubstantiated claims, such as that he was a lawyer and that a fortuitous meeting with Andrew Carnegie had inspired his program.) His loose relationship with the truth notwithstanding, Hill might be the ur-exemplar of a particular streak of American thought, one that toes the line between bootstrapping entrepreneur and con man, showing how you could be lazy and get rich doing it. He writes in *Think and Grow Rich*, "You are the master of your destiny. You can influence, direct and control your own environment. You can make your life what you want it to be. . . . Both poverty and riches are the offspring of thought." The self-empowerment borders on self-deification; he belongs in the Smithsonian. A few decades later, in the 1963 book *The Power of Your Subconscious*, Joseph Murphy claims that he "resolved a sarcoma by using the healing power of my subconscious mind." He tells the story of a young woman seeing an expensive handbag in a shop window, deciding it was hers, and, miracle of miracles, receiving it as a gift from her boyfriend later that night.

Author and podcaster Amanda Montell notes, "Manifestation always experiences a spike in the culture whenever we really need it." In 2020, the year COVID descended and we were all quarantined and scrolling, Google searches for "manifesting" went up 600 percent. We were vulnerable, looking for answers. Teachers stepped in to fill the market's demand.

The terrain of the subconscious (the term these manifesting programs deploy) is rocky, and there are many guides ready to clear your path. *A Course in Miracles*, *The Secret*, and To Be Magnetic are all basically the same. The good news: your fate is all up to you. The bad news: your fate is all up to you. You can become your own spiritual ATM. Conspicuously absent from these monologues is the role of structural inequality, or privilege, or plain old-fashioned luck. Your life sucks? Your subconscious mind is telling you so. You've been too negative, too limited in your beliefs. You can get whatever you want, be it a partner, a handbag, or a clean bill of health. Rewrite your subconscious script, rewrite your life, they say. I bristle at their messages. It is simplistic, trite, with a conservative nobody's-fault-but-your-own subtext.

But if I'm being honest, a part of me bristles, because what if it really is that simple?

I sign up for a weekend workshop to find out. This is in addition to a monthlong course I'm already in the middle of. I learned of the manifesting course Cassandra Stefka* leads every month from a former writing student, who is brilliant, wry, and shockingly gorgeous. When she was in my class I googled her, because I knew she had to be somebody, and she is—a working actress who has been on premium cable TV shows. Walking into the airy Williamsburg loft where this weekend's workshop is being held, I see facsimiles of my former student everywhere: twenty- and thirtysomething willowy-limbed women, with long, sleek hair trailing down their backs, wearing wide-legged pants and silky pajama shirts over crop tops, the

---

* Name and identifying details changed.

kind of outfit that on them looks ethereal and on me would look like I had escaped from a nineteenth-century institution. Most everyone crowds to the front and is wearing white, which I learn is a Kundalini yoga thing—the hue expands your auric field. I am wearing all black and choose a meditation cushion in the back row.

What do these women want? That is what I want to know. To my left is a woman who has flown in from Toronto for the weekend, and at lunch I meet a woman who has traveled from Montana to learn from Stefka in person. What they want, I learn, is relationships, their own businesses, children, optimum health, and vitality. Money. Security. Love. Stefka has promised them the key.

Stefka is in her early thirties and has a background in traditional Chinese medicine, acupuncture, and Kundalini yoga. She launched her manifesting course in 2019. Membership exploded during COVID. "The class helps people step into their power. Period," she explains. "We have morning meditation live streams every morning. Because that's how you change your mind and your subconscious. I give a talk online once a week and do a Q&A."

The meditations are Kundalini-inspired, which is new to me. They include breathwork and a series of waving your hands over your head in a swirling pattern to raise your vibration for thirteen minutes, which I find physically impossible. I ask my former student if she can do this, to which she says she can: "I'll wave my hands over my head for however long if it's going to get me what I want!" she says with a laugh. There are also daily 5-7-9 writing exercises, in which you write out what it is you hope to manifest five times in the morning, seven times in the afternoon, and nine times at night. I've been feeling burnt out, so my manifestation this month is to realize heightened energy levels. In my notebook I write three times a day that "I am energized and alert," trying to cast a spell over my drained body. Were anyone to stumble onto my notebook for this month, they would be frightened. With other students, we're to check in daily to let each other know when we've done our meditation and our 5-7-9 writing. At one point, I venture to open a discussion about some of my misgivings: "I worry about toxic positivity." Crickets.

The monthlong course costs $150. It is cheaper than the average uninsured cost of a single session of therapy, and more explicit and tangible in its goal. (One woman in my cohort says this is her thirty-sixth straight month of participating. This doesn't seem like an endorsement of its efficacy; rather, the opposite.) I'm about halfway through the monthly course when I arrive at the immersion weekend. Whether it's the writing or the hands waving above my head, I'm sleeping and feeling better than I was at the beginning of the month.

"I know what women are missing," Stefka tells us. We are seated on our meditation cushions, looking up at our guide, who is sitting on a platform in front of a giant gong at the front of the room. The floor is strewn with white rose petals, and we have been gifted goody bags with face oil, tinted lip balm, and cans of CBD-infused sparkling water. "Women are missing female friendships and community. I wanted to create a space where women could relate to each other from a place of power, not insecurity. When you decide to take ownership of your life, one step at a time, one day at a time, inside an amazing bubble of support, 90 percent of success is who you surround yourself with." Looking around the room at the nodding heads and scribbling pens in our fresh gift notebooks, I see what Stefka is talking about: what these women want is to feel less alone. And to be recognized, fully, for the smart, complete people they are.

Which is what anyone wants. When you tap into your intuition—which you have, which is your birthright—you can feel less alone. You feel more connected to yourself, to your gifts and your potential, to the moment, to the world. But here's the problem: it's hard. It's hard for about a zillion reasons, including but not limited to: we live in a culture that champions rational thought and sees extra-rational ways of knowing as silly; we live in a capitalist system that wants us constantly spinning our wheels toward productivity and achievement rather than getting quiet and hearing what actually resonates with us; we are overstimulated by a constant stream of sights, sounds, and distractions. Mostly, we are very tired. Developing intuition is work. You have to decide that this is something you want, and you have to work at it, by doing things that don't look like "work" in our capitalist understanding. This kind of work looks like checking in with yourself, like getting quiet, like going for a walk. It is the work of discernment, which, as anyone who works in the field of discernment knows—picture an art connoisseur at Sotheby's, for example—takes years to achieve. And you get there by small daily practices. And the worst part of all? The intuitive messages you get might not be fun, or easy to enact. It might be that you need to change the way you're used to eating,* or who you're used to dating, or the career path you've been forging. Real intuition is not the kind of quick fix we have been conditioned to expect.

In other words, when you start experiencing your own intuition, it will not let you bypass that which is unpleasant. This is the big difference between developing true intuition and what the manifesting crowd is selling. Dream as you might for the right romantic partner to come into your life, if you haven't excavated and dealt with your shit, you won't be able to meet them in a meaningful way. Delving into the unconscious is a worthy endeavor, as it often reveals a lot of grody ideas and other people's inheritances we didn't ask for. *I really don't need or want the full set of silver, Grandma!* But there it is, collecting dust and getting tarnished until you remember it is there, polish it, and send it packing. Skating over the subconscious will never provide the same profit. And it will be frustrating when the same unpleasant circumstances keep rearing their heads: the same shitty dudes, the same feelings of inferiority that keep showing up. They are not to be avoided. These life circumstances are our true teachers, and they don't have Instagram accounts or accept Venmo. As Pema Chödrön put it, "Nothing ever goes away until it teaches us what we need to know."

You can't bypass life's difficulties, and you can't avoid dumb bad

---

* My intuition has been telling me that I need to stop eating meat for years now. I still eat meat!

luck either. Writer Cyndie Spiegel knows that better than anyone. Spiegel had crafted a career around the power of positive thinking, authoring the bestselling *A Year of Positive Thinking*. Then, in 2020, her nephew was murdered. Her mother died. She was diagnosed with breast cancer. Her brother had a stroke and was hospitalized for months. So how to look on the bright side when there is no bright side? "After my mom died, positive thinking did not exist for me," she says. She sees the limitations of the one-size-fits-all promise of manifesting. "I come from poverty in New Jersey," she tells me. "We are not people who manifest." She laughs. "We're asking too much of people. It's like asking me to run a marathon when I haven't even taken a step. We cannot expect people to overhaul their thinking when they are in the midst of very challenging real-life circumstances." Beyond that, Spiegel also sees the problem of short attention spans. "With social media culture, we're so used to getting everything in fifteen-second clips. So if I'm following all these quick tips, I might start wondering why it's not working for me. A consistent relationship to our intuition is something most of us have not honed. You don't do intuition one time, or do it for a week, or for thirty days," she says. She advocates for the unglamorous, consistent work of developing intuition to lead to a richer, more aligned life beyond manifesting and positive thinking. "I think storytelling and listening to the stories of others and not being in silos is huge. Therapy is another. Sitting in quiet is another way. Reading, being curious. If you're not curious, you will not believe what you feel."

It is no wonder that when a thirty-day program comes along that provides structure and promises results, it is tempting to sign up. Plus, we need teachers. While intuition is to many people their own inner wisdom, learning to hear it takes coaxing. When deciding with whom to study, if that is something that appeals, use your brain but don't shut off your intuition. If the teacher prickles suspicion in you, listen to that.

—

In her 1970 book *The Sovereignty of the Good*, philosopher and novelist Iris Murdoch wrote that beauty might be the only thing that can save us from ourselves. Our inner lives are too often consumed by "the fat, relentless ego." Murdoch called for noticing the beauty in our midst as a means to transcend our self-consciousness:

> Beauty is the convenient and traditional name of something which art and nature share, and which gives a fairly clear sense to the idea of quality of experience and change of consciousness. I am looking out of my window in an anxious and resentful state of mind, oblivious of my surroundings, brooding perhaps on some damage done to my prestige. Then suddenly I observe a hovering kestrel. In a moment everything is altered. The brooding self with its hurt vanity has disappeared. There is nothing now but kestrel. And when I return to thinking of the other matter it seems less important. And of course this is something which we may also do deliberately: give attention to nature in order to clear our minds of selfish care.

Murdoch called it unselfing. The experience of losing yourself, your agenda, your to-dos, to be in transcendent communion with something beautiful, something bigger. Cyndie Spiegel calls these "microjoys." Finding moments to unself can develop our intuition. In these moments we are outside of our rational minds and in the thrall of the moment. This might be what all of the thinkers of accessing unconscious processes—Bargh with his dolphins, Guralnik with trying to pin down the question, Mugianis's ceremonies, Cummins's positive suggestions—are getting at. How do we leave the familiar anguish of ourselves behind? How do we tap into a richer version of experience that's running right alongside the mundane?

Intuition itself, for me, is this experience. It draws me out of the canals of my well-trod thought patterns and shows me: *here, this, this is what matters*—the cherry blossom confetti blowing in the wind, my sons' shoulder blades, the crossing guard ferrying kids across the street. Simple beauty, love made manifest in the world. And it's free, and available right now, this very instant. A kestrel will never tell you how to think. A kestrel will take you to that sublime place—where you, in all your you-ness, cease to be the main character. And paradoxically, from that place of dissolving, you can begin to hear yourself a bit more clearly. Can you find your kestrel? And when you do, can you see it?

CHAPTER 7

PREMONITIONS

In 2007, Dolores Rivera* was living in Maryland and working toward a PhD when she had a dream that saved two lives. She had come to Jesus a few years before and was now involved in her church, serving as a leader of the youth group. One night she dreamt of a teenager from the youth group with a gun in his hands. It seemed like he was going to use it to shoot someone. She woke up immediately and had the sense that the dream was very real.

The dream stayed with her, but she didn't tell anyone. Sometimes embarrassment prevented her from sharing the visions that came to her at night—what to make of such dramatic nocturnal messages? She went about her day. That afternoon, she got a breathless call from the church's pastor. One of the kids from the youth group was missing. Rivera knew who it was without having to ask. And, more importantly, she knew why. She disclosed the dream she'd had hours earlier to the pastor and the boy's mother. The adults located the boy. He had a gun, and he was trying to find his mother's ex-boyfriend, who had raped his sister. Rivera's dream had come to fruition, and her premonition prevented any further tragedies from occurring that day.

---

* Name changed.

Rivera had had predictive dreams like this before. Warning dreams, she calls them. She dreamt that her sister fell and was injured, and the next day her sister tripped while running and had to get twenty stitches. She had a dream about her cousin and a motorcycle. Her cousin was living in Florida at the time and dating a guy who, unbeknownst to Rivera, had a motorcycle that her cousin was considering riding. By now Rivera's authority had been cemented in her family. You get a call from Rivera, and you don't do whatever it is you were about to do.

In 2007, a family friend was murdered, along with his wife and son. The police had not found the killer. They were releasing details about the suspect, a person of color. A few days later, she had a dream: "I entered the home during the murder scene and walked up the stairs. I was in the middle of the event. It was in slow motion. I was at the top of the stairs. And the person who killed the family stopped and looked me right in the face. And I woke up. I told my mom what the person looked like. And I drew a picture of the person." The man she drew was white, unlike the young man of color the police were looking for. "The next day they found the real killer, and he looked exactly like the person I saw in the dream," she says.

Rivera is telling me this in the Oyster Bar at Grand Central Station. Her office, where she is an executive at an investment firm, is a few blocks away. She has squeezed in this lunch during a stacked day of meetings. Her hair is swept up and she wears rectangular glasses and a colorful blouse. She is mild, polite, unassuming. Other people with these kinds of visions would have taken their story to Maury Povich, but Rivera seems like she'd be the last to do so. "I don't identify as an intuitive person," she tells me. "If anything, I'm very cerebral." She describes herself as introverted and guarded. She seems a little embarrassed about the whole thing and, more than that, lonely. She has often wondered why she has been given this ability.

I ask how this burden feels to her, as a Christian. It is not without precedent. The Bible refers to at least fifteen stories of premonitions in dreams. Since Rivera has been able to use her dream intuitions constructively, they feel difficult but worthwhile to her. She is not alone in this uncanny ability. People throughout history have presaged horrors. On August 12, 2022, the writer Salman Rushdie was stabbed onstage at an event in Chautauqua, New York. In his memoir about the attack, *Knife*, Rushdie writes,

> Two nights before I flew to Chautauqua, I had a dream about being attacked by a man with a spear, a gladiator in a Roman amphitheater. . . . I was rolling about on the ground trying to elude the gladiator's downward thrusts, and screaming. . . . I sat up in bed, shaken by the dream's vividness and violence. It felt like a premonition (even though premonitions are things in which I don't believe). After all, the Chautauqua venue at which I was booked to speak was an amphitheater too.

Rushdie had told his wife he did not want to go. But, like all sensible people who know the difference between the fantasy world of dreams and waking reality, he relied on his rational mind and went. "You don't run your daily life because of having a bad dream," he explained to Terry Gross in an interview on *Fresh Air*. He doesn't believe in premonitions, he told Gross, then added, "There's a lot of things in which I don't believe that have happened."

So what, practically speaking, is a premonition? How are they related to intuition? Do premonitions only forebode the terrible, or can one receive positive premonitions? And what the hell are you supposed to do when you have one? How do we live with the unexplainable, and what are the benefits of threading more mystery through our lives?

—

Early in her career, Laura A. King, the University of Missouri psychology professor, was part of a research team that was studying how people make meaning out of life transitions, and interviewed parents of children with Down syndrome. The team asked their sample of eighty-seven parents to tell them the story of how they found out they would be having a child with Down. One researcher pointed out a trend the team had not anticipated: many parents began their story with intuitive foreshadowing. They would say things like, "My husband opened up *What to Expect When You're Expecting* to the Down syndrome page." Many said they'd had a premonition, and that it made their experience more meaningful.

King, ever the scientist, explains the phenomenon this way: "Do I think God or the universe was sending these parents a message? No. If opening to the Down page in the book happened to you and you don't have a kid with Down syndrome, you completely forget it. If you flip to the page in the book and your kid *does* end up with Down syndrome, then wow. You remember." Or, as a neuroscientist would say, we experience memory bias. She goes on: "When we have these intuitive, magical experiences, it's not your obligation to argue those experiences away. It's just to be present. We have the capacity to notice connections between important events. It is how we survive." Your job is not to prove whether or not your premonition is real or a coincidence. It's just to notice, and to connect the dots, if that makes sense to you.

We all have that experience the parents King studied had—some kind of premonition pans out and feels all the more important because we somehow anticipated it. When my husband and I had been dating for a while but were not yet engaged (the whole thing was taking entirely too long, I thought; he disagreed), I told him one groggy morning that I dreamt he had given me a blue engagement ring. We had never discussed rings, ergo my frustration. A few days later he presented me with a sapphire he'd been sitting on for some time and asked me to marry him. That dream made our engagement all the more magical, and imbued extra meaning into a ring that is already very precious to me. I dreamt it before I saw it.

Like Dolores Rivera's night visions, like my dream of a blue ring, many people experience dispatches from the future in their sleep.

Theresa Cheung and cognitive neuroscientist Julia Mossbridge are the authors of *The Premonition Code*. Cheung has written a number of bestselling books on dreams. She calls dreams "nocturnal intuition—it's what's invisible and unexplained and mysterious. It's what makes life fulfilling and exciting and like an adventure." When you dream a vision of the future, it may reflect a future you are working toward in the present, she believes. Don't like what you see? Change the present.

But how to know when you are receiving an intuitive download of the future and when it's a plain old anxiety dream? Mossbridge and Cheung described a qualitative study of precognitive dreamers who reported their experiences. They found an interesting trend: anxiety dreams, like not being able to find the classroom on the first day of school, had "a rich emotional state upon awakening," Mossbridge tells me. Dreamers reported their dreams feeling real and urgent, and all the associated knots in the stomach and racing heartbeat were present. But intuitive precognitive dreams that did, in fact, come true "produce[d] upon awakening a more neutral *knowing*. Like 'my father will die today.' It feels like it already happened," she explains. So examining the emotional residue a dream leaves you with can be useful in determining whether it is anxiety or intuition: If it's more emotionally laden, that's probably anxiety. More neutral? Premonition.

Writer Jean Hannah Edelstein provides an illustration of the neutrality associated with premonitions. Her father was a carrier for Lynch syndrome, a rare genetic disorder linked to an increased risk of developing cancer. In 2013, her father was dying from Lynch-related cancer. "I didn't get tested because I knew I had it," Edelstein says. "Then, I would be on a medical pathway I wasn't ready for, and I knew it would be deeply upsetting to my father. Being in a state of ambiguity at the end of his life was less difficult for me than telling him I had Lynch syndrome. I used my intuition there to make the decision not to get tested during his life," she says. After he died, Edelstein got tested. As she already knew, she was positive. "When I got the results, I wasn't surprised," she says. Edelstein writes beautifully about her Lynch diagnosis in her memoir *This Really Isn't About You*.

Biologist Rupert Sheldrake defines a premonition as an advance warning, precognition as "knowing in advance," and presentiment as "feeling in advance." But here is where premonitions get really wild: they throw our notions of linear time into disarray. To wrestle with premonitions, you also have to hit the mat with the space-time continuum, which is the point at which many say, "I'd prefer not to." And I get it. It kinda makes your head explode. Sheldrake writes that the concept of precognition and presentiment "defies our certainty that cause always precedes effect. It also flies in the face of our idea of the present, suggesting there are no sharp divisions between future, present, and past. . . . Premonitions and precognitions may be able to tell us something very important not only about the nature of life and mind but also about the nature of time." Mossbridge describes precognitive dreams and premonitions as "passing yourself notes through time." So when I feel like I'm always living in the past or the future, and having such trouble staying in the present moment, maybe I am actually . . . on to something?

"The evidence for precognition is as good as evidence that says aspirin is a blood thinner," Mossbridge, who has run experiments on precognition, tells me. In other words, the evidence is solid, according to her. But science is a conservative field—start talking about psi, the umbrella term for precognition, psychic ability, telekinesis, and mediumship, and you are automatically dismissed as a crank. All of a sudden you are no longer a respected contributor to the field but instead the kind of scientist who would be a character in a Dan Brown novel. Science is supposed to be the most rational of fields—and yet there is bias here too.

Daryl Bem is perhaps the most famous scientist to have attempted to measure psi. A psychology professor at Cornell, he had been studying psi phenomena for three decades when he ran what is known as a ganzfeld (from the German words for "entire" and "field") experiment in 1994. One subject attempts to mentally transmit an image to another subject, who receives it in a state of sensory deprivation. The telepathic communication he studied is one facet of psychic ability.

Daniel Engber wrote of Bem's work in *Slate* that "for most observers, at least the mainstream ones, the paper posed a very difficult dilemma. It was both methodologically sound and logically insane." If nothing else, Bem's paper set off a crisis about replication and "priming" (sending subconscious cues to subjects) in the academic psychology community, with Daniel Kahneman commenting, "I see a train wreck looming." (Which sounds an awful lot like a premonition.)

Temporal intuitions contain inherent paradoxes. If you get a vision of the future that you want to avoid, as Cheung suggests, and you take steps to prevent it from coming true, does that mean it was *not* actually a premonition? "These are all future potentials, where everything happens all at once. You begin to realize what a timeless being you are," she says, suggesting that our current reality is not the be-all and end-all—there might be more than meets the eye. "You can rise above the present moment," she says, "and it's mighty empowering."

—

Jessica Utts, a statistics professor at the University of California, Irvine, served as a consultant on the Stargate Project, the U.S. government's eighteen-year attempt to harness psychic ability for defense. The classified program began in 1977 and was declassified in 1995, culminating in a CIA report to Congress. It began in the Cold War out of fear that Soviet spies were already far ahead of the Americans in utilizing psychic ability in intelligence gathering. Stargate had two branches—strategic, which Utts worked on, and operational, which was under the auspices of the military. Jon Ronson's hilarious account *The Men Who Stare at Goats* documents the attempts of soldiers to become psychic. Utts was brought in as a consultant, along with Ray Hyman, a University of Oregon psychology professor and skeptic of the paranormal, to evaluate the nearly twenty-year data sample intelligence agencies had amassed. "What I did was not the sexy side of parapsychology," she tells me over Zoom from her home in California.

Utts's role as a statistician in the controlled experiments that Stargate ran on psychic ability was critical, as instances of psychic ability are often dismissed as coincidence. She explains: "If something has a one-in-a-million chance of occurring in a given day to a given person in the United States, with our population of 350 million, that means there are still 350 people for whom that amazing coincidence might occur," she says. "With the Stargate experiments that I've been involved in, we controlled for those probabilities."

The experiments tested the ability to receive messages with the mind through time and space, which they called "remote viewing." The experiment used sets of four distinct photographs all with imagery as dissimilar as possible (think: photographs of Big Ben, an astronaut floating in space, Marilyn Monroe on the subway grate, Machu Picchu). One of the images is the "target," which uses their mind to convey to the "receiver," who is in a separate room (or sometimes up to a hundred miles away, depending on the experiment). Other times, the target was simply placed in a secure location. In the Stargate experiments, the receiver was in a locked room and told to describe what they were seeing. Sometimes they could draw what they received. Then a "judge" would be shown the four images—the target plus the three decoys—and asked to select which one they believed the receiver had described. If it matched the target, it was called a "hit." The majority of participants in these experiments were military and intelligence personnel.

"If getting hits was just coincidence, we'd expect correct guesses one-quarter of the time," Utts explains to me. You could randomly guess four times, and statistically one of those guesses would coincide with the target. "Instead we found people got it right about one-third of the time," she says. In the report presented to Congress in 1995 she wrote, "At this stage, using the standards applied to any other area of science, it is concluded that psychic functioning has been well established." She urged Congress and the scientific community to stop using resources to determine *whether* psychic ability works, but rather to study *how* it works.

Hyman, on the other hand, remained unconvinced: "I admit that the latest findings should make Professor Utts and some parapsychologists optimistic," he said. "Where parapsychologists see consistency, I see inconsistency. Although I cannot point to any obvious flaws in the experiments, the experimental program is too recent and insufficiently evaluated to be sure that flaws and biases have been eliminated." When the report was presented to Congress in 1995, the project was defunded, despite objections by Senators Claiborne Pell and William Cohen, the ranking member of the Senate Intelligence Committee from 1983 to 1991, who called for further research.

I asked Utts whether, in studying the data, she found any applicable lessons for everyday psychic development in civilians who are not trying to intercept government secrets. "I think this is a skill that could be taught and you could get better at with practice. What you can teach people is to not have such an analytical overlay," she says. In other words, the trick to developing psychic ability is for people to "get out of their own thinking and let whatever it is come through," she says. Utts's research showed that you can become more psychic by trusting your first impressions, being open to the sensations that arise, and resisting the brain's urge to cogitate and rationalize.

Utts believes that people at either end of the belief spectrum—those who believe everything and those who believe nothing—are both equally ignorant and misinformed. She also believes that there is a difference between skepticism and denial. "Skeptics are good. Skeptics question things and start with a low probability that anything [psychic-wise] could be going on. But then they are willing to update their probability based on the data." It's the deniers, those who refuse to engage with the data, who are the problem. Parapsychology is so stigmatized in the mainstream scientific community, she says, because "it challenges the prevailing paradigm, even though it really shouldn't. I think people have the mistaken impression that it conflicts with what we know about science, but I don't think that's true. We have so many unanswered questions already, like consciousness, for example. We don't understand consciousness at all."

As she engaged with the data that said psychic potential is real, the unanswered question of how it works always bothered her. "Is it time? Is it space? Where is this stuff coming from?" she wonders. But she recently heard an explanation that to her makes sense. "William James had the theory that our brains are not the creators of consciousness, but the receivers," she tells me. "The human brain is like a television or a radio, receiving thoughts rather than creating them. If that were the case, then you could see where this information could come in. And if you're not filtering it out, like we normally do, then you would be able to receive it. To me, that's the best explanation I've come up with." She pauses. "But how you would begin to prove something like that? I don't know."

———

Like Dolores Rivera, the writer Rudyard Kipling experienced flashes of the future in his dreams. Once, looking down at the stone floor of Westminster Abbey, he recognized the sight from a dream. "But here is where I have been," he noted. "How, and why, had I been shown an unreleased roll of my life-film?"

Deirdre Barrett seeks to answer Kipling's question. Can dreams foretell the future? Barrett sees the space-time continuum as a bit more tethered to earth. "Dreams can be predictive in an intuitive sense," she says. "Our intuition can pick up on all kinds of things our rational mind doesn't know, like noticing a person seeming ill or knowing someone may be dying and they haven't yet told us." Barrett's research has found examples of people dreaming that they had slow-developing diseases like cancer or neurological conditions. "Our immune system usually does know something is there and it's making antibodies," she says. Dreaming of illnesses that do indeed come to pass may be "our body sensing disease processes that we're not consciously picking up on yet," she says. One Christmas, I was visiting my in-laws with my family and dreamt they had COVID. They tested positive two days later. Perhaps I was picking up on the subtle signals Barrett describes. Our bodies are complex, and they communicate in ways our conscious minds cannot (or would rather not) process.

But what about the many who claimed to have prophesied 9/11 in dreams? To these large-scale, global events, Barrett says, "We underestimate all the possible coincidences in the world. The World Trade Center were dramatic buildings that people looked at and noticed. It would be surprising if people *didn't* dream about them." Barrett doesn't participate in supernatural explanations. And I hear her about the role of coincidence, especially as it relates to cultural icons common to our vernacular that show up in dreams. But when I think about Rivera's dreams, their specificity and how they have come true, that feels different. Perhaps it's the packaging: Rivera is reticent about her uncanny ability. As I go on investigating dreams as a portal to intuition, Barrett warns me, "you'll definitely find people who believe that dreams are communicating with the future." Her words feel like equal parts warning and admonishment.

—

Not all premonitions come in the form of dreams, and it's not only humans that have the capacity to foretell. In 1997, a major earthquake hit the town of Assisi, Italy. Locals observed strange behavior in animals just before the rumblings began. Dogs barked throughout the night. Birds stopped singing. A week before the quake, people noticed that the nearby town of Foligno had been "invaded by rats." How did the rats know to leave the sewers and head twelve miles away, to safety, a week before the earthquake, when their human counterparts were blithely going about their daily business?

These tales of animals knowing that doom is coming and sensibly heading out of harm's way is the stuff of legends. Yet it has historical roots. Ancient Greek historian Diodorus Siculus documented an exodus of snakes, weasels, and rats from the city of Helice in 373 BCE before a massive earthquake. Pliny the Elder (23–79 CE) wrote that "one of the signs of a coming earthquake is 'the excitation and terror of animals with no apparent reason.'" Some reported "a multitude of worms" evacuating from the dirt a week before the Lisbon earthquake of 1755, which flattened the city.

In more recent history, the December 26, 2004, earthquake off the west coast of Sumatra was one of the strongest ever recorded, a 9.1 on the Richter scale. The quake unleashed tsunamis throughout the Indian Ocean, claiming more than 225,000 lives. But many animals, according to observers, protected themselves. "Elephants in Sri Lanka and Sumatra moved to high ground before the waves struck," writes Rupert Sheldrake in *Dogs That Know When Their Owners Are Coming Home*. "They did the same in Thailand, trumpeting before they did so. According to a villager in Bang Koey, Thailand, buffalo were grazing by the beach when they 'suddenly lifted their heads and looked out to sea, ears standing upright.'" Some dogs refused to go for morning walks, and a nesting colony of flamingos moved to higher ground. "In the Andaman Islands, groups of tribal people moved away from the coast before the disaster, alerted by the behavior of animals," Sheldrake writes.

Animals seem to possess an uncanny ability to anticipate looming geological or natural disaster that humans are blind to. (Sheldrake also documented many instances of dogs making some real Lassie-like saves, such as informing their diabetic owners that they were on the verge of hypoglycemia, alerting epileptic owners to oncoming seizures, and even detecting nascent cancers.) Humans would benefit greatly from paying more attention to the intelligence of animals. In 1974, China's State Seismological Bureau determined that there would be a major earthquake in Liaoning Province in the coming years. The government recruited citizens to be on the lookout for strange behavior in animals. In early February, there was a sharp up-tick in reports of cattle, pigs, and horses behaving erratically. Heeding these warnings, city officials evacuated citizens on February 4. At 7:36 p.m. that evening, the city was rocked by a magnitude 7.3 earthquake. "More than half of the buildings in the city were destroyed," Sheldrake writes. "Tens of thousands of people might have lost their lives had it not been for the timely warning." Despite the efficacy of the program (and the relatively low cost, especially when compared with disaster recovery), it was defunded after a few years. Harnessing the wisdom of the natural world and extra-rational ways of knowing is perhaps too big a leap of imagination for policymakers. But it is one of several attempts to systematize premonitions and psychic ability for civic welfare.

In *The Premonitions Bureau*, journalist Sam Knight tells the story of John Barker, an English psychiatrist who sought to use everyday people's dreams and visions to foretell and prevent disaster.

On October 21, 1966, a coal mine collapsed, causing a landslide in the Welsh village of Aberfan. One hundred forty-four people were killed in the slide, 116 of them children. Many people claimed to have dreamt about the disaster before it happened, including some of the schoolchildren who lost their lives. Barker arrived on the scene and was convinced that there were supernatural warning signs. He and science reporter Peter Fairley placed an ad in London's *Evening Standard* to collect premonitions from everyday people. Inevitably, they got a lot of hooey. But some were on the money. A teacher and a telephone operator became regular sources, both separately predicting a fatal train derailing. Barker and Fairley set out to collect this intelligence and present it to the UK's Medical Research Council, in the hopes of setting up a national early warning system. Despite their best efforts, the government did not bite. It's too easy to dismiss seers as crazy, or benefiting from coincidence. Knight recognizes the paradox, writing, "Premonitions are impossible, and they come true all the time. The second law of thermodynamics says it can't happen, but you think of your mother a second before she calls."

And yet, like when you think of your mother and then receive a call from her, we don't have to look too far to experience premonitions. For Dr. Dustin Ballard, it was his Labrador retriever that made him stop in his tracks. As she was nearing her last days, she would settle herself under bushes in the yard by herself. "Her intuition was to take herself out and die under a tree in nature," he recalls. She was preparing to die, and showing her human companions it was time.

Ballard works in emergency rooms, so he has seen his fair share of panic. "I've had a lot of people ask me, 'Am I going to die?' You can tell it's usually anxiety driving those questions," he tells me from his home in Marin County, California. But one patient stood out to him as completely distinct. He was a healthy sixty-year-old man who came into the ER with a headache. A CT scan revealed a tiny brain bleed, so small it wasn't causing any neurological dysfunction. The plan was to get his blood pressure under control and transfer him to a hospital that could perform neurosurgery. "I told him the diagnosis and the plan," Ballard recalls. "And he looked at me and very calmly said, 'I am going to die.'" The doctor reassured him that this was a tiny bleed and they were transferring him to be near a neurosurgeon, just as a precaution. The patient insisted that he was going to die. When Ballard followed up a few days later, the man's condition had quickly deteriorated. He died less than a week after walking into the hospital.

"That experience got me looking into premonition," Ballard tells me. As a doctor, he was concerned that he and his team had missed something that would have been treatable. In this case, he was already carrying out the most cautious course of care. But perhaps doctors can evaluate patients' premonitions and know what to look out for. This patient registered his impending death with a flat affect, "some sadness, some melancholy," Ballard recalls. He was more resigned than anxious. The doctor tells me that if he found himself confronting a patient like this again, "in a situation where there was something actionable for me to do, in terms of diagnosis of treatment, the patient's affect would have changed my clinical course."

As Mossbridge and Cheung observe, the emotional tenor around a premonition can be very revelatory: high emotionality often suggests anxiety, whereas neutrality aligns with premonition.

How is premonition related to intuition? I ask Ballard. There's pattern recognition intuition, of course, but premonition seems distinct: it is the ability to presage an event that has no precedent, for which there is no pattern. This type of intuition Ballard calls "reptilian intuition." He tells me the story of his friend's aunt who randomly started making and freezing dinners for her husband. She had a feeling something bad was going to happen to her, and a month later she had an aneurysm that put her in the hospital. She ended up recovering, but in the meantime her husband had a stockpile of meals to eat while she was out of commission. "That has nothing to do with pattern recognition," he says. Instead, he hazards that there is some signal the aneurysm sent to the woman's reptile brain—the amygdala, our certainty checker, the oldest structures, just above the spinal column, meant to keep us alive. That signal can be a surge of epinephrine that sends a signal to the frontal lobe, which starts making decisions even before it knows what it is responding to. The body's biological imperative for survival can sometimes tip us off to something afoot in the form of premonition. "Intuition is the highest level of instinct," Ballard says.

—

She calls it "the bees." When disaster preparedness expert Lucy Easthope senses an impending disaster—be it a fire, flood, or chemical warfare—the bees start buzzing. Easthope has been at the helm of every major emergency involving the deaths of British citizens since 9/11, from storms to terrorism to plane crashes to the COVID pandemic. She is a professor of risk and hazard at the University of Durham, a professor of mass fatalities and pandemics at the University of Bath, and a member of the UK's Cabinet Office National Risk Assessment Behavioural Science Expert Group. And before each tragedy, the bees start their awful swarming, warning of impending doom.

She experiences these "precogs," as she refers to her precognitions, viscerally in her body: a thrum of anxiety in her bloodstream, cramps in her stomach, constriction in her throat. In her bestselling memoir *When the Dust Settles*, she writes that her bees involve "klaxons in the head, sweaty palms, rapid breathing and a whole load of feelings centered around the gut. And more specifically the bowels. The Ancient Greeks considered the bowels the centre of our emotional responses." In the course of her career, where she has postmortemed every major disaster to determine what went wrong, she has acquired the highest level of expertise and pattern recognition, the intuition of science. But she also possesses a faculty that transcends merely putting in the hours. Her body is a divining rod.

"The day before the Grenfell fire, I landed in hospital with acute pancreatitis," Easthope tells me over Nutella pancakes in a hotel restaurant a stone's throw from Buckingham Palace. The bees showed up in that case as an infection in her body, predicting the worst residential fire in Britain since World War II. Easthope is warm, self-deprecating, and passionate. You wouldn't expect someone who has spent her adult life witnessing tragedy to be so downright jolly. Her mind jumps from one thing to another, the connections obvious to her but not always to her interlocutor. She often interrupts herself to offer a counterpoint to what she just said, a side effect, perhaps, of briefing high-level military and government officials and the peanut gallery on X, where she has a healthy following under the handle @LucyGoBag—she can always anticipate what the opposition might say.

She was in that exact kind of meeting on June 13, 2017. She was leading a session for emergency planners where she brought up her concern about the potential for a major fire occurring in a public housing block due to faulty gas safety. Easthope's precogs were not always received enthusiastically. She became famous for her "wildcard thinking," seeing out on the horizon what most cannot. In early

2020, for example, when news of COVID first started coming out of China, Easthope could see into the future what few could: the up-tick in suicides from isolation, the dogs that were adopted and then abandoned when lockdowns lifted. By the time the pandemic eased up, her predictions had come true: the UK experienced a record high number of suicides and abandoned puppies.

Like military generals, government public safety officials often fight the last war. When it came to the potential for a fire in public housing, Easthope was concerned about an outdated rescue proto-col that would have residents stay put in their apartments until the fire was under control. Easthope presented her colleagues with the scenario of "a major fire in a high-rise. . . . The residents would be a highly diverse community, many of whom didn't speak English well. The fire would burn at a terrific temperature, making the remains of victims difficult to identify."

The day of the fire, the bees' buzzing had reached a fever pitch. Easthope was on edge and feeling lousy, and her skin was yellow-ing. From her hospital bed she watched breaking news reports of a massive fire in Grenfell Tower, a public housing block in North Ken-sington. Her body, her anxiety, the bees—they all predicted the fire, which would claim seventy-two lives. (Easthope is quick to point out that it's not about her; it's about the victims.)

I've been trying to disentangle intuition and anxiety. But what happens when anxiety *is* intuition, as it so often is for Easthope, in her line of work?

Over breakfast, we discuss what to do with that feeling. "If you're going to allow your intuition to flourish, I think you also have to have a strategy for what you then do with it," she says. The bees need someplace to go. Easthope found a career where forward-looking preparedness bordering on hypervigilance is rewarded. But even in her everyday life, Easthope obeys the bees. "I'll go to a restaurant and walk out. I'll move my kids across the train carriage if I get a bad vibe from someone nearby," she says. Many of us feel these urges but tamp them down, for fear of seeming crazy or offending someone.

"I'm hell to live with," she says, laughing. "I'm not doing my bench presses every day, and I'm not meditating every day," Easthope tells me. "But I do hone my gut every single day."

And it has saved her life, and those around her, literally. In her memoir she tells the story of going with her husband and two young daughters to a theme park that had seen better days. The family considered the roller coaster, but Easthope made the executive decision that they were all better off retiring to their hotel room. Something about the whole scene made her bees buzz. They left the park. Hours later, the roller coaster crashed, resulting in injuries to park-goers. Once the accident Easthope has sensed coming on occurs, and her bees are validated, a peculiar calm washes over her. She experiences a catharsis—"But the most bitter, horrific catharsis," she clarifies.

Since childhood, Easthope has been deeply empathetic. She grew up in Liverpool. In 1989 she lost friends and classmates in the Hillsborough tragedy, in which ninety-seven people died at a match in Sheffield after too many Liverpool fans had crowded into one section. She was sickened by the media coverage of the event, which suggested that the victims were somehow responsible for their own deaths. That episode shaped her stance on disaster planning: to center victims and hold government response accountable. She married Tom, an airline pilot whose training drilled into him the value of listening to one's gut. "Where there is doubt, there is no doubt" is the motto Tom and his fellow pilots live by; if they have an inkling, even if they cannot explain it, the plane does not take off.

Easthope's form of visceral prediction is not limited to events on the world stage. She is a mom to two daughters, but carrying pregnancies to term was not easy. She had five miscarriages. "I always knew when my babies had died," she says. "I knew to the hour." When she went to the doctor she was often dismissed with *Oh, are you an anxious mummy?* "Then they'd do the scan and tell me the baby had stopped growing two days ago," aligning with the moment she knew. "We need to be able to say we're not crazy."

Easthope's professional intuitive genius is attuned to safety.

"Bluntly, it is about first impressions," she writes. She has honed her ability by following through—when she gets the icky feeling, she turns on her heel and walks out. But she has also sharpened her vision in two directions. While her job demands forward vision of future disaster ("I'm like a Parisian fashion house: I'm always two seasons ahead," she said on a podcast), a big part of her work involves retrospection. She and her colleagues sift through the wreckage to see what went wrong and where disaster could have been, if not avoided, then reduced. "When you work in safety and look back over a disaster," she tells me, "the major failings were pretty obvious ten steps before the incident." Analyzing past mistakes has made it second nature for Easthope to look for those patterns. So much so that her precogs are true premonitions.

Not all of us will find a career so perfectly suited to our natural inclinations and preternatural abilities. But Easthope does have quite a bit to teach us about intuition.

First, she shows us that sometimes anxiety *is* intuition. And while you and I might not be predicting the world's horrors, we've all been around people who make us itchy. Sometimes the vibes just make us anxious, perhaps because people are unpredictable or don't respect our boundaries or are energy vampires. Our intuition might tell us to flee, and that is the right diagnosis. But oftentimes we can't. Why? Because life: they are our coworkers, our neighbors, our family members. So what then?

In these moments, when intuition can't be a sword severing us from the nasties all around us, intuition can be a Swiss Army knife instead. There are people in my life who, despite my fantasies of a giant trapdoor opening in the floor beneath them, are immovable facts. I must see them, interact with them, coexist with them, even though the mere thought of them raises my heart rate. So how can intuition be useful in these moments?

The Swiss Army knife of intuition can help me deal with this reality in the healthiest way possible. When you consider intuition as triage, it can inform the best next step. When I see a certain name in my inbox, my anxiety will want to pounce to open it, to see what bad news it likely contains and rush to put out the fire. But intuition can help me resist the urge to open the message right away. Instead I can let it breathe for a few hours. When I've been in meetings with people who make me anxious, I place an object between us—a water bottle or a pillow across my chest if one is available (super normal, I know)—and picture it as a shield. My intuition tells me to wash my hands of these people, literally—I go to the bathroom and wash my hands for an inordinate amount of time to clear residual energy. Palo santo and open windows are my friends in these moments too.

Can I trust myself? This is the question that has anchored my attempt to understand intuition. Sometimes it's really hard to distinguish when it's plain old familiar anxiety and when it's something more, something along the Easthope lines of prediction. More than any other facet of intuition, researching premonitions made me incredibly anxious. When considering premonitions, you are the hammer and every passing fear is the nail. One can find premonitions of death around every corner, perhaps because that is our one sure ultimate destination. One of my biggest fears is missing the red flag, not heeding the warning. Being like Salman Rushdie, having the dream and then going anyway. It's a layered prison: being afraid of the bad thing happening, then feeling bad that the bad thing happened, because I should have acted differently.

Also, I fear that my premonition radar is somewhat askew. Unlike the mothers who have grabbed Lucy Easthope after losing their children in a tragedy and whispered, "I knew it," I once conducted an interview with Ross Ellenhorn *about intuition* while my phone logged a half dozen missed calls from my husband. Our son needed to go from the pediatrician to the hospital to get a steroid for labored breathing. During this time, I sat on the edge of my seat, hanging on Ellenhorn's every word, totally unaware of the peril young Truman was facing. When I finally looked at my phone after ninety rapt minutes, Scott's futile attempts to reach me culminated in sending me a selfie in the back of an ambulance. If ever I should have sensed something was off, that was the time.

Once you start looking at premonitions, you can see them everywhere: Theo doesn't want to go to school today—is he keen to some impending disaster I am not? I dreamt of my mom—should I tell her to go to the doctor?

In the midst of researching this chapter on premonitions, I went on a trip to Italy with a group to celebrate my best friend's fortieth birthday. The plan was to take a red-eye and then rent a car and drive three hours on mountain roads to our destination. The trip was a dream, but getting there was, for me, a nightmare. Since experiencing a car accident at seventeen, I have been an uneasy passenger. And I'd been having nightmares about the drive—the car getting stuck in reverse, careening off the edge of a mountain pass. Was this anxiety or intuition? I'd been trying to cleave them apart. If I use the pattern recognition heuristic, this driving dilemma is firmly anxiety, as it is a canalized pattern of fear resulting from past trauma. But as Ballard pointed out, there is a primal intuition that does not conform to patterns. Lucy Easthope's words and experiences reverberated. Sometimes anxiety *is* intuition. I was more tied up than a Celtic knot.

I applied Mossbridge and Cheung's rubric of determining whether this was anxiety or a true premonition. The dreams felt quite emotional: scary, keyed up, visceral. Therefore, I decided that this dream and the feelings I felt along with it were anxiety, not intuition. It's easy to put fear in the driver's seat. But this is not intuition, I don't think. Intuition wants to enlarge our lives, not keep us small and ground down by our routines. Was I really going to miss the trip of a lifetime because premonition had become my lens? I felt uneasy about the travel. I always feel uneasy about the travel. So, while my nausea at the thought of it was real, it was not to be trusted as predictive. This is the same old same old. Know thyself, know thy foibles.

With the help of half a tab of Klonopin, I climbed into the back seat of a rental car (upgraded to an Alfa Romeo—if you are looking for signs, this seems like a good one) and buckled up. We had the time of our lives. There is another version of this story where I didn't go, looked on enviously at the pictures on Instagram, and told myself that the only reason they survived was because I wasn't there. That is not a good story. I like the one that happened a lot better, the one where I am laughing with friends and slurping bowls of pasta.

Easthope's job trained her to review what went wrong prior to a disaster. How could the crisis have been averted? We can all bring that act of retrospection into our lives. When you look back over the wrecks of your life, take your pick: a relationship that didn't work out, a job that sucked, a friend who wasn't trustworthy—what were those "environmental breadcrumbs" you picked up on but didn't listen to? Was there a moment when you knew, perhaps by charting and analyzing what mistake you knew you were making? (We all do it!) Where did you rationalize? Where did you look away?

It's actually not that hard to be intuitive. We are by design. It's just that we second-guess ourselves so much.

After a bout of COVID, I had a cough I couldn't shake. An ongoing cough is good for getting a seat on the bus but makes one a social pariah. After three months I finally went to the doctor. I did a course of steroids, and still the hacking persisted. I called my health provider's referral line to see when I could get in with a pulmonologist or an ear, nose, and throat (ENT) doctor. The earliest appointment on the pulmonologist's books was two months away. But an ENT in the hinterlands of Brooklyn had one available . . . that day.

I found the immediate availability of an appointment with a specialist startling, and after telling the agent that I couldn't make it all the way across town in ninety minutes—perhaps intuition, perhaps a knee-jerk "I'm too busy!" response—I doubled back and said I'd rearrange the rest of my day and go see the good doctor.

You don't need to be an intuitive genius to see the writing on the wall. Upon arriving at the ENT's office, I did put it together that excellent specialists usually don't have availability that very day for a reason. The office was dirty, noisy, and chaotic; the doctor's nurse clearly hated him; the doctor had a full hot-drink setup at his desk and poured creamer into his tea as he berated me for being hesitant to have a camera threaded up my nostril; he claimed to have given me an allergy test when in fact he did not; and he diagnosed my post-COVID condition as acid reflux (just no).

Why didn't I leave? I'd been studying intuition for more than a year and I knew, immediately, that this doctor was no good. I think I just talked myself out of that fact. I wanted relief for the cough, I had taken an Uber, I had rearranged things. The costs seemed sunk. But it's better to divest when you see a bad outcome, no matter what came before.

Seeing those environmental breadcrumbs is not all that hard. It's so easy to defer to those we perceive to have more authority than us. I've done this sort of thing countless times—staying with a babysitter when I was a new mom because the sitter had come highly recommended, even though I didn't think she was all there; seeing a dentist who tried to drill a cavity without Novocaine while playing recordings of his own original music, only because Scott had been going to him for years. I picked up on the breadcrumbs. But vesting myself with the power to trust my own experience and act on it is where the rubber meets the road.

Easthope also highlights just how individual intuition is, how there is no one-size-fits-all. A piece of conventional wisdom I had absorbed as fact is that to be intuitive one needs quiet. One needs to be still to hear one's inner voice. But the nature of Easthope's high-pressure job doesn't seem to allow many moments of Zen. I ask her about the role of quiet for her intuition. "Yeah, no," she says, laughing. "If the bees are bad"—the buzzing of her intuitive anxiety—"that's when Netflix is great." She shows that distinct ways of knowing are valid. What Easthope is saying is that you can be incredibly intuitive without locking yourself in a dark closet. Intuition can be woven throughout the day, not separate and apart from the business of living. Sometimes we actually need distractions and noise when our intuition is really thrumming. We have to find ways to self-soothe.

But perhaps most consequentially, Easthope trusts her gut because she hones it every day. When she doesn't like the look of a place, she leaves. She gets a bad vibe from someone in a train? She moves. We can all do this. Because we all get these little messages. But usually we gloss over them and keep forging ahead so quickly because we tell ourselves we are silly, or we don't want to look weird or cause a scene. But what would change if you trained your intuition by following through with action, however small?

When I look at the matrilineal line of my family, the two undeniable qualities all of these badass women share—and the central tension of my life—are intuition and shame. The fulcrum that can balance these two, I've realized, is self-belief. That comes from learning to listen to one's intuition. When you start to notice the environmental breadcrumbs Easthope refers to, along with the biofeedback of your body, you can begin creating your own intuitive language and act on those feelings. They can change your life in small ways that can lead to huge transformations.

I walk my son to school on the same side of the street every day, because it's the most efficient route by about seven yards, the length of one crosswalk. And with a five-year-old, every yard counts. A curious thing happened recently. After drop-off, I did the unthinkable: I crossed the street. A pink dogwood was in full bloom on the other side of the street, and I wanted a closer look. For the past week, I'd craved a closer look, but that thought lasted about a nanosecond and was then buried under my mental playlist of to-dos and resentments to polish. But for some reason, on this day I heeded the call of the dogwood, of my intuition's desire.

I gawked at the pink blossoms for a few moments and continued on. My intuition had led me to that beauty, which was life-affirming on its own. But as I traveled farther on that elusive side of the street, I passed one of those little free libraries where people leave books. I picked up one that looked appealing, *French Exit*, by Patrick deWitt. It's a hilarious novel about a codependent formerly wealthy, currently disgraced mother-and-son duo who flee New York for

Paris. Highly recommend. I enjoyed it because it reminded me of my friend Christopher, this kind of story being very much his thing. I had the idea to mail it to him. Again, that is the kind of idea I'd typically dismiss, as a trip to the post office is less than appealing. But it felt like a good intuition to follow. I mailed him this lucky talisman, passing along the benefit of a brief intuitive reverie. You could call this slowing down to smell the dogwoods, noticing the beauty all around. But answering the call of my intuition set off a chain of events—I saw the dogwood, I enjoyed my neighbor's discarded book, I felt more connected to my community. The book made my days brighter, and I passed that on to my friend. This is just a tiny, everyday example of how opening up to my intuition and training myself to listen to it set off a virtuous cycle that made life a bit more sparkly. And it's a reminder that heeding intuition's call is not just about curtailing misfortune.

It can also lead you in positive, unexpected directions. Abiding one's intuition might not always be so pleasant and might well be in conflict with another's intuition about the same circumstance. Sometimes it will be difficult to act on, or it might result in tough conversations. One person's intuition might not reflect someone else's reality. I bring this up because sometimes we dampen our own intuition to make room for someone else's. This could well be based on some kind of shame about one's inner experience or needs. But shame gets leveled through experience. Intuition is a process, not a destination. Through opening oneself up to new experiences and recognizing *I am okay, even when I make a mistake, I can do wrong without* being *wrong*, we can start to shrink shame. Intuition, in this way, is emergent. *I can be open and learn. I can weather the blows. Maybe, just maybe, I am not actually fucked.*

We are all born with these intuitive inclinations. "Children have strong intuitions," Easthope says, "and we squish it out of them." Kids will be hesitant to hug the creepy uncle, and then the family will pile on and say *"Give him a hug!"* Sometimes they will be resistant to eating certain foods, as Easthope's youngest daughter was, only to be diagnosed with an allergy that entirely validated her gastronomical choices. Children do not possess the self-consciousness to be ashamed for listening to themselves. We teach them that. By listening to our intuitions and acting on them, we are honoring the wisdom we once had before adults and the world got to us. And we can teach our kids to listen to themselves by extending the respect of listening to them.

—

The thing is, none of us really know what is going to happen. And that makes life both terrible and wonderful. The scientists who dismiss clairvoyance as coincidence are the same ones who prognosticate over the future of AI. We want badly to know what to expect (because we are always expecting) and to avoid calamity where possible. Some premonitions that come true are probably coincidences. Some, like Rivera's warning dreams, seem so specific as to defy mere probability. We all suffer from memory bias, too, recalling the warnings that came true, chucking into the bin the ones that did not. Do they cancel each other out? Some did come true. That feels important too.

Premonitions are not either/or; they are both/and. Attempts to scientifically "prove" them, while admirable, while understandable, are to me a bit misguided. Which isn't to say that this facet of human experience isn't worthy of rigorous study—it certainly is. But it also feels like trying to pinpoint the coordinates of the origin of a poem. Some things are just mysterious. And to parse them is to approach them not on their plane. Perhaps instead of drawing premonitions down to our earthly realm of metrics and data, we can rise to meet them in their realm, the celestial. The noetic. The unknowable. It's what makes life wonderful.

When we attempt to master intuition, to parse it and systematize it, the worst thing that can happen is that it becomes a form of myopia: *How am I doing on my journey to my wildest dreams?* This is where manifesting feels like a corrupted form of intuition; it's too focused on the individual. Back at the Oyster Bar, Dolores Rivera said something that stuck with me. She was reflecting on her visions, and what it all means. "I believe intuition is not just for us," she said. "I believe there needs to be action too. There's something meant for us to do. And it might not be in that moment. It might be in a couple days," she said, and pushed back her chair, ready to dash to her next meeting. "But if you dream about someone, reach out. What's the harm?"

CHAPTER 8

PSYCHIC ABILITY

On a Sunday afternoon in June, a few dozen people descended to a black box theater in the East Village to watch Nelly Reznik perform her bespoke blend of stand-up comedy and communicating with the dead. Reznik's work as a psychic medium is a premise that lends itself quite naturally to jokes. Let's face it: talking to ghosts is pretty funny, as far as jobs go.

Reznik is thirty-seven years old, with dark, curly hair and an orientation toward deadpan misanthropy. Dressed in loose linen pants and a sleeveless shirt, she stands in the spotlight and tells the audience what to expect. The way she connects with energy and with spirits is like turning a dial on a radio—she finds the right frequency. "Tuning in to your energy is the psychic part. Communicating with those in spirit"—the dead—"is the medium part," she says. When she talks to ghosts, she is both the means and the mode of communication itself: "As a medium," she tells the audience, "I'm like a telephone wire if that telephone wire was a Jewish woman who lived for gossip, regardless of whatever plane of existence the gossip is coming from." This kills.

Reznik's work is the work of communication. And being the middle person between the living and the dead can be awkward. She often has to navigate thorny conversations—a deceased parent who wants to apologize to a child who does not want to receive an apology, for example. She once tuned in to a client's deceased brother who had committed murder, and connecting with him left her drained and disoriented. "I have to be prepared for anything," she says. "I don't know whether the client will be interested in getting information about a new job prospect or communicating with a child who has died." In the course of the thousand-plus readings she has given, she has seen a lot.

Once she tunes in—which she does in an instant, seamlessly transitioning from stand-up patter to playing ambassador between dimensions—she is conveying messages from the great beyond to us here on earth. "I receive information through what can best be described as a game of charades, Pictionary, and broken telephone all at the same time, at the weirdest and worst party you've ever been to," she explains. She receives phrases and images from spirits, meant for people in the audience, which she then must convey into language specific enough for the person to recognize their ghost. One such spirit, a man who "acted like a kid, very hyper, running all around," was a woman's brother who had recently passed. After the show, the woman approached Reznik in tears, telling her how powerful the experience was. Another spirit appeared to Reznik dressed in a mechanic's jumpsuit—he was an audience member's cousin's husband who loved working on cars. "I love when the randos show up," Reznik laughs. She identified that in life the man had two daughters and a son, and pinpointed his personality: private, reserved.

Reznik practices evidential mediumship. She provides specific details to the client about their beloved deceased. In a reading she gave me, she tuned in to my maternal grandmother, who talked about the ulcerative colitis she dealt with at the end of her life, dynamics within our family, and advice for parenting my kids. All mediums are psychic, but not all psychics are mediums. She explains the subtle but important distinctions: "Intuition is *Don't get on that subway car*. It's guidance. Psychic ability often gives you reasons, like *Don't get on that subway car because it's not safe*. Mediumship is a message from the spirits, like *My dead grandma is telling me not to get on that subway car because it's not safe.*" Intuition, according to Reznik, is the foundation for all psychic work. It's *this, not that; go here, not there.* It's gentle direction. Psychic ability drills down more to the reasons for the *why* of things and, as Reznik explains, "usually isn't even all that necessary" when you are just orienting yourself toward which way to go. There is much we can learn from someone as versed and experienced in intuition as Reznik. She contends that anyone can tap into their own psychic ability, and that it is like building a muscle: it happens through practice and repetition.

Yet there are few words in the English language as polarizing as "psychic," and few professions as stigmatized. Say it and some immediately recoil and reject anything that person may have to say. I'm not here to convince you. I did, however, approach the psychics I interviewed with the same level of respect I extended to the neuroscientists I spoke with; I do not question whether or not what academics and researchers do is real. If our minds are open, all of these practitioners have news we can use. For a lot of people, including me, a session with a psychic can be profoundly impactful. "Nelly did in ninety minutes what it took twenty-five sessions of therapy to do," Anna McDonald, an antiques dealer and mother of two, tells me. To have your energy seen and reflected by a psychic, without having to do anything at all, can be very powerful. Why and how does it work? No one really knows. But if you've ever had a positive experience with a mode of healing that others call bunk—whether that's craniosacral therapy, acupuncture, prayer, you name it—you know it doesn't matter. If it works for you, it works.

What Reznik and a great many other practitioners do today is not about fortune-telling and soothsaying. *"Will I have children? Will I get married?* That's what most people think psychic ability is," Reznik said on a podcast. The future, as she sees it, is unwritten, and present action can impact what the future looks like. Whether or not we get married or have kids or achieve our wildest dreams are interesting questions, for sure, but not necessarily the most useful in the long run. "What I'm trying in my practice is relational," Reznik says, "people taking responsibility for their own shit, fully. *How can I live a better life? What does that mean to me?*" These are the kinds of questions Reznik counsels her clients with. (She is enrolled in a master's program in social work so she can become a licensed therapist.) They are not as black-and-white or transactional as fortune-telling. "I'm not knocking fortune-telling, because that's how a lot of psychics were able to survive, and it has roots in Roma cultural practice," she clarifies.

Nat Strafaci, a licensed therapist and psychic medium who co-teaches a course on intuition with Reznik, which I took, explains that, from their perspective, harnessing intuition is about "stepping into being the leaders of our own lives. It's not surrendering to whatever happens next. It's not a modality, but a way of being in the world. It's about self-autonomy and self-determination." In other words, as I've been learning, intuition can be synonymous with confidence and trusting oneself.

But also, psychics come in a wide variety of styles and personalities. You may be a "dog lover" but really prefer your spunky Chihuahua to your neighbor's drooling Great Dane. One weekend late in the summer, I attend a weekend-long workshop at a healing center in upstate New York to learn from psychic mediums. What I experienced on this weekend is, I think, what many people associate with psychics, and I get why they are turned off.

I take a seat in an audience of fifty-odd white people, majority boomers, almost uniformly women. Everyone here has lost a loved one—parents, children, spouses. I feel a little apprehensive, as this scene is a bit more self-consciously "spiritual" (there are a lot of flowing garments and crystal necklaces in the audience), a bit more maudlin than Reznik's down-to-earth style. The medium who leads a gallery reading of the group tunes in while playing a song by Enya about loss. Even though I find it emotionally manipulative, there is not a dry eye in the room.

Like Reznik, this psychic is an evidential medium. "I love science," she says. "I have very little faith and I'm constantly asking for proof." That tension of seeking proof for the immaterial is striking. "Thank the spirits for showing up," she tells us. "Gratitude is an attracting energy."

The entire audience is on the edge of their seats as the medium decides which spirit to follow. "You're all like puppies in a pet store!" she jokes. She connects with the father of two sisters who have come together. "That's him!" they concur.

But the next day, a most curious thing takes place. Gerry Gavin, a gentleman with a kind, open face, stands at the front of the room to channel an angel. He says he came to know this ethereal presence when he was in his early forties and living in a very haunted house. "In the process of learning how to help the energy in our home to reconnect with its higher self," Gavin writes on his website, "I found myself reconnecting with what seemed to be a 'memory' of knowing how to communicate with the world of spirits, the energy of the earth and eventually Angels." This led him to meet his guardian angel and greatest teacher, Margaret.

Margaret has intel for us on earth, and she has chosen Gavin as her vessel. When Gavin channels her, he gives his body and voice over to her. When Margaret appears, Gavin's deep voice rises a few octaves higher to a tinkling register and his vocabulary changes to that of a sweet old lady. Margaret tells us how excited she is to be here with us today. Then, in the middle of her platitudes, the lights go out. Everyone claps. Margaret, coy as ever, waves off our applause, saying via Gavin that it actually has nothing to do with her and more to do with the electrical system on this stifling hot August weekend. "If it were really Margaret," the woman seated next to me turns to say, "she'd know to turn the A/C on."

Margaret gives a brief lecture about finding ways to live more from the soul, from our higher selves. She wants us to realize that there really is so much love all around. She opens the floor up to questions. I've never had the opportunity to ask an angel a question, but if ever there was an interlocutor to ask the driving question of my inquiry—is it anxiety or intuition?—Margaret is it. I shoot my hand up, lest I be boxed out by the other puppies in this pet shop.

"When you are getting intuitive messages," Gavin/Margaret tells me, "you are not going to be anxious. You are going to get love." Anxiety, on the other hand, is more from the subconscious and is not a divine message, according to Gavin/Margaret. This feels right (though a bit general), and it is the work of differentiating the energy behind the feeling. Intuition is more loving, anxiety is more spiky, I surmise from the angel.

The next question is from my enemy of the weekend, a man named Joe, in a Tommy Bahama shirt and complicated strappy sandals, who, of course, has no idea he is my enemy. He proceeds to ask a personal question about a project he's working on. Typical Joe, I think, bogarting the Angel Margaret for his sole use. "Your success comes from believing it is a success," she tells him. Later, I realize I've done the exact same thing. Joe, I am you. Margaret saw us both and diplomatically gave us answers everyone could use.

Here's what I've learned over the weekend: boomers do not like it when they cannot hear the program. "Speak into the mic!" has been a most common refrain. Despite arriving in the bodies of Subaru-driving coastal elites, in their past lives the attendees were Aztec warriors and witches persecuted at Salem, as reported in the share-out after the group past-life regression hypnosis on Sunday morning. Not a potato picker among them, isn't that something. The center does not make coffee available—anywhere on the campus—until 8 a.m., which should be a crime against humanity. In chakracise, a combination of aerobics and energy clearing, it is very difficult to figure out which way is counterclockwise when you *are* the clock—try it now! Nowhere since the year 2002 have I heard more people peddling their physical DVDs and CD-ROMs.

These were not my teachers, not my people. But that knowledge is also quite valuable. Just because one philosophy or teacher does not resonate with you does not mean that there isn't someone out there who does. For the former Aztec warriors and Salem witches this weekend, this style seemed to really land with them, which is great. It's funny, the lines I see myself drawing. While a materialist would dismiss anything remotely psychically attuned as hogwash, I am developing my own thresholds, which are always shifting. A few months ago I would've drawn the line at past lives. Now, who knows? I asked the Angel Margaret a question and got a pretty decent answer.

Similarly, if you dabble in the psychic arts, you might encounter different modalities, or ways of tapping into psychic energy. These might include mediumship or tarot or Reiki. But here's the thing: there's nothing inherently right or wrong about mediumship or tarot or Reiki. Those are just instruments. All the modalities are tools for the psychic to ascertain information and energy. It's like art—it's all getting toward truth and beauty. The composer and the sculptor express themselves differently, based on their inclinations and natural facilities. The same goes for the consumer of art, and her preferences. Just because I don't like acid jazz does not mean I should dismiss the concept of music entirely. Just because the Angel Margaret and chakracise didn't do it for me doesn't mean I need to summarily dismiss psychic work entirely. Art is a way toward transcendence; psychics are a way toward insight.

—

There's something definitively human about looking to psychics to explain the mysteries of life.

For as long as people have been alive, they have communed with the dead. They have done so across time, countries, and cultures. For oppressed and marginalized people, this kind of connection often meant more than just speaking to those on the other side; it was a vital form of resistance to colonial power. In *Brujas: The Magic and Power of Witches of Color*, Lorraine Monteagut writes that in Puerto Rico, "brujería was first documented on the island in the 1500s, as a response to the colonizers' religion and as a method of keeping

Indigenous and African traditions alive. Providing private modes of healing and dissent, brujas and brujos stepped in to help the people when governments and mainstream medicine fell short." Enslaved African Americans brought to the United States the traditions of West Africa that eventually evolved into the practices of hoodoo and conjure. William Wells Brown, a writer and abolitionist who was born into slavery, wrote in his 1880 memoir that "nearly every large plantation had at least one, who laid claim to be a fortune teller, and who was granted more than common respect by his fellow slaves." Black Americans sustained these practices in the South after emancipation and brought them north in the Great Migration and set up shop in cities throughout the United States.

But white mediums have always received the most mainstream attention. They popularized speaking to the dead with the rise of Spiritualism, a religion and social movement that captivated nineteenth-century America. In her book on a contemporary Spiritualist community in Maine, *The In-Betweens*, the journalist Mira Ptacin writes that Spiritualism is rooted in two basic ideas: that people have a duty to follow the Golden Rule "and also that we humans can talk to the dead if we want to." Many trace the origin of Spiritualism in the United States to 1848, when Kate and Margaret Fox, ages twelve and fifteen, made contact with the spirit of a murdered peddler whose body was found in a house in Hydesville, New York. His name was Mr. Splitfoot. People who were present said they heard rapping noises. A year later, the sisters performed for a paying audience at the Corinthian Hall, in Rochester. The Fox sisters were the first celebrity mediums, garnering huge crowds. The fact that they were young and white ensured their mainstream popularity.

Spiritualism drew contemporary luminaries such as Elizabeth Cady Stanton, Frederick Douglass, William Cullen Bryant, Sojourner Truth, James Fenimore Cooper, and William Lloyd Garrison. The religion really took off in the 1860s, when the Civil War claimed at least 752,000 lives. "Mourners needed an outlet and they needed hope," Ptacin writes, "something different from the you're-born-a-sinner, fire-and brimstone afterlife they'd been told to fear and respect. Spiritualism offered the perfect balm. It rejected traditional Christianity. It demanded less and promised more." The wife of Franklin Pierce hosted the Fox sisters at the White House after losing her son Benjamin in a train crash, and Mary Todd Lincoln brought "countless" mediums to 1600 Pennsylvania Avenue to connect her and Abe with their deceased sons William and Edward.

After living the lives of child stars, by the end of the nineteenth century the Fox sisters were suffering from alcoholism and had burned through their money. A reporter from the tabloid *New York World* offered them $1,500 for an exclusive. They published a confession in the paper revealing their Mr. Splitfoot methods (cracking their joints to make rapping sounds). The confession "was a gut punch, but it wasn't a deathblow" to Spiritualism, Ptacin writes. The Foxes cast a shadow on the veracity of mediumship. A few years before her death, in 1889, Margaret Fox recanted her words, saying she was broke and desperately needed the money. Certainly there were fraudulent mediums then and now. Author Dean Radin writes in *Real Magic*, "Each time a medium was unmasked as a fraud, it led to growing skepticism—which persists to this day—and to the notion that *all* mediums were necessarily frauds and fakes. This wasn't true then, nor is it true today." In all professions, from plumbers to presidents, there are bad actors. So, too, with psychics. But the difference is that criminality is presumed at the outset. The only job akin to this is lawyers, perhaps. (Reznik and all other psychics working in New York state are required to post a disclaimer that their services are for "entertainment purposes only." You could argue any religion should have the same requirement, but instead they get tax-exempt status. It's curious and somewhat arbitrary which faith society deems acceptable and which it does not.)

Skeptics position themselves as rational, rigorous, grounded on planet Earth, unlike the airy-fairy fraudsters they doubt. Writes Rupert Sheldrake:

No educated person wants to be thought superstitious, precisely because being superstitious undermines his or her claim to be educated. To go against this taboo involves a serious loss of intellectual standing, a relegation to the ranks of the uneducated, the childish, and superstitious. . . . Skepticism about anything historically associated with witchcraft, including psychic powers, has dominated the scientific and academic world for generations. Whatever intellectuals may think in private, skepticism is usually an integral part of their public image.

Kenny Biddle is the chief investigator for the Committee for Skeptical Inquiry, and the scales have fallen from his eyes. When we speak, over Zoom, he's wearing a T-shirt emblazoned with the phrase I DOUBT IT! across the chest. He has an enthusiastic, broadcast-ready voice, and his office is furnished with overstuffed bookcases, a whiteboard, cameras, printers, and a microscope, the tools with which he does his doubting. He wasn't always so critical, as he used to spend his spare time ghost-hunting. In the late 1990s he got into photography and began to see how the anomalies ghost hunters held up as proof were actually mistakes of the camera. On a ghost hunt in Gettysburg, he got mistaken by other prowlers as a ghost, and no amount of dissuading could convince them otherwise. A skeptic was born.

Biddle has since published articles debunking UFOs, aliens, ghosts, and psychics. He assists with testing applicants who enter a challenge offering $500,000 to anyone who can prove "these superpowers." One person claimed to be able to move clouds across the sky at will, and did not receive prize money when his claim did not come into fruition.

"I cannot stand when people are taken advantage of. They're exploiting your missing child, maybe your daughter who passed away in a tragic accident. I think it's disgusting, unethical, unprofessional, and they are charging hundreds of dollars," Biddle says. He believes that mediums prevent the bereaved from moving on, and that it's all too easy for them to find even the most granular information about someone online and pass it off as divination. He's passionate because he wants to prevent people from being preyed upon. "I don't want people to get taken advantage of and lose money. Some people lose thousands and thousands of dollars, and they don't recoup because they are too embarrassed to say anything," he says.

Reznik, ironically, is one of those people who lost thousands of dollars to charlatans and didn't recoup because of shame. And to add another layer of irony, being scammed helped lead her to discover her own psychic ability. She was working at the AmeriCorps VISTA program when she became incredibly close with her coworker Henry. "We were twenty-eight, and he was the main person in my life. We had that rare understanding between two people that's hard to explain, but when you touch it just feels electric. Your nervous system realizes it's safe," she says. When he died of a fentanyl overdose, it was shocking. Reznik had lost one of the only people in her life to truly see her. She was caught in a storm of grief and depression, living at home with her mother in New Jersey, making $12,000 a year. In this state of vulnerability, she saw a street psychic who took advantage of her.

The "psychic," whom we'll call Pamela, told Reznik she'd had a curse placed on her, and that she would have to pay Pamela several hundred dollars to research it. She also told Reznik that Henry was in a kind of purgatory and the only way she could help him was by paying her. Then she was on the hook for hundreds more dollars for the crystals that would remove the curse. After making a payment, Reznik would be clear for a few weeks. But, according to Pamela, since Reznik was so spiritually unencumbered, this left her open to other spirit attachments—bored ghosts who want to hang out and hang on to you. The only way to get rid of them? You guessed it: cough up some more cash.

This is the basic outline of how scammers work—there's a curse that only they can fix, and it can be fixed only by giving them money. Which is all to say: charlatans do exist, and buyers should beware.

Some speculate that street psychics, the kind you see in storefronts offering five-dollar palm readings in neighborhoods with rents of tens of thousands of dollars, are fronts for criminal activity. Steer clear of these places at all costs. No good psychic will try to hook you in for more. The dozen or so psychics I have visited charge between $100 and $300 for a session, and none of them have tried to sell me a curse-clearing candle, or even offered a follow-up.

Reznik was so ashamed, she couldn't tell anyone. These kinds of scams are similar to the ways in which people become enmeshed in cults: it happens gradually. Then you have sunk costs and are mired in isolation and embarrassment. But at the same time Reznik was seeing Pamela to deal with her grief, she was also devouring books and podcasts about death, loss, and psychic ability. She started meditating and had some powerful insights. She regularly had visions of a mask, which she came to realize represented Pamela. Reznik had dreams where Henry came to her vividly. She started having other dreams where "I felt like dead people were talking to me," she explains.

The trauma of Henry's sudden death opened her up, the way any profound experience—loss, parenthood, falling in love—can widen our aperture, stretch our edges, increase our empathy and sensitivity. Many psychics describe coming into their ability through loss and trauma. Reznik believes the survival instincts ingrained in her ancestry are at least partly responsible for her psychic ability—these were people who could see signs and act. The granddaughter of Jewish holocaust survivors from Ukraine, Reznik was born in Latvia two years before the fall of the Soviet Union. At two years old, her family came as refugees to Bensonhurst, Brooklyn.

"My childhood is kind of a blur to me, but I was extremely sensitive," she says. "When I look back at myself, I see a raw nerve. As a kid, I experienced my psychicness as anxiety. People who are highly empathetic often have to be hypervigilant when they are young." She was bullied throughout elementary school. When she was twelve, her family moved to New Jersey, which was "jarring," leaving the babushkas of Bensonhurst for the suburbs. Throughout, she was picking up on things. Her natural sensitivities made her a sponge for other people's energy, and that porousness was debilitating. Figuring out she was psychic, in her late twenties, made her experience of the world more manageable.

Around this time she happened upon a podcast about evidential mediumship, where a medium did a reading with a client on the episode. She was struck. "This was so different than how it was with Pamela," Reznik recalls. "This was what psychic ability can actually be like. They're having the conversation with the spirit person in real time, instead of reporting back on it later. They're getting better, specific information, and not digging around, trying to manipulate the client," she says. "I started to recognize myself in how mediums described their experiences."

She found a medium who practiced in the Lower East Side. In her session, she said to the medium, "My friend died. I think I'm being scammed." Reznik had never said those words out loud before. This medium tuned in to Henry—his personality, the way he slouched. After that, she was hooked on evidential mediumship and never went back to Pamela. In the end, though, she lost thousands of dollars to the scammer. "I'm a very free person because I have been through that. I was angry, but I'm grateful, even though it took a lot from my life. I think I'd be a very different medium now if it hadn't happened. It took away a lot of my fear, a lot of my ego," she says. The experience informed the way Reznik works. She is interested in empowering her clients to live to their fullest potential.

—

An intuitive master can teach us much about everyday intuition. For people who want to leverage their sensitivities, to go from being ruled by them to utilizing them as a tool, Reznik has a lot of thoughts. First, you need to familiarize yourself with what intuition feels like to you. In her intuition class with Nat Strafaci, Reznik led students through a meditation where we touched into our solar plexus, the area just below the rib cage that many psychics believe is the seat of intuition. Indeed, the solar plexus is home to a concentrated cluster of fibers that are part of the vagus nerve. We set the intention to activate this center of feeling. After meditating on this area for a few minutes, Reznik led us through a series of statements, some true, some false, to get a sense of what truth—as opposed to lies—feels like in this part of the body.

When I stated facts about myself, such as "My name is Liz, I live in Brooklyn, and I love chocolate ice cream," I felt a warm expansion settle over my chest. When I stated falsehoods, on the other hand, like "My name is Alicia and I live in Denver and I love fettuccine Alfredo," I felt a constriction across my body. The difference was subtle but marked. Other students in class reported seeing images or feeling tingling sensations. Intuition shows up differently for different people.

"A key to developing your intuition is that you have to trust it is happening before it is happening," Reznik told us. It's a leap of faith. The biggest thing is to gather data on yourself—you have to realize first what anxiety feels like to you, versus what intuition feels like. And to do that? You have to practice. "And don't be precious about it," she said.

Experts in other fields apart from the psychic arts echo Reznik's sentiment. Chris Voss, the FBI hostage negotiator and bestselling author, leads with his intuition and extolls the virtues of practice, repetition, and analysis. And this can be as simple as stating what you see. "The more you articulate your gut, the more you're going to find out how good it is," he tells me. "You see somebody who looks like they're having a hard day. They're stressed, they're preoccupied. They're avoiding you when they shouldn't be avoiding you. Don't say *how are you?* Instead, say *tough day.* Just speak out loud what your gut is." That tactic of verbally mirroring what you intuitively pick up on has freed innocent victims from kidnappers and earned Voss millions in business deals. To improve intuition, Voss insists on analyzing the results with a cool head: "You've got to move forward to see if your gut was correct or wrong, and then be completely open to the feedback. Data improves design."

The process of data collection is crucial when it comes to developing intuition generally—as you now know from tracking what anxiety feels like to you and how it is distinct from intuition—and for psychic development specifically. As a younger person, before Reznik was working as a psychic, she would often find herself agitated or drained in crowds. Unwittingly, she was picking up on other people's energies. A big part of her work is maintaining her boundaries, so as to activate her porousness at the right times, like when tuning in to a reading, and not being a sponge when walking around out in the world. Because she has learned to turn it off and on, she is not bothered by errant spirits at a party, for example. I ask her about this in an interview at a noisy restaurant. She likens it to the dining room we are in. "You know how there is a lot of background noise right now but you and I can still hear each other? It's like that," she explains.

Differentiating between background noise and useful information is a pragmatic, everyday intuition skill for anyone. Too often, we take on other people's shit before we even realize it. The beautiful part of that is a fully developed sense of empathy; the crappy part of that is that it is exhausting and confusing. Not long ago, I had a situation involving a work agreement with an associate with whom I was friendly. When I tried to clarify the terms, I got back long explanations, none of which were overtly negative, but they left me feeling odd, jagged, irritated. When I worked on the project, I felt anxious, but not anxious like I normally do, where I want to chain-smoke and make very rapid decisions. I felt more foggy and floaty. Unable to concentrate on the project, I went for a walk, and by the time I got back to my desk I was resolved to sever this contract. When I did, I felt a flood of relief, and received an email back from the client right away saying that this was what she wanted, too. Do you have to be psychic to pick up on weird social signals? Certainly not. But had I not been interviewing Reznik and learning about the way she discerns what is hers from what is not, I would have done what comes naturally, which is feel terrible and decide it was all my fault. In this case, I realized I was picking up on my client's energy and taking it on as my own. This discernment is a life's work—to be able to clearly feel into what is me and what is not me. But it is a worthy endeavor, as it allows you to harness your sensitivities into a superpower instead of feeling flattened by this deep feeling all the time.

What I experienced with that client is an example of "clairempathy"—feeling how someone else is feeling. Psychics often reference the clairs, or ways of picking up information. They are like senses, or learning styles; you will probably relate to some more than others. There's clairvoyance (clear seeing), clairaudience (clear hearing), claircognizance (clear knowing), clairintellect (clear thinking), clairempathy (clear emotion), clairtangency (clear touching), clairalience (clear smelling), clairgustance (clear tasting), and other clairs not on this list that you might experience. They are useful shorthand for how you know what you know, and I believe we can conceptualize them broadly. Take clairvoyance, for example: the image that might spring to mind is someone gazing into a crystal ball. But clairvoyance can be much more than that. It can mean getting images, yes, but it also might mean noticing visual signs in your life. I vividly remember standing on the street and reading an annoying email. I looked up, and right before me was graffiti reading PLEASE GO AWAY. Coincidence? Maybe, but noticing that little visual message made me smile and shrank my irritation, preventing me from getting totally hijacked. Reznik experiences clairaudience as literally hearing phrases and conversations—think of how many psychics were institutionalized for "hearing voices." Clairempathy can be picking up on other people's emotions, feeling what other people are feeling—or just getting a specific feeling about something yourself. Clairintellect? You just know.

Spend some time—a week, a month—noting how you experience intuition. Is it a constriction in your throat, a drop in your stomach, a warm expanse across your chest (clairsentience)? Perhaps when meeting a new client or contractor you might get a distinct download like "This person is going to screw me over" or "This person is going to be a wonderful collaborator" (clairintellect). But even more broadly, ask yourself: When you have an intuition, do you feel it in your body? Does it come to you in a sentence? Do you get visual flashes or notice objects in your visual field that take on a special significance? Consider what you *do* feel and experience, not what you *don't* feel and experience, Reznik encourages us. I've yet to experience clairaudience, but I have smelled in my dreams a few times. What does it all mean? Maybe just that there are lots of ways of knowing.

While these are the building blocks of a psychic practice, on their own they are tools for living a more integrated, engaged life. As a psychic medium, Reznik by definition communes with the dead in her work. Though this might seem like a niche skill, Reznik believes that we all have work to do when it comes to our ancestors. "We are our ancestors," she says. "Your instincts are your ancestors' instincts." Reznik attributes her tendency to hide when things get difficult to her inheritance from ancestors who were persecuted across the generations. Epigenetics reflects this, as does the idea of inherited trauma. She applies this idea to her work in comedy: "My intuition is telling me to get out there and market myself. But if I wasn't aware, I would listen to my programming, which would be to accept whatever measly offering I get and to stay quiet and small," she says. That protective impulse is not intuition, she believes, but something ancestral. When we heal ourselves, we are breaking cycles, but also healing the past, looking back. This is another way of carrying out our intergenerational errands.

Meditation is key to familiarizing yourself with your energy. This doesn't mean you need to become a monk and shut yourself off from the world. But getting quiet and still, even for just a few moments, will reveal what is lying underneath all the noise and activity of life. How do you *actually* feel? Sometimes when I meditate I experience something that feels like joy, plain and simple. Sometimes I feel something that is more like grief. But whatever it is, it is often buried under an avalanche of to-dos, autopilot, and exhaustion. When I can just be with whatever is going on, it makes me more aware of my inner life, and therefore more attuned to my reactions. That irritation I thought I was sensing in a friend's text message might actually be my own frustration with something completely unrelated. Or maybe I am picking up on *her* frustration about something else and sensing it through our interaction. That agitation I felt earlier might actually be my son's boredom, and on and on. Meditation allows us to get intentional and go deeper with learning the textures of our energy. It doesn't need to look the same for everyone. For those who have experienced trauma, stillness can be threatening, so keeping the hands occupied with repetitive activities like doodling or knitting while meditating can soothe the nervous system. Through this lens, to meditate isn't to retreat from the world, but to become more skillful at navigating it.

I've noticed that when I need my intuition most—when I'm wound up about a decision or deep in my head about the meaning of things or mired in the mundane realities of the boring business of living—that's when intuition can be hardest to find. When I'm wrapped around the axle of anxiety, unraveling to the more expansive intuitive state can seem nearly impossible. Reznik provides some guidelines for how to use intuition in heated moments: "'Should' does not exist in intuition," she says. If the information you're getting feels a little too much like the running inner critique of how you *should* be (thinner, more productive, married—you name it), that is more likely society's script, or the noise of the collective unconscious, as Orna Guralnik might say. Similarly, our deeply patterned, automatic reactions are rarely intuitive. "Intuition is never a triggered response," Reznik says. "When you are triggered, you can't make it go away. When you're activated, you're activated." Intuitive responses can feel similar to a trigger response (the flood of shame or a prickle of fear, for example), "but it will just be to give you information. It won't have the same emotional charge. It will give you the information, but it won't be the emotion itself," she explains.

"You can't use intuition to help you answer the question 'Should I key my ex-boyfriend's car?' I mean, do it, YOLO," she says, laughing, "but that's not intuition." We all get triggered, all damn day. "In my world, triggers are a good thing. We heal through triggers," Reznik says. This discernment is ultimately pragmatic for everyday life, and it takes a lot of practice. As Julia Mossbridge and Theresa Cheung said, intuitions are more neutral in tone; anxiety comes with more emotional agitation.

As you develop intuition, keeping it low-stakes and playful is key. "If you want to develop your intuition," Reznik tells a group of students gathered on Zoom, "don't start with 'Should I go to grad school?' or 'Should I have a baby?' You probably already have pretty strong feelings about those questions. Practice more with 'What kind of pizza should I get?'" And let yourself be wrong. We're going to get it wrong sometimes, and that's okay. Developing intuition to me means developing self-belief; if you practice getting it wrong and not descending into despair, you can try again. "You can't bully intuition," Reznik says. Oftentimes, there is no right answer.

Strafaci emphasizes presence over correctness. "You can't be wondering *Am I right?* and practicing intuition or psychic ability at the same time," they say. That second-guessing and self-consciousness only gets in the way of hearing and seeing clearly. Practicing intuition in the here and now, free of meta-critique, is another way of engaging with this moment as it is, as we are.

—

Psychics often get asked why, if they possess this sixth sense, they aren't millionaires or living with total ease. The psychic Sylvia Browne was a guest on *Larry King Live* when he asked her why she doesn't just use her ability to place a winning bet. "Because we can never do anything for ourselves, Larry," she said. "Did you ever hear of a surgeon operating on themselves? It's never been for us. If that were the case, I wouldn't have had a bad marriage. I have the same problems as everybody else does."

Psychic Brandi Auset echoes that sentiment. She often hears "'Why don't you play the lottery?' 'Tell me how many fingers I'm holding up.' First and foremost," she says with a laugh, "I don't do fucking parlor tricks. Second, that's not my gift. There are people who are gifted with guessing, who are gifted with numbers. There are people who are gifted with spirits and ghosts, and there are people who are gifted with reading other people's energy. It's how your intuition shows up for you. We all have different gifts." And we all suffer from the myopia of self. No matter how gifted, an individual is always subject to blind spots. When an intuitive attempts to read for themselves, Auset explains, "you'll only get half of the picture. You can't see the forest for the trees. That's why we have readings. That's why we have therapy. I can't see everything myself."

These detractors are tapping into an important question, though. Why wouldn't a highly intuitive person use their intuition to avoid the less ideal aspects of life? Is it possible to use intuition to bypass life's difficulties? Reznik was once asked on a podcast whether she ever gets forewarnings about how a gig is going to go and, if the premonition is foreboding, cancels. "If I get a bad feeling," she says, "I'm not going to cancel. The way you get good at comedy is by doing things that suck. You cannot use your intuition and get ahead in life by avoiding every bad situation. I might get an intuitive feeling of *Just be prepared for this* or maybe *Don't do this joke.* But I can't just cancel."

Intuition, in Reznik's opinion, is not meant for evading life's inevitable challenges. Things are often going to suck, and if we were to yield to every intuitive hit of vague negativity, we would likely never get out of bed. Instead, Reznik wants us to think of intuition as a method for growth. And growth is rarely comfortable. What Nelly Reznik knows from using intuition at a high level and from talking to hundreds of people who have died, who know something about life, is that we are not here to retreat. "We are here to have experiences, and to evolve," she tells me. "We're here to grow."

CONCLUSION

In 2019, several years before I started this project, I went with a friend to a tarot-for-intuition workshop one Tuesday evening. It was listed on Eventbrite, cost $30, and took place three subway stops from my house. I'd recently gotten interested in reading tarot and had a deck and a guidebook I'd dip into occasionally. The opportunity to learn from an expert was appealing. My friend and I walked up the stairs of a former schoolhouse converted to loft apartments, and we saw a dozen or so other people who had signed up, all pretty young and eager. Our teacher that evening was a self-described urban shawoman with purple hair, draped in diaphanous garments, burning sage. Before long she was talking about past lives. She urged us to buy the tarot decks she had for sale, and since everyone else was, I did too. I asked about the difference between intuiting the messages of the cards and projecting our own meaning into the cards, and she brushed me off. I left crestfallen. I wanted pragmatic intuitive tools, not the trappings of spirituality.

The next morning, I wrote as much in my journal. "I just want a tarot class for regular people. I want everyday intuition." I didn't know what it meant then. As I've learned, intuition can make things come out of your mouth that you don't understand. But then they are etched. E. L. Doctorow famously said, "Writing is like driving at night in the fog. You can only see as far as your headlights, but you can make the whole trip that way." You can also live a whole life that way. I followed the headlights through the fog to that sentence.

We live in a culture that teaches us that we can master the future, when the reality is that the floor falls out from under us all the time. It's not only our culture but our very biology, too, in our sweet amygdalae that claw for certainty. But stepping into intuition means giving up the illusion of certainty and confronting what is right now, or the immediate next. It means surrendering the hope of a superior future and living in action. To touch into intuition is to touch the divine. It's awe, mystery, and paradox, all rolled into a single moment.

As I read back over earlier drafts, I could see the shame I was fighting. I could see how much I polarized rationalism as male and intuition as female, doubling down on the binary, because I was tired of being made to feel silly. I was also ventriloquizing the messages I'd absorbed from a long line of Mennonites about how vain it is to think you have something to say. Ergo, the self-deprecation, the tap dancing, the fear of authenticity, the fear of self-substantiating. There's a self-centeredness to shame, a self-absorption. And, let's face it, it's boring. Is that self-deprecation again? I don't know. But I know I want to move on to something else. The connection that comes from intuition—to yourself, to the world, to your ancestry—is the antidote. I wish I could say that those earlier versions of me are today unrecognizable, but they are all too recognizable. I can relapse in the blink of an eye.

So: Is it anxiety or intuition?

I set out on this project to answer that question because there was another question lurking behind it: Can I trust myself? Can I trust myself to know the difference, and to make good decisions powered by intuition?

The means by which I tackled that question was an answer in itself: I sought the advice of experts. As a nonfiction author and curious person, that's what you do. I went to books, studies, articles, and interviews, collaged the perspectives of hundreds of people from hundreds of backgrounds. But at a certain point it becomes a form of procrastination. After a while, I realized I was outsourcing the expertise. I am advocating for people to make themselves the ur-expert, while still deferring to people with letters behind their names when appropriate. Don't get me wrong: I love to see the letters *M* and *D* when I need an antibiotic. But I don't need antibiotics all the time. At a certain point, intuition asks us to step into our own inner authority.

So here's what I know:

Intuition is personal. It will look different for different people. You have to pay attention to how yours shows up. We all have it, and it can be trained. Doing so will bring you closer to a life aligned with your highest potential. It might force you to look at areas and habits that are not working, which may be uncomfortable. But intuition allows you to be with the uncomfortable on your own terms. Rationalizing what you know to be true, no matter how unpleasant, only delays the inevitable. Explaining intuitive information away is the greatest form of magical thinking. Rational frameworks prioritize certainty, while intuitive thinking is flexible. The mind can be your enemy or your ally, and you have the power to change it—that's what neuroplasticity is all about.

But what's richer still, working with the mind can actually just be fun and full of discovery. Intuition won't let you bypass difficulty or avoid it—that's usually anxiety, yearning for certainty. I had to confront my own internalized biases around extra-rational ways of knowing; I was quick to call things I didn't understand "woo-woo." We won't always be able to act on our intuitions in the moment, but we can plant seeds toward their becoming. That's how gardens grow. Appreciating how we humans loathe uncertainty is vital in identifying anxiety. Intuition has less cortisol. Intuition: a comment. Anxiety: a question. I know what my *no* feels like, and how it's different from my *yes*. It's okay to start small. You will likely have better intuitive abilities in some areas of life than others. Investigating why might be revealing. Learning to trust yourself can be the antidote to shame. There are many ways of knowing. Your way is not wrong. You can trust that.

We can never escape who we are. But we can approach the old hurt and the crusty habits with a fresh perspective. People have asked me if, after all this research and immersion, I feel more intuitive. I say yes. But the truth is, I've always been intuitive. You probably have been, too. The difference is that now I trust it.

But in the end, what is it all for? Intuition, I think, is the motor of creativity and connection. It's Kayvon Pourazar dancing through grief. It's Dimitri Mugianis singing over the person on his mat. It's Nelly Reznik performing and connecting with the dead at a comedy club. It's Dolores Rivera dreaming reality into existence and reaching out to the people who come to her. It's Lucy Easthope's bees informing better preparedness strategy. It's Maria Konnikova at the poker table, evaluating her decision to raise or fold. It's Toccarra Cash facilitating conversations between young women about how they see themselves. It's Briana Scurry defending the goal for the game-winning save, abiding the voice telling her to look up. It's Melissa Coss Aquino spinning injured instincts into characters in a novel. It's my grandmother taking us on walks through the cemetery and writing poems at the kitchen table at night after the dishes were put away. It's my mother applying to college. It's me, at my own kitchen table, on my own intergenerational errand, writing to you. And it's you, in your life, trusting yourself to take the next step, following the wraith of right direction.

My greatest wish for my mom and my sister and myself in the parking garage that fateful day—and for you, whatever your proverbial parking garage and its lost ticket may be—is for us not to be fucked. Or to say, *Okay, fine, we are fucked, ultimately.* We all are eventually. But today? Maybe not. Then to let out a little sigh and to smile. To take a deep breath, turn on the radio, and be guided toward the ticket to our freedom.

ACKNOWLEDGMENTS

Thank you to all the brilliant experts and everyday intuitive geniuses who indulged me in answering questions about their fields
and experiences waaaay below their pay grades, the equivalent of an
interviewer asking me, "So, exactly what *is* a paragraph?" I marvel at
this generosity, and may this be a lesson to us all to 1) pay it forward
and 2) just ask! I met so many fascinating people on this research
journey that writing a book is a Trojan horse to have these conversations. Thank you.

Karen Rinaldi, my dream editor, the person meant to shepherd
this project into the world. No one has ever told me to cut the shit
in such a loving, meaningful way, and I'm forever grateful. I would
write another book just to have long conversations about it with you.
Rachel Kambury, you are a star.

Will Palmer, once more into the breach! Thanks for your metic-
ulous eye and not registering my use of the English language as a
crime against humanity. Kim Witherspoon, Will Watkins, and Jessica
Mileo, agents extraordinaire! Susannah Cahalan for an introduction
that changed my life. Jordan Monaghan for transcription assistance.

Katie Smith Roberts and the Delta, where I wrote the proposal for
this book and knocked around ideas. Geoffrey Goldstein for use of his
house, aka G-Work. Saltonstall and Lesley Williamson, both heaven
on earth. Kamilla Delaney and Eva Reich for making Fridays possible.

The Brooklyn Public Library holds system and the Columbia
University reference librarians.

My writing group! Frances Dodds, Jean Hannah Edelstein, and Ruth Curry, you asked all the right questions and slogged the slog. I love you, and our group text is my lifeboat.

Brooklyn Habit for keeping me caffeinated and allowing me to lurk.

Frances Dodds, for misappropriating the robot. Namwali Serpell, for a fortuitous introduction. Anna McDonald, for all the afternoons of conduction. Ruth Buchanan, for so many lunches at East One. Joe Buffa for the endorphins. Helen Rubinstein, for rewiring my brain toward gratitude every day for years and counting. Brooke Dawson, my wife for life. Swan Huntley, Zoe Banks, Raina Lipsitz, Denny Dipps, Rafia Zakaria, Karyn Marcus, Anya Yurchyshyn, Sarah Perry, Marin Sardy, Kenan Halabi, Eva Price, and Rachel Magida.

Christopher Backs, graphic designer, web mistress, daughter dearest, genius behind the illustration on page 23, the true brains behind the operation. You deserve your own acknowledgments section. Fortune smiled upon me that summer in Montauk, and your spirit and hilarity make my day, every day.

Readers who provided valuable feedback on early drafts: Phil Eil, Jean Murley, Sally Franson, Christopher Backs, Valerie Seiling Jacobs, Jessica Grose, Ben Lorr, I am forever in your debt.

My parents, Susannah Greenwood, Mike Rubin, Jan and Tom Thomas.

All my wise women—Janette Greenwood, Melissa Coss Aquino, Sindy Grappy, Jan Thomas, Joyce Pope, and Bonnie, RIP.

Mei Ting Xie, for allowing me to be an elder to you.

The Thomas and Cable women, the ones I know and the ones I don't, for cutting this path for me to follow.

Theo and Truman, I love who you are and I love you more every day. Thank you for bringing me into my intuition. Always listen to the voice of truth inside you. It won't steer you wrong.

Scott, my heart and my home, the answer to my question. My intuition led me to the right place that snowy night, and every night after.

APPENDIX OF TIPS

INTUITION, DISTILLED!

CHAPTER 1: EVERYDAY INTUITION

Become your own laboratory: Intuition is personal, and it shows up differently for all of us. Paying attention and taking notes about how you feel is key. Intuition can be subtle, so it's almost easier to begin with thornier feelings. What does anxiety feel like to you? Where do you feel it in your body? What does it sound like?

Historically, how has intuition shown up for you? How did you know it was intuition and not something else? Find your baseline. Because intuition can change and evolve. Begin to build a vocabulary around what it is for you, today, and be open to how it might shift.

This can be as simple as keeping a note on your phone about intuitions you have, how they feel, whether you acted upon them, and what happened. If nothing else, this just adds a fun shape to the day.

Develop your personal intuitive lexicon: One framework I've found helpful is, when I have something that feels like an intuition, I ask: *Am I feeling this from the neck up or from the neck down?* If the idea is coming from my forehead and is speedy and wants me to act *now now now*, that is usually anxiety. If it's in my chest as a warm, grounded sensation, that's more of an intuition.

Tone is important, too. Sometimes an intuitive inclination will keep cycling back into my mind in a quiet, gentle way, whereas anxiety is ruminative and loud. I kept thinking about a random post about a recommendation for a children's book series I saw on a parent listserv I subscribe to, and even though it was a few weeks old, I responded to it. Unbeknownst to me, a friend had posted the question, and I only learned that from my response. I once decided to do a long-put-off errand one afternoon after little visions of it happening kept coming to me, and I ended up running into a good friend. The gentle nudge, as opposed to the badgering *You should be doing x*, indicated intuition to me. How does it work for you?

Sally Franson calls this learning her *yes* and her *no*.

Derya Altan realized that, for her, anxiety is a question and intuition is a comment.

Some people also really enjoy looking for signs, synchronicities, and coincidences to reify their inner knowing. What makes you feel like you are on the right track?

Start small: What do you actually want to eat for lunch? What kind of exercise—if any—does your body crave today? How will that fourth cup of coffee feel in your body? Which side of the street do you feel drawn to walk on, and which side is more ingrained? You have ten minutes: Would it feel better to scroll your phone or shut your eyes?

Literally no judgies, just questions to begin to discern your intuitive instincts from your habits.

Keep it super low-stakes and playful: Try, for example, to let your intuition guide you to the perfect outfit, or the order in which you do your chores. Don't overthink it, just go with it.

CHAPTER 2: BECOMING EXPERTS IN OURSELVES

Neuroscientists agree that intuition is synonymous with domain expertise. Becoming experts in ourselves is the first step in recognizing our personal patterns. Some questions to consider:

- What categories, in addition to hungry, angry, lonely, tired (HALT), cloud my thinking?

- What are my anxious thought patterns? E.g., do I catastrophize, fall into black-and-white thinking, ruminate, etc.?

- When and where are my thoughts most clear, expansive, and reliable?

Familiarizing Ourselves with Uncertainty: In addition to providing our most ancient fight/flight/freeze responses, the amygdala has evolved to be "our certainty checker." Brains hate uncertainty, but, alas, we live in a very uncertain world. This accounts for 95 percent of our insanity, I'd say. (The other 5 percent is social media.) Try as we might, we will never be comfortable with uncertainty. Our brains are literally designed to search for certainty, no matter the circumstance. Recognizing this tension, however, is a vital part of the process. We can acknowledge our discomfort with uncertainty, and the behaviors we engage in to mitigate our uncertainty, when it starts to creep in. And by looking at our thoughts through the lens of how we are coping with uncertainty, we can begin to sort anxiety from intuition.
Ask yourself:

- *How do I try to establish certainty?* E.g., looking at the weather report; texting friends to verify whether or not they still like me; checking my bank account; and on and on.

- *When do I do this?* Literally: Is there a time of day when you start clawing for certainty? I almost always start checking things at night, perhaps because drifting off to sleep is a time of great mystery, and I want to feel grounded.

Also, what are the circumstances in which I reach to establish certainty? Perhaps it's waiting for a friend to show up at a restaurant and double-checking the plans half a dozen times to make sure you're in the right place, or trying to read your bloodwork results without the help of a doctor and diagnosing yourself with a half dozen rare diseases, all gleaned from Reddit message boards (not that I would know).

- **What do I do when things feel uncertain?** Do I numb out or distract myself? Do I compulsively plan?

CHAPTER 3: THE LIMITS OF RATIONALITY

Know when to apply rationality or extra-rational ways of knowing: Economist Russ Roberts differentiates between "tame" problems and "wild" problems. Tame problems are simpler and adhere to pro-con lists: where to go on vacation, how to invest your money, which car to buy. Rationality applies here. But wild problems, like whether and whom to marry, your career path, whether to have children—relying on rationality alone won't address the whole picture. Here, intuition can better serve you.

Try to be aware of your blind spots: We all have 'em. Ask trusted friends and family for their opinions (and gird your loins for their responses) about what qualities your ideal partner, or place to live, or job might have. The answers might surprise you.

Pay attention to your mood: Studies have shown that people will make intuitive decisions when in a good mood and rational decisions when in a neutral or bad mood. Ask yourself how you are feeling when you are considering something, and then cross-reference that decision when in a different mood.

Sleep on it: As with mood, giving yourself some time and space can help you come to the best conclusion. Stepping away from a problem and returning with fresh eyes allows you to see more clearly, and will also help you to better align with what you truly want. When faced with uncertainty, our anxious tendencies want us to take action right away so we can quickly exit uncomfortable ambiguity. Hang out in uncertainty for a beat. Better yet, do it while asleep.

Get out of silos: Expose yourself to novel inputs—art forms, ideas, sensory experiences, opinions, places. Rationality is cerebral, adheres to black and white, and can be self-reinforcing. Intuition is polyphonic and multifaceted, so drawing in a variety of experiences mimics that state.

CHAPTER 4: INTUITION OF THE BODY

Develop interoception: Interoception means the awareness of the inner workings of our bodies, and there are a plethora of ways to build this skill. Scientists recommend "heavy work," which means tasks that engage our muscles and bodies. For kids, this could look like pushing a loaded laundry basket across the floor. For adults, it can be doing household work with a finer attunement to how it feels: gardening without earbuds in, for example, and feeling how the blood courses through your arms after ripping out weeds for twenty minutes. Restorative yoga, mindful body scans, dancing, weightlifting—you name it. The key is to put your body first and to notice sensations without judgment.

Eat intuitively: The principles are simple: eat what you want, when you want, and notice when you feel full. Easier said than done! Monitoring hunger and satiety is a good place to start.

Track your triggers: Intuition is not one-size-fits-all, and for many people who have become alienated from their bodies, pulse-tracking devices are incredibly helpful for showing when their heart is stressed. These tools are a bridge between being alerted to dysregulation to recognizing it internally.

What would make ten-year-old you happy?: Or you at whatever age you can access a version of yourself prior to trauma, shame, and the funkiness of growing up. What would make that youngster happy? The answer to that question is likely the intuitive one.

Differentiate between fear and anxiety: Fear is in the present moment (*The tiger is eating me, oh no!*). Anxiety is almost always about the future (*I'm afraid I'm going to be eaten by a tiger*) or the past

(*I'm such an idiot for getting eaten by a tiger*). I call that past-tinted anxiety douche chills. When your hackles go up about something in the present moment—the vibe you get from a person or feeling afraid walking on a certain street—that is intuitive fear that should be listened to.

Pay attention to your jokes: If you start making out-of-the-blue jokes about something you dread happening, that could be intuition. The only time Julie Holland ever got assaulted working in Bellevue Hospital was moments after she had made an offhand joke about that very thing happening.

What does the moment need?: Kayvon Pourazar said he designed his Guided Bodily Reverie sessions by asking that question, and you can apply it to so much of life. It expands our outlook to something much more inclusive: not *What do I need?* or *What do you need?* but *What could most benefit this ensemble of players—energy, environment, people—right now?* Tapping into the energy of the moment is intuition in its purest form.

CHAPTER 5: WOMEN'S INTUITION?

You, and your way of knowing and being, is not wrong: Say it loud for the people in back! Medicine, religion, capitalism, and patriarchy have conspired to promote the idea that there is only one right way to be, which happens to be male, straight, white, linear. Ways of knowing that threatened these social hierarchies were (and are) deemed "old wives' tales," "woo-woo," and so on. Reclaiming intuition is a revolutionary act of saying, *Why yes, I am, in fact, quite right as I am.*

Intuition is never a "should": Intuition might lead you in a direction that says you'd be better served in a different relationship, or geographic location, but it won't badger you with guilt-infused *shoulds.* Getting a whiff of a *should* (e.g., *I should call my mean relative even though they will make me feel bad; I should wear this blue blazer even though I want to wear the rad jumpsuit,* etc.) can be a tip-off to something that is not intuition but a social pressure or guilt trip.

There's a great venue for distinguishing *should* from intuition: your closet. Marie Kondo was on to something with the idea of sparking joy, but consider this: What are the *shoulds* occupying valuable real estate in your closet? You will probably know immediately what works, today, for real, and what doesn't and is charged with some kind of shame and *should* for the lifestyle/job/body you "should" have. I have held on to dresses I wore before I had kids in the hope that someday I will contract an intestinal parasite and be able to wear them once more. I have a stack of skinny jeans that I keep hoping will come back into style. I have a green blouse I paid too much money for that I want so badly to be the kind of person who owns a steamer so she can wear it with panache. These are all *shoulds* that weighed me down, and one day when I worked up the gumption to go through my closet intuitively, I saw it all so clearly. These were garments of guilt, and looking at them every day was making me feel like shit on an unconscious level. Filling up some FreshDirect bags and bringing these items to a clothing swap gave me a high like no other. Donate your guilt-inducing garments and their attendant *shoulds* straight to the Goodwill.

Go to the doctor if you are worried: Get answers. As Philippa Gordon says, finding out nothing is wrong is not a waste of resources; it's a good outcome.

Intuition is another piece of the puzzle: When Talia Kovacs was diagnosed with complications in pregnancy, she saw her intuition as another piece of data, alongside scans and lab work. Her intuition was no better or worse than other metrics, but another factor to weigh. You can apply your intuitions the same way—they're not the be-all and end-all, nor should they be dismissed. When Truman was three, he self-reported that he had shoved beads up his nose. No one saw beads go in or saw beads come out. I was panic-stricken for a moment, considering plastic had lodged up his precious nostrils. But after checking in, I got the intuition that he did not, in fact, have beads stuck in his passageways and that he was fine. I still took him to the doctor, but that intuition helped me stay calm in the unpleasant Beadgate incident.

What would you tell a friend?: It's often easier to dispense the kindest, most loving advice to our friends than to ourselves. Intuition is expansive and wise, so what you would say to a friend is more likely to come from an intuitive place.

Find elders and be an elder: Throughout history, knowledge about women's health and lives was handed down from elders to younger generations. Connecting with elders honors that chain of knowing that has been obliterated in many cultures. We need elders to guide us on the path ahead, which we can't always see clearly from where we stand. And we need to extend a hand back to younger people. Distilling the lessons of our lives helps to crystallize what is important. Toccarra Cash notes how healing it is, in the sessions she runs on body image for participants, to connect with their younger selves. You can connect with your older self through meditation: First, envision yourself looking back at you ten years ago and think of what message today-you would dispense. Then conjure an image of yourself ten years from now, looking back at you today: What would older you tell contemporary you?

CHAPTER 6: DIPPING INTO UNCONSCIOUS WATERS

Give your unconscious mind an assignment before you go to bed: Whether it's a problem at work or a creative project where you feel blocked, the unconscious mind loves complexity. Religious people might call this prayer; neuroscientists call it delegating to the back office of the brain. Wherever you fall on the spectrum, ask for help before going to bed.

What is the question you are asking? What is the intergenerational errand?: Orna Guralnik says that we are attracted to certain romantic partners because the object of affection speaks to a question from the past that we have chosen the person to answer. What might your question be? Therapy is a great place to find out. And we ask questions in all areas of our lives, not just with our romantic partners.

What question have you asked vis-à-vis your career? Your hobbies? In your parenting style?

Psychedelic exploration: Despite popular depictions of brain-melting and ego-annihilating trips (which are very available, should you so desire), psychedelics can be titrated. You can begin with smaller doses and build up. Psychedelics disrupt habitual modes of thinking and allow you to see things from a new perspective. And the experience itself can build self-belief. Obviously, you need to take into account your own mental health profile and any contraindications, and there are more and more psychedelic therapists and processors available to help you navigate those choices.

Write down your dreams upon waking: This cathartic exercise allows you to clear any accumulated psychic sediment from the night and begin the day with clarity.

Hypnosis: For those of us who have been at odds with our own minds via nasty inner critics and thought distortions, hypnosis can harness that storytelling potential toward the positive. There are a number of self-hypnosis recordings available for free online; the app Insight Timer is a great place to start.

Unself: Intuition, at its most corrupted, can become a form of myopia: *What do I want, and how do I get there?* But in its truest, most essential form, intuition helps us trust ourselves enough to get out of our own damn way. Transcending the self and our postage-stamp-size purview of reality is important to cultivating the spirit and knowing what intuition feels like. You can do it through art, nature, connection with friends—anything that takes you away from you to see the beauty of the world around you. Make beauty and the world your greatest teachers.

CHAPTER 7: PREMONITIONS

High emotionality = anxiety; neutrality = intuition: This simple formula comes from researchers who have analyzed premonitions in dreams

202 / APPENDIX OF TIPS

and ER doctors who have seen patients predict their own deaths. When you wake up frantic from a scary dream, that is more likely garden-variety fear working itself out in the subconscious. Waking from a dream with neutrality, the feeling that something has already occurred, is more likely to be a premonition. And play with proof! I awoke from a dream one morning with the certainty that a trip I had planned with my husband for our anniversary was going to have to be rescheduled. I emailed myself (time stamp, receipts) the dream that morning, and sure enough, a few days later we had to postpone for a funeral. The funeral was very sad, but the evidence I had the forethought to send was a small consolation.

Look at animal behavior: Throughout history, animals have predicted oncoming earthquakes and moved themselves to safety while their human counterparts stood there agog and got knocked on the head with falling plaster. Sparky acting strangely? Pay attention.

Sometimes anxiety is **intuition:** Antsy feelings can be communicating something to us, and we needn't always write it off as mere anxiety. If you can act on a bad vibe, do it. Turn on your heel and leave the bar, switch train cars, throw out the package of iffy deli meat. But other times, there are people who make our skin crawl and, because they are our neighbors or coworkers, we can't easily evade them. We should acknowledge these feelings as real, and use the Swiss Army knife of intuition to help us determine how best to cope.

Make intuition your Swiss Army knife: When anxiety is intuition, how can you use your intuition to protect yourself? Do you need to respond to the email right away? How can you limit your interactions with people who make you uneasy? What little ritual can you engage in to feel protected? Mine include placing an object that I envision as a shield between me and whichever scoundrel; washing my hands; and putting certain text threads/contacts on mute so that I'm not interrupted by their names flashing across the screen and can deal with them at my leisure.

Reflect and retrospect: Disaster preparedness expert Lucy East-hope readies herself for the next calamity by reviewing the last.

What were the "environmental breadcrumbs" you picked up on and ignored? What would you do differently next time?

Listen to children: Kids are incredibly intuitive, because they have not been leveled with shame and taught to mistrust their instincts. If a child doesn't want to give a certain family member a hug, or refuses to eat certain foods, there might be something to it. Before rushing to make them do something they don't want to do because you know better, try to hear them out.

Reach out: Dolores Rivera has vivid dreams about friends and family, and sees her intuition as part of a web of connection. "Intuition isn't just for us," she says. If you dream about someone or they pop into your mind out of nowhere, Rivera implores us to reach out. Perhaps this is your intuition nudging you to connect with others.

CHAPTER 8: PSYCHIC ABILITY

Know your clairs: Intuitive information can come in many forms, including but not limited to clairsentience (clear physical feeling), claircognizance (clear knowing), clairvoyance (clear seeing), clairaudience (clear hearing), and clairgustance (clear tasting). Keep track of how you pick up information and what it feels like.

Visit a psychic: Psychics work through a variety of modalities: tarot, Reiki, mediumship, reading energy. It might take a bit of experimenting to see who and what works for you. Avoid storefront psychics and remember that no good psychic will lead you to believe you are cursed and rope you in for multiple payments. I highly recommend the psychics I interviewed for this book—Rebecca Auman, Brandi Auset, Nelly Reznik, and Manu del Prete—but your mileage may vary!

Notice and voice first impressions: Psychic information can often seem random as hell because it just shows up, free of context. For example, I took an herbalism class and the instructor passed around a tea and asked us to say out loud whatever words came to mind. I said "red." The potion was green. Turned out the tea we were drinking was red clover tea. At the time, I was undercaffeinated and less censorious than normal, and I allowed my first impression to speak. Even though it did not make logical sense, it turned out I was on to something. Practicing with friends pulling tarot cards for each other is a fun, low-stakes way to let first impressions speak.

Protect your energy: Sometimes we take on other people's junk. Highly sensitive and empathetic people tend to do this. Here is where our expertise in ourselves comes in to help us, big-time. When you know what your specific flavor of joy, anxiety, sadness, and so on feels like, you can more deftly know when your energy is meshing with others'. You can protect your energy by envisioning a shield around it and other people's slings and arrows bouncing off it.

Intuition will not let you bypass: Life is hard, and honing your intuition won't magically solve everything. If you keep getting "intuitions" to stay small and play it safe, that is more than likely your sweet amygdala working overtime to protect you from uncertainty. Sometimes intuition will be difficult to act on, or reveal difficult truths. But the more we develop a trusting relationship with ourselves, the more we can step out into vulnerability and know that, ultimately, we will be okay.

AND BEYOND

Mindfulness-Based Stress Reduction eight-week class: especially for developing pattern recognition and instituting pauses throughout the day. https://mbsrcollaborative.com

Connect with the natural world: "Don't be a fool. Go back and stand under that one red flower and walk straight ahead for that last hard mile. Go up and knock on the old weathered door. Climb up to the cave. Crawl through the window of a dream. Sift the desert and see what you find. It is the only work we *have* to do.

"You wish psychoanalytic advice?

"Go gather bones." —Clarissa Pinkola Estés, from *Women Who Run with the Wolves*

Find ways to get out of your head: Exercise is a good one, but sometimes if I'm doing exercise I've done a million times before, I'm just scrolling through my to-do list in my mind. A class like boxing, or dance with choreography I have to follow, gets me out of that hemisphere of my thinking brain. Doing something with your hands or learning something new can be another way. Here, when you are not in your default mode, your intuition might show up in a pleasing and surprising way.

Meditate: This doesn't have to be anything fancy; it can just be sitting still and taking a few deep breaths. Capitalism and patriarchy don't want you to slow down and hear your inner voice. This teaches us how to be with uncertainty without leaving. Give productivity demands the middle finger and go sit!

Heed the call: If a friend pops into your mind, text them. If you feel pulled into a store you're walking by, go in. If you find yourself thinking about a random movie you saw years ago, give it a rewatch. Our lives are so busy that it's really easy to just forge ahead. Experiment with actually heeding your intuition's call—and prepare to be astonished!

NOTES

CHAPTER 2: BECOMING EXPERTS IN OURSELVES

10   "preparation for everything": https://www.youtube.com /watch?v=Wh3mcKPscbA.

10   "I knew right then that that was the one I was going to save": *Fresh Air*, July 27, 2022, https://www.npr.org/2022/07/25/1113437267/soccer -champion-briana-scurry.

10   "before she kicked the ball": Ibid.

11   describes the brain thusly: *Nineteen Ways of Looking at Consciousness*, by Patrick House, p. 18.

11   "contains embodied brains": *Being You*, by Anil Seth, p. 6.

13   present in great apes: https://www.smithsonianmag.com/science -nature/brain-cells-for- socializing-133855450/.

13   "The von Economo neurons": Quoted in "The Growing Picture of 'Intuition' and Possible Implications for Bowen Theory," by Christopher F. East.

14   a lasting sense of fulfillment: https://www.headspace.com/articles/flow-state.

14   slip into flow more readily: https://positivepsychology.com/flow-activities.

15   "a dynamic cascade of insight": "Flow as Spontaneous Thought: Insight and Implicit Learning," by John Vervaeke, Leo Ferraro, and Arianne Herrera-Bennet, chap. 24 of *The Oxford Handbook of Spontaneous Thought*, ed. Christoff and Fox.

15   "little or no conscious deliberation": Hogarth, 2001, p. 14, quoted from "Flow as Spontaneous Thought," p. 321.

16   "AI is going to make various decisions": Interview with Matthew Lindauer, August 18, 2023.

17   A seminal 2002 study: "Effects of early experience on children's recognition of facial displays of emotion," Seth D. Pollak, Pawan Sinha, *Dev Psychol.*, 2002 Sep;38(5):784-91, doi: 10.1037//0012-1649.38.5.784.

19   Dr. Jerome Groopman concurs: *How Doctors Think*, p. 20.

21   the FFA is really a center for storing expertise: https://web.mit.edu /bcs/nklab/media/pdfs/OP236.pdf.

22   "practicing so much it feels like magic": *Voices in the River* podcast, "The Paradox Between Science and Mystery," https://podcasts .apple.com/us/podcast/the-paradox-between-science-and-mystery /id1709712815?i=1000643954124.

28   ambiguity as an integral part of intuition: *The Gifts of Imperfection*, by Brené Brown.

32   how she has learned to differentiate: Interview with Sally Franson, August 19, 2024.

CHAPTER 3: THE LIMITS OF RATIONALITY

35   *Moral Algebra*: Quoted in *Gut Feelings*, by Gerd Gigerenzer, p. 5.

36   "reason acquires its possessions through work": Quoted in "Spontaneous Thinking in Creative Lives," by Alex Soojung-Kim Pang, *Oxford Handbook of Spontaneous Thought*, p. 134.

36   "the big decisions": *Wild Problems*, by Russ Roberts, pp. 3, 32.

37   It is "a neural process": "The Growing Picture of 'Intuition' and Possible Implications for Bowen Theory," Chris East, PsyD, *Family Systems*, January 17, 2022, p. 6.

39   "Linda is a bank teller": https://lloydmelnick.com/2017/04/19 /thinking-fast-and-slow-part-1-the-lynda-problem/.

40   once we have gathered data: Bargh, p. 168.

42   "think or act depending on different situations": Ibid., 878.

42   "sense of our closeness": https://psychclassics.yorku.ca/James/Principles /prin9.htm.

43   felt better both *before and after* making intuitive decisions: Ibid., p. 1506.

44   "a gut response": *How We Change*, by Ross Ellenhorn, p. 58.

46   "I moved the needle": https://www.salesforce.com/blog/robin-arzon -peloton-smb.

47   "messages from the great beyond": Pinker, *Rationality*, pp. 304–5.

48   half of Americans: "Thinking Preferences and Conspiracy Belief: Thinking and the Jumping to Conclusions—Bias as a Basis for the Belief in Conspiracy Theories," *Frontiers in Psychiatry*, 2020, p. 2.

48   people who hold paranormal beliefs: "Paranormal Belief, Thinking Style Preference and Susceptibility to Confirmatory Conjunction Errors," *Consciousness and Cognition*, 2018.

49   "a sense of meaning and purpose": "Ghosts, UFOs, and Magic: Positive Affect

and the Experiential System," by Laura A. King et al., *Journal of Personality and Social Psychology*, 2007, p. 917.

50   "too much cognition": Interview with Hugo Mercier, December 1, 2023, p. 4.

CHAPTER 4: INTUITION OF THE BODY

59   "knowing what you feel": *The Body Keeps the Score*, p. 95.

59   our more intuitive powers: *The Master and His Emissary*, by Iain McGilchrist, pp. 437–40.

60   "silent interoceptive processes": "The Paradox of Listening to Our Bodies," by Jessica Wapner, *The New Yorker*, July 26, 2023.

60   "feel in charge of your body": *The Body Keeps the Score*, p. 98.

62   "the right card": Interview with Tim Dalgleish, September 11, 2023.

63   "telling me something about how I feel": Interview with Kristen Lindquist, September 30, 2023.

63   the heartbeat discrimination task: https://www.sciencedirect.com /science/article/pii/S0301051121002325.

64   "a different form of rationality": Dalgleish interview. Quote adjusted for clarity.

66   hundred million nerve cells: *Mind-Gut Connection*, by Dr. Emeran Mayer, pp.11–12.

67   "a massive supercomputer": All Mayer quotes from interview, March 22, 2021.

67   "emotional memories": *Mind-Gut Connection*, p. 183.

68   "shouldn't trust your intuition": Interview with Dr. Michael Gershon, November 16, 2023.

68   "an instinctual sense": Interview with Elyse Resch, March 19, 2024.

70   the state of increased sensitivity: https://www.healthline.com /health/hypervigilance#:~:text=Hypervigilance%20is%20a%20state %20of,these%20dangers%20are%20not%20real.

71   "instinct injured": *Carmen and Grace*, by Melissa Coss Aquino, p. 3.

71   "hide from their selves": *The Body Keeps the Score*, pp. 98–99.

73   "proud and happy": Interview with Sarah Perry, July 24, 2023.

73   "constraining in times of peace": All quotes from interview with Stephanie Foo, May 13, 2024.

74   "pain or death": *The Gift of Fear*, p. 327.

75   "I really didn't listen": Interview with Julie Holland, July 13, 2023.

75   making onyx-hued jokes: *Gift of Fear*, p. 82.

77   "we need to re-up": https://twitter.com/hubermanlab/status
      /1614285522440179719?lang=en.

77   better impulse control: https://www.entrepreneur.com/leadership
      /how-to-be-less-impulsive/437489#:~:text=Delay%20gratification
      %20by%20even%20a%20few%20minutes&text=The%20point%20is
      %20to%20be,no%2Dgo%20moments%20each%20day.

79   "feel more like yourself": Interview with Laurie Dawson, August 16, 2023,
      p. 21. Quote adjusted for clarity.

CHAPTER 5: WOMEN'S INTUITION?

81   "check Mr. Sandoval's phone": https://radaronline.com/p/ariana-madix-
      declaration-raquel-leviss-revenge-lawsuit-read.

82   "the female state": *All in Her Head*, p. 289.

82   "represented deviations from the ideal": *All in Her Head*, p. 36.

82   theoretically to be applied to women: https://www.ncbi.nlm.nih.gov
      /pmc/articles/PMC8812498.

83   "women don't have that kind of rational thought": Interview with Tabitha
      Stanmore, January 22, 2024.

83   "to be a person of intelligence": *Initiated*, by Amanda Yates Garcia, p. 12.

84   "exclusion from universities": *Witches, Nurses, and Midwives*, by Ehrenreich
      and English, 1973.

84   the worst witches of all: Grossman, p. 121.

84   "medicine became professionalized": *All in Her Head*, p. 169.

84   75 to 85 percent of them women: *Waking the Witch*, by Pam Grossman, pp.
      84–85.

85   "validating each corresponding contrary": "Inversion, Misrule, and the Meaning
      of Witchcraft," by Stuart Clark.

85   objective rationality: "Knowing Otherwise: Restoring Intuitive Knowing as Femi-
      nist Resistance," by Fee Mozeley and Kathleen McPhillips, building off Foucault.

85   "change to suit male convenience": *Witches, Nurses, and Midwives*, by Ehrenre-
      ich and English.

85   "big enough for love": Ibid.

85   "in competition with others": *Initiated*, by Amanda Yates Garcia, p. 17.

86   "One man's woo-woo": https://www.nytimes.com/2010/01/27/dining/27yoga
      .html.

86 "the first opportunity": Brandi Auset interview, January 30, 2024.

87 "my racial solidarity": https://www.glamour.com/story/gabrielle
-union-describes-being-raped-at-gunpoint-in-book-excerpt.

87 "an edge to read people": https://www.medicaldaily.com/your-gut
-feeling-way-more-just-feeling-science-intuition-325338.

88 "something is wrong": Interview with Jo Anne Kelly Richards, January 10,
2024.

88 "certain nonverbal skills": "What's Behind Women's Intuition?," Psychologyto-
day.com, February 22, 2015

88 "someone that has more power": Interview with Rose Hackman, April 19,
2024.

88 the position of dominance: *BBC Woman's Hour*, March 20, 2024.

90 "calling it science": https://www.nytimes.com/2022/08/26/opinion
/sunday/maternal-instinct-myth.html.

91 Grandmothers' identification scores: "What's Behind Women's Intuition?,"
Psychologytoday.com, February 22, 2015.

92 "innate predispositions": "Fathers Are Just as Good as Mothers at Recognizing
the Cries of Their Baby," by Erik Gustafsson et al., *Nature Communications*
vol. 4 (April 2013): 1698, doi: 10.1038/ncomms2713.

92 child-rearing ability: https://www.ncbi.nlm.nih.gov/pmc/articles
/PMC4103311.

92 "I literally don't know": Interview with Jen Glantz, August 5, 2024.

93 more accuracy and precision: "Emotional Sensitivity for Motherhood: Late
Pregnancy Is Associated with Enhanced Accuracy to Encode Emotional Faces,"
by R. M. Pearson, S. L. Lightman, J. Evans, *Hormones and Behavior*, vol. 56, no.
5 (2009): 557–63. doi: 10.1016/j.yhbeh.2009.09.013.

93 were able to decode . . . better at spotting crimes: Fullgrabe, 2002. From Marc
Bornstein, p.11, referenced in *Mom Genes* by Abigail Tucker and in an interview with Tucker, September 19, 2023.

94 "not trusting your own ability": Interview with Talia Kovacs, January 31, 2024.

95 "practice, mastery, and experience": Bellenbuam interview, February 9, 2024.

95 "I don't think intuition is intrusive": Tucker interview, September 19, 2023.

98 more evolutionarily advantageous: https://faculty.utah.edu
/u0030555-KRISTEN_HAWKES/hm/index.hml.

98 "women who were truth tellers": *BBC Woman's Hour*, May 6, 2024.

99 "messaging has been magnified": Interview with Toccarra Cash, February 27,
2024.

101 over the course of her career: https://rebeccaauman.com/your-guide.

102 "Knowing what you want": https://podcasts.apple.com/us/podcast/voices-in-the-river/id1709712815.

103 "constantly be on guard": Interview with Rebecca Auman, January 29, 2024.

104 "what the outside world is demanding": Interview with Amber Tamblyn, February 6, 2024.

CHAPTER 6: DIPPING INTO UNCONSCIOUS WATERS

108 "hallucinatory, primitive, irrational": *Subliminal*, by Leonard Mlodinow, p. 17, quoting from John F. Kihlstrom et al., "The Psychological Unconscious: Found, Lost, and Regained," *American Psychologist*, June 1992.

108 "a dump for moral refuse": Snowden, 62.

108 "neurosis or even physical disease": *Jung: The Key Ideas*, by Ruth Snowden, pp. xvii, 58.

109 "unconscious action . . . function outside awareness": *Subliminal* by Leonard Mlodinow, pp. 32–34.

109 "more reality bound": *Subliminal*, by Leonard Mlodinow, p. 17, quoting from John F. Kihlstrom et al., "The Psychological Unconscious: Found, Lost, and Regained," *American Psychologist*, June 1992.

110 While our conscious . . . assists in their sole imperative: Interview with John Bargh, April 24, 2024, and *Before You Know It*, Bargh, pp. 127–34.

110 "Unconscious processes create consciousness": Ibid.

111 behind the closed doors: https://bookreadfree.com/39861/1013580.

112 "That's the only . . .": Interview with John Bargh, April 24, 2024.

112 "as was possible": Interview with Dimitri Mugianis, July 7, 2023.

115 "things that provoke . . . drive is": Interview with Orna Guralnik, December 14, 2023.

115 "A good time to engage in therapy": Ibid.

116 "will play out": Hollis, p. 77.

116 "'Neuroplasticity' is the word": https://time.com/6315438/psychedelics-play-essay.

117 prolonged positive impact: https://nyulangone.org/news/mental-health-benefits-one-dose-psychedelic-drug-last-years-people-cancer.

117 major depressive episodes: https://www.hopkinsmedicine.org/news/newsroom/news-releases/2022/02/psilocybin-treatment-for-major-depression-effective-for-up-to-a-year-for-most-patients-study-shows.

118 psychedelics are a magic bullet: https://culanth.org/fieldsights/the
-pollan-effect-psychedelic-research-between-world-and-word.

119 the effects users report: https://www.nature.com/articles/s41398-022-02039-0.

119 "Psychedelics increase . . . some of the effects": Interview with Kalina Christoff, May 28, 2024.

121 Chuck Richards . . . "the rest was history": Interview with Chuck Richards,
March 25, 2024.

124 "they put something in our heads": Interview with Michael Pollan, March 25, 2024.

124 Emily Dickinson captured this experience: https://www
.poetryfoundation.org/poems/45706/i-felt-a-funeral-in-my-brain-340.

125 would make any Freudian salivate: https://www.lauriloewenberg
.com/i-dream-i-have-sex-with-my-mom-help.

125 "emotions and metaphors": Interview with Lauri Loewenberg, May 2, 2021.

125 "what we've already done": Barrett, p. x.

125 the Battle of the Bulge: Barrett, pp. 66, 182.

126 "free to hallucinate": Barrett, p. 185.

127 "release the pressure": Interview with Lauri Loewenberg, May 2, 2021.

128 a large Irish Catholic family: Interview with Shauna Cummins, April 17, 2024.

128 "our intuition will scream something": Interview with Pablo Milandu, March
7, 2024.

129 "you'll be OK": Email from Shauna Cummins, April 8, 2024.

130 Andrew Carnegie had inspired: https://en.wikipedia.org/wiki/Napoleon_Hill#.

130 "Both poverty and riches": *Think and Grow Rich*, p. 30.

130 "the healing power of my subconscious": *The Power of Your Subconscious*, by
Joseph Murphy, p. 7.

131 "a spike in the culture": "The Cult of Manifestation," *Sounds Like a Cult*, April
9, 2024.

131 Google searches for "manifesting": https://www.theguardian.com
/lifeandstyle/2022/mar/20/making-dreams-come-true-inside-the-new
-age-world-of-manifesting.

132 "Because that's how you change your mind": Interview with Stefka (name
changed), August 10, 2023.

135 "positive thinking did not exist": *Entrepreneur*, January 17, 2023, https://www
.entrepreneur.com/growth-strategies/i-built-a-public-persona-around
-positive-thinking-until/442529.

136 "the fat, relentless ego": https://philosophybreak.com/articles/iris
-murdoch-unselfing-is-crucial-for-living-a-good-life.

136 "clear our minds": https://www.themarginalian.org/2019/10/21/iris
-murdoch-unselfing.

CHAPTER 7: PREMONITIONS

139 "the person I saw": Interview with Dolores Rivera, August 14, 2023.

139 "I'm very cerebral": Ibid.

139 fifteen stories of premonitions: *The Premonition Code*, p. 58.

140 "the Chautauqua venue": *Knife*, p. 7.

140 "There's a lot of things": *Fresh Air*, April 16, 2024.

141 parents of children: https://www.sciencedirect.com/science/article
/abs/pii/S0092656600922852.

141 Many said they'd had a premonition: Interview with Laura A. King, July 24, 2023.

141 "It is how we survive": Ibid.

142 "like it already happened": Email from Julia Mossbridge and Theresa Cheung,
May 28, 2024.

142 Writer Jean Hannah Edelstein provides: Interview with Jean Hannah Edelstein, August 19, 2024.

143 "the nature of time": *Dogs That Know Their Owners Are Coming Home*, by Rupert Sheldrake, p. 249.

143 "passing yourself notes": Interview with Julia Mossbridge, May 28, 2024.

143 "precognition is as good as evidence": Ibid.

144 a state of sensory deprivation: https://en.wikipedia.org/wiki
/Ganzfeld_experiment.

144 "methodologically sound and logically insane": https://slate.com/health
-and-science/2017/06/daryl-bem-proved-esp-is-real-showed-science-is-broken
.html.

144 "a train wreck": https://www.nature.com/news/polopoly
_fs/7.6716.1349271308!/suppinfoFile/Kahneman%20Letter.pdf.

144 "it's mighty empowering": Interview with Theresa Cheung, May 28, 2024.

145 "our population of 350 million": All quotes from interview with Jessica Utts,
July 11, 2024.

145 "remote viewing": https://en.wikipedia.org/wiki/Stargate
_Project#Background.

146 "psychic functioning has been well established": https://www
.ucdavis.edu/news/psychic-spying-research-produces-credible-evidence.

147 "Our intuition can pick up . . . things our rational mind doesn't know": Interview with Deirdre Barrett, March 26, 2024.

148 Not all premonitions . . . blithely going about their daily business: *Dogs That Know Their Owners Are Coming Home*, by Rupert Sheldrake, pp. 265–66.

149 the Lisbon earthquake of 1755: https://en.wikipedia.org/wiki/1755 _Lisbon_earthquake.

149 detecting nascent cancers: Sheldrake, pp. 250–59.

150 "people might have lost their lives": Sheldrake, p. 269.

150 schoolchildren who lost their lives: https://www.theguardian.com /books/2022/may/04/the-premonitions-bureau-by-sam-knight-review -astonishing-adventures-in-precognition.

150 "think of your mother": Ibid.

151 For Dr. Dustin Ballard . . . "diagnosis of treatment": Interview with Dustin Ballard, August 7, 2023.

152 every major emergency: https://www.newyorker.com/magazine/2023/05/22 /lucy-easthope-profile-disaster-response.

153 "the centre of our emotional responses": *When the Dust Settles*, p. 179.

154 a record high number of suicides: https://www.gov.uk/government /statistics/near-to-real-time-suspected-suicide-surveillance-nrtsss -for-england/statistical-report-near-to-real-time-suspected-suicide -surveillance-nrtsss-for-england-for-the-15-months-to-august-2023#.

154 abandoned puppies: https://www.dailymail.co.uk/news/article-11664867 /Number-puppies-abandoned-soared-73-Covid-lockdown-shock-new-figures -show.html.

154 "the remains of victims": https://www.newyorker.com/magazine /2023/05/22/lucy-easthope-profile-disaster-response.

155 the roller coaster crashed: *When the Dust Settles*, pp. 183–86.

155 "we're not crazy": Interview with Lucy Easthope, September 27, 2023.

156 "I'm like a Parisian . . .": *Difficult Women* podcast, April 11, 2022.

156 "major failings were pretty obvious": Ibid.

162 "squish it out of them": Interview, April 26, 2024.

CHAPTER 8: PSYCHIC ABILITY

166 Reznik practices evidential mediumship: Interview with Nelly Reznik, June 20, 2024.

167 "what most people think": *Therapy Is Gay* podcast, May 8, 2024.

168 "a way of being in the world": Intuition Immersive class one cohort 2, September 29, 2024.

169 "the energy of the earth": https://www.gerrygavin.com/about/.

172 "mainstream medicine fell short": *Brujas*, p. 4.

172 "granted more than common respect": Quoted in "Dream Books, Crystal Balls, and 'Lucky Numbers': African American Female Mediums in Harlem, 1900–1930s," by LaShawn Harris, *Afro-Americans in New York Life and History*, vol. 35, no. 1 (January 2011): pp. 74–110.

172 "we humans can talk to the dead": Ptacin, p. xv.

173 "Spiritualism offered the perfect balm": Ptacin, p. 12.

173 their deceased sons William and Edward: Ptacin, p. 13.

173 "frauds and fakes": *Real Magic*, Dean Radin, p. 61.

174 "an integral part of their public image": *The Sense of Being Stared At*, by Rupert Sheldrake, quoted in *Listening in the Dark*, p. 178.

174 "these superpowers": Interview with Kenny Biddle, April 23, 2024.

175 "too embarrassed to say anything": Ibid.

175 "Your nervous system realizes it's safe": *MUM* podcast, October 23, 2024.

176 fronts for criminal activity: https://www.reddit.com/r/nyc /comments/2z1u1r/how_do_psychics_survive_in_new_york_city.

176 "dead people were talking to me": *MUM* podcast.

176 "I was extremely sensitive": Interview with Nelly Reznik, June 27, 2022.

178 to a concentrated cluster of fibers: https://www.sciencedirect.com /topics/neuroscience/esophageal-plexus#:~:text=Vagus%20Nerve.

178 "Experts in other fields": Interview with Chris Voss, October 24, 2024.

180 other clairs not on this list you might experience: chrome-extension:// efaidnbmnnnibpcajpcglclefindmkaj/https://reikilifestyle.com/wp-content /uploads/2024/10/The-Clair-Senses.pdf.

181 "Your instincts are your ancestors' instincts": Interview with Nelly Reznick, June 20, 2024.

182 meditating can soothe: Interview with Nat Strafaci, September 29, 2024.

184 "a surgeon operating on themselves": https://www.tiktok.com /@sylviabrownegroup/video/7229033219306310955.

184 "I can't see everything myself": Interview with Brandi Auset, January 30, 2024.

CONCLUSION

188 "you can make the whole trip": https://www.theguardian.com/books
/2015/jul/22/el-doctorow-in-quotes-15-of-his-best#:~:text=Writing
%20is%20like%20driving%20at,the%20whole%20trip%20that%20way.

FURTHER READING

Carmen and Grace, by Melissa Coss Aquino

The Premonitions Bureau, by Sam Knight

When the Dust Settles, by Lucy Easthope

Dogs That Know When Their Owners Are Coming Home, by Rupert Sheldrake

Purple Crayons, by Ross Ellenhorn

The Mind-Gut Connection, by Emeran Mayer, MD

Intuitive Eating, by Evelyn Tribole and Elyse Resch

The Gift of Fear, by Gavin de Becker

Women Who Run with the Wolves, by Clarissa Pinkola Estés, PhD

Cunning Folk: Life in the Era of Practical Magic, by Tabitha Stanmore

Waking the Witch: Reflections on Women, Magic, and Power, by Pam Grossman

Witches, Midwives, and Nurses, by Barbara Ehrenreich and Deirdre English

All in Her Head: The Truth and Lies Early Medicine Taught Us About Women's Bodies and Why It Matters Today, by Elizabeth Comen, MD

Finding Meaning in the Second Half of Life: How to Finally, Really Grow Up, by James Hollis, PhD

Emotional Labor: The Invisible Work Shaping Our Lives and How to Claim Our Power, by Rose Hackman

WishCraft: A Guide to Manifesting a Positive Future, by Shauna Cummins

Microjoys: Finding Hope (Especially) When Life Is Not Okay, by Cyndie Spiegel

The In-Betweens: The Spiritualists, Mediums, and Legends of Camp Etna, by Mira Ptacin

What My Bones Know: A Memoir of Healing from Complex Trauma, by Stephanie Foo

Being You: A New Science of Consciousness, by Anil Seth

Ten Trips: The New Reality of Psychedelics, by Andy Mitchell

The Master and His Emissary: The Divided Brain and the Making of the Western World, by Iain McGilchrist

Brujas: The Magic and Power of Witches of Color, by Lorraine Monteagut, PhD

Before You Know It: The Unconscious Reasons We Do What We Do, by John Bargh, PhD

The Empath's Survival Guide: Life Strategies for Sensitive People, by Judith Orloff, MD

INDEX

Descartes, René, 58, 85
Dickinson, Emily, 124
Diodorus Siculus, 149
Doctorow, E. L., 187–88
dogs, 148, 149, 151, 154, 254
Dogs That Know When Their Owners Are Coming Home (Sheldrake), 149
Douglass, Frederick, 172
Down syndrome, 140–41
dreams, 124–27, 201
  intuition and, 124–27, 142, 147–48, 203
  premonitions and, 138–40, 141–42, 143, 147–48, 150, 201–2
dual-processing models of cognition, 37–39, 47

earthquakes, 148–50
Easthope, Lucy, 157, 158, 162–63, 190, 202
  as a disaster preparedness expert, 152–54, 155–56, 159, 160
  Grenfell fire and, 153, 154
  sensing impending disasters, 152–53, 154–56, 160–61
  When the Dust Settles, 153, 155
eating, 68–69, 197
Edelstein, Jean Hannah, 142–43
Edison, Thomas, 129
ego death, 121
Ehrenreich, Barbara, 83–84, 85
elders as mentors, 97–101, 200
Ellenhorn, Ross, 44, 116, 117, 157
Emotion, 42

Emotional Intelligence (Goleman), 88
Emotional Labor (Hackman), 88
emotions, somatic markers and, 59–60
Engber, Daniel, 144
English, Deirdre, 83–84, 85
Enlightenment, xv, 36, 85
enteric nervous system (ENS), 66–67
epigenetics, 181
Epstein, Seymour, 47
ER medicine, pattern recognition and, 18–19
Estés, Clarissa Pinkola, 87, 99, 204
Evening Standard, 150
expertise
  domain, 18, 31, 194–95
  fusiform face area and, 21
  intuition as, 10–11, 17–18, 21–22, 86
  uncertainty and, 30

facial recognition, 21
Fairley, Peter, 150
fathers, 91–92
fear
  differentiating between anxiety and, 73, 74–75, 197–98
  intuition and, 74, 75
  trance state of, 129
  unprocessed trauma and, 76
fear learning, 16–17, 31, 70
Feldman, Mallory, 63–64
FFA (fusiform face area), 21
Finding Meaning in the Second Half of Life (Hollis), 116

ABOUT THE AUTHOR

ELIZABETH GREENWOOD is the author of the critically acclaimed nonfiction books *Love in the Time of Incarceration: Five Stories of Dating, Sex, and Marriage in America's Prisons* and *Playing Dead: A Journey Through the World of Death Fraud*. She lives in Brooklyn with her family.